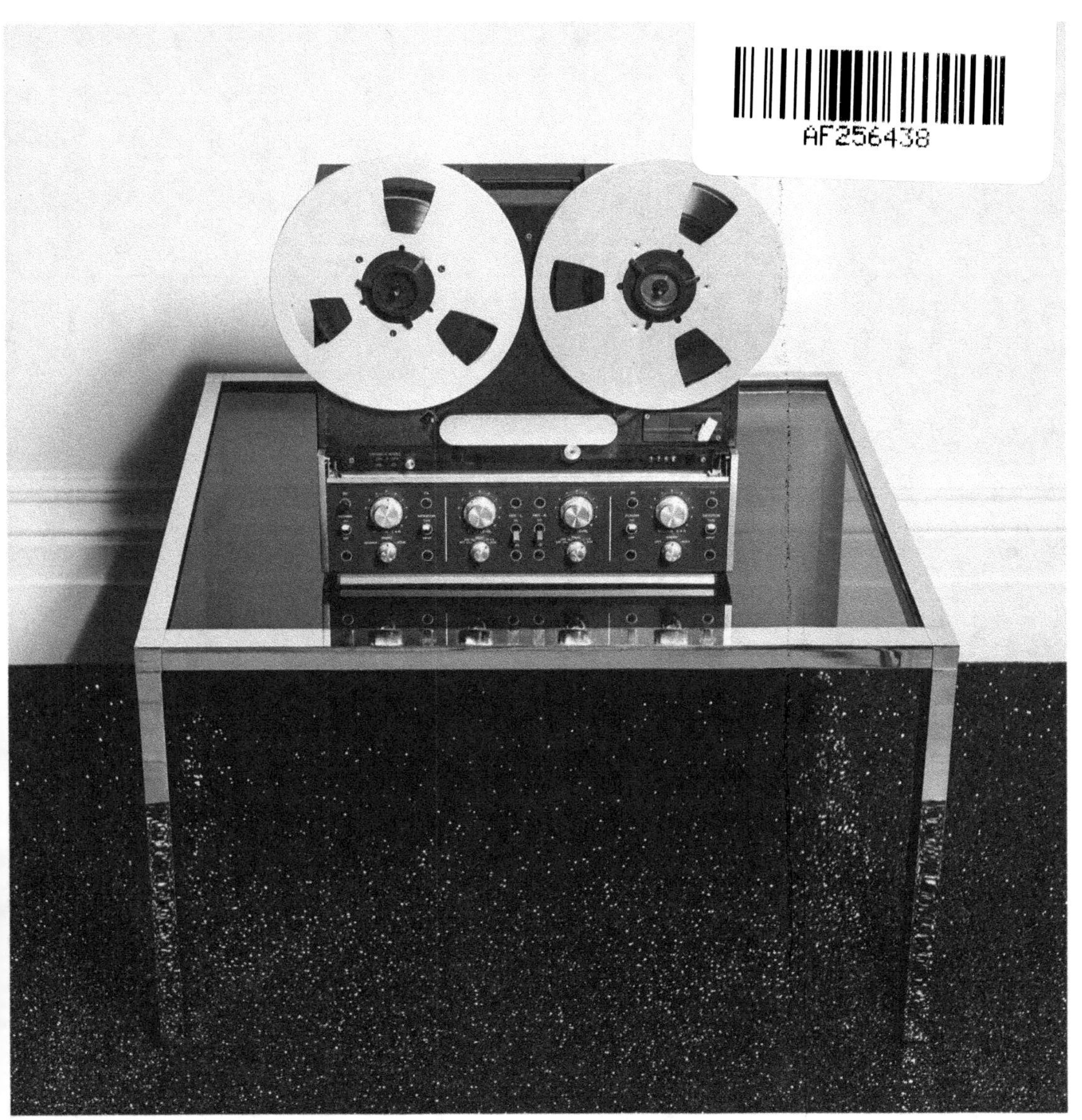

CELINE

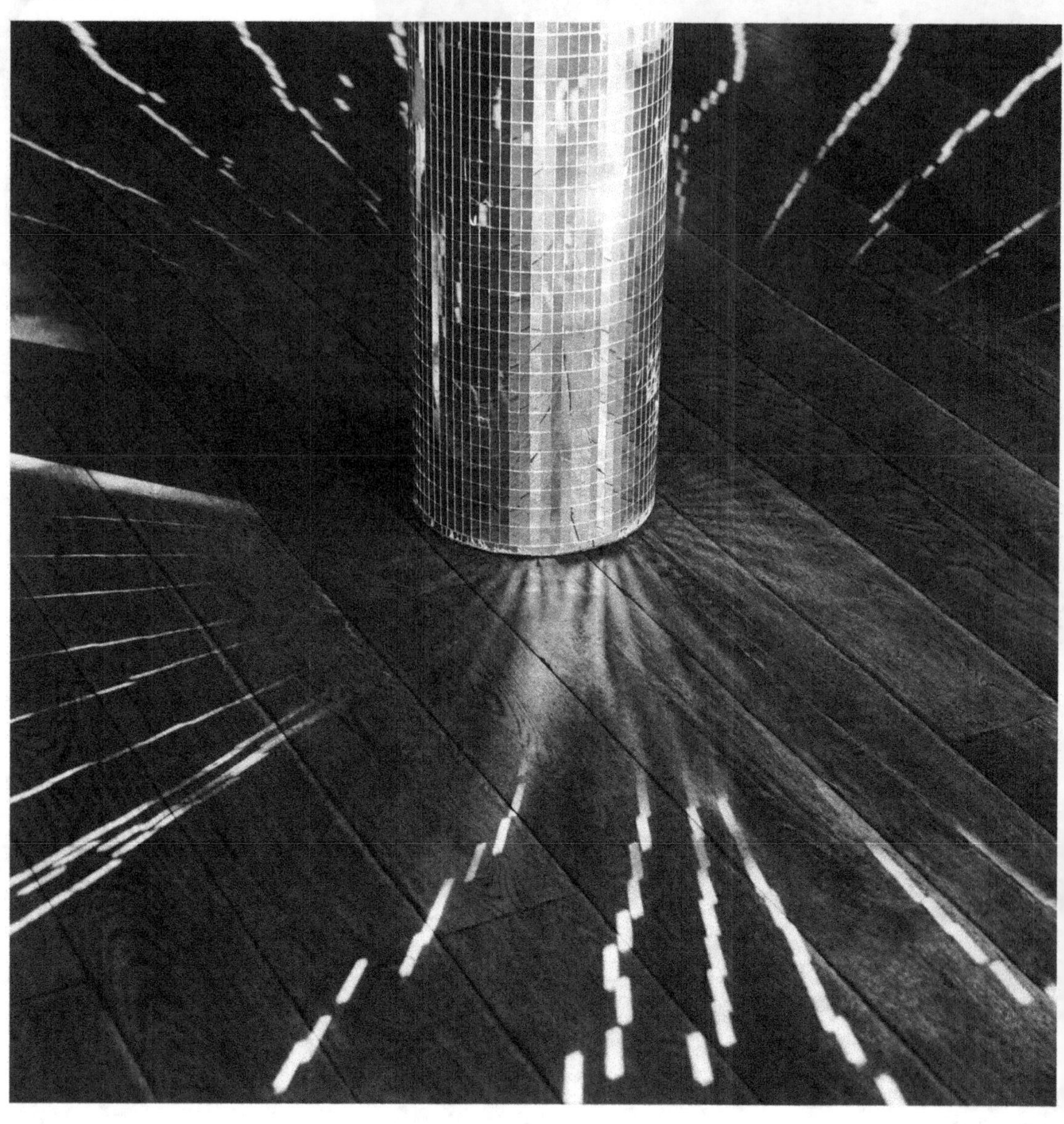

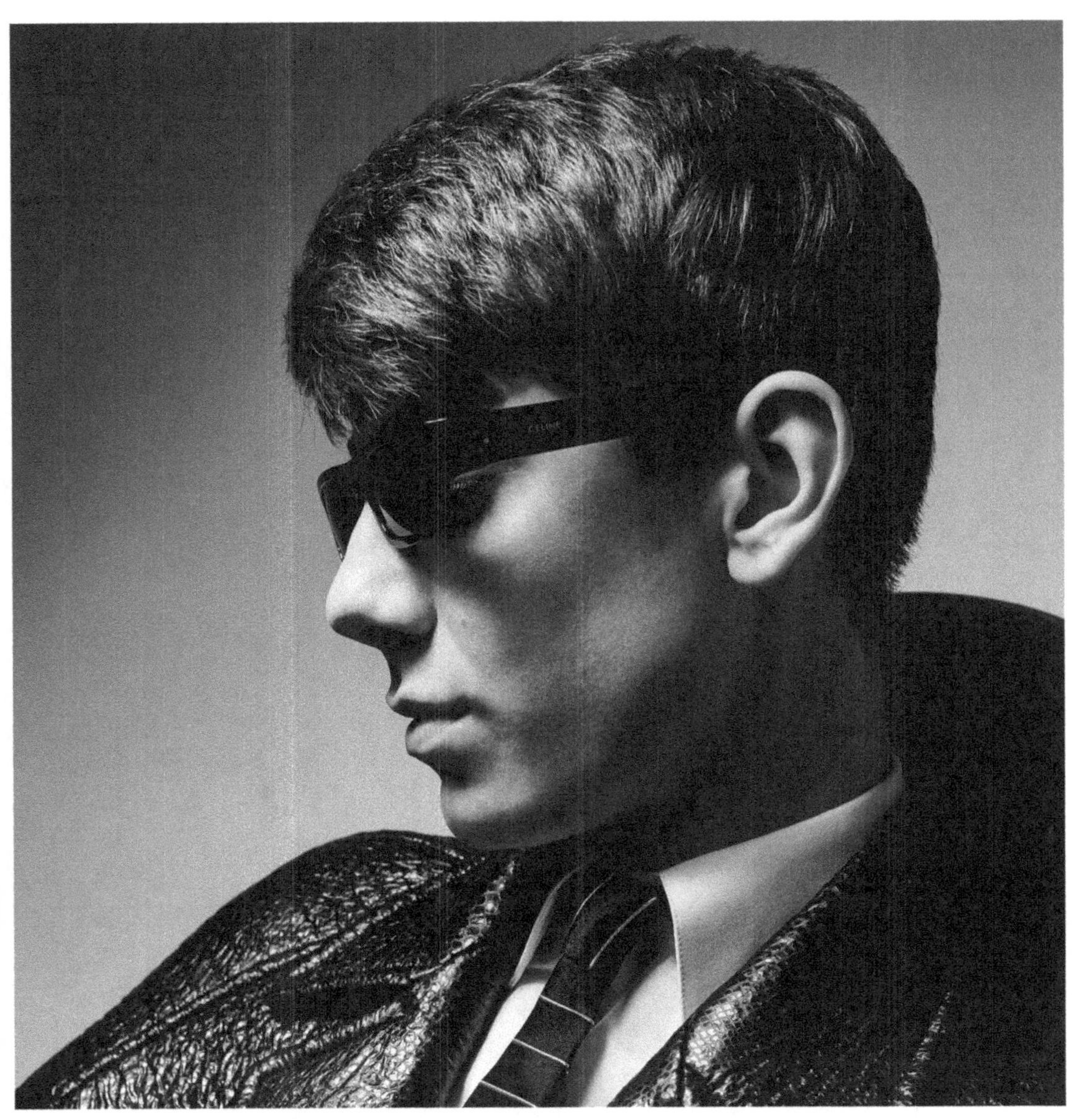

CELINE

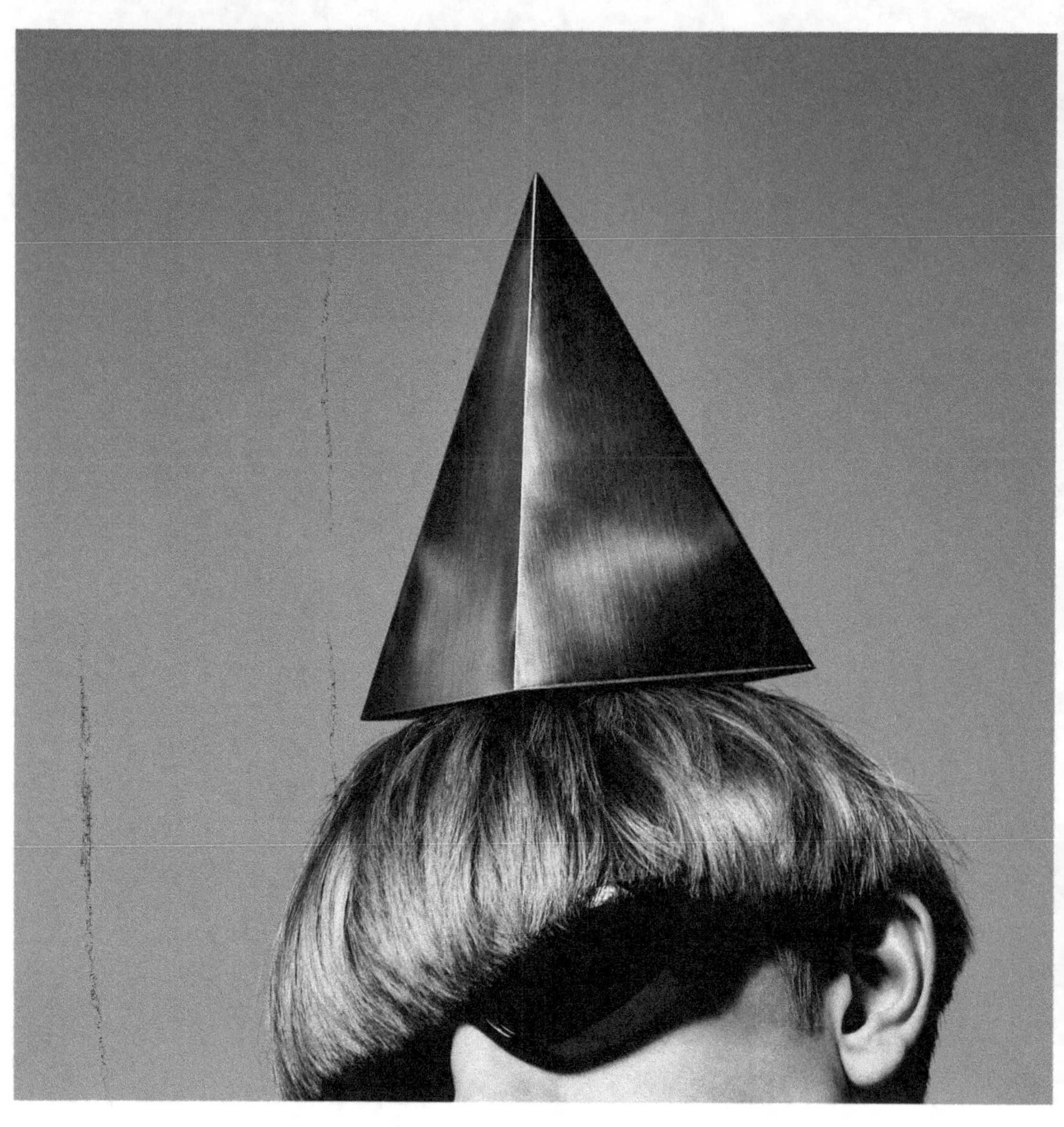

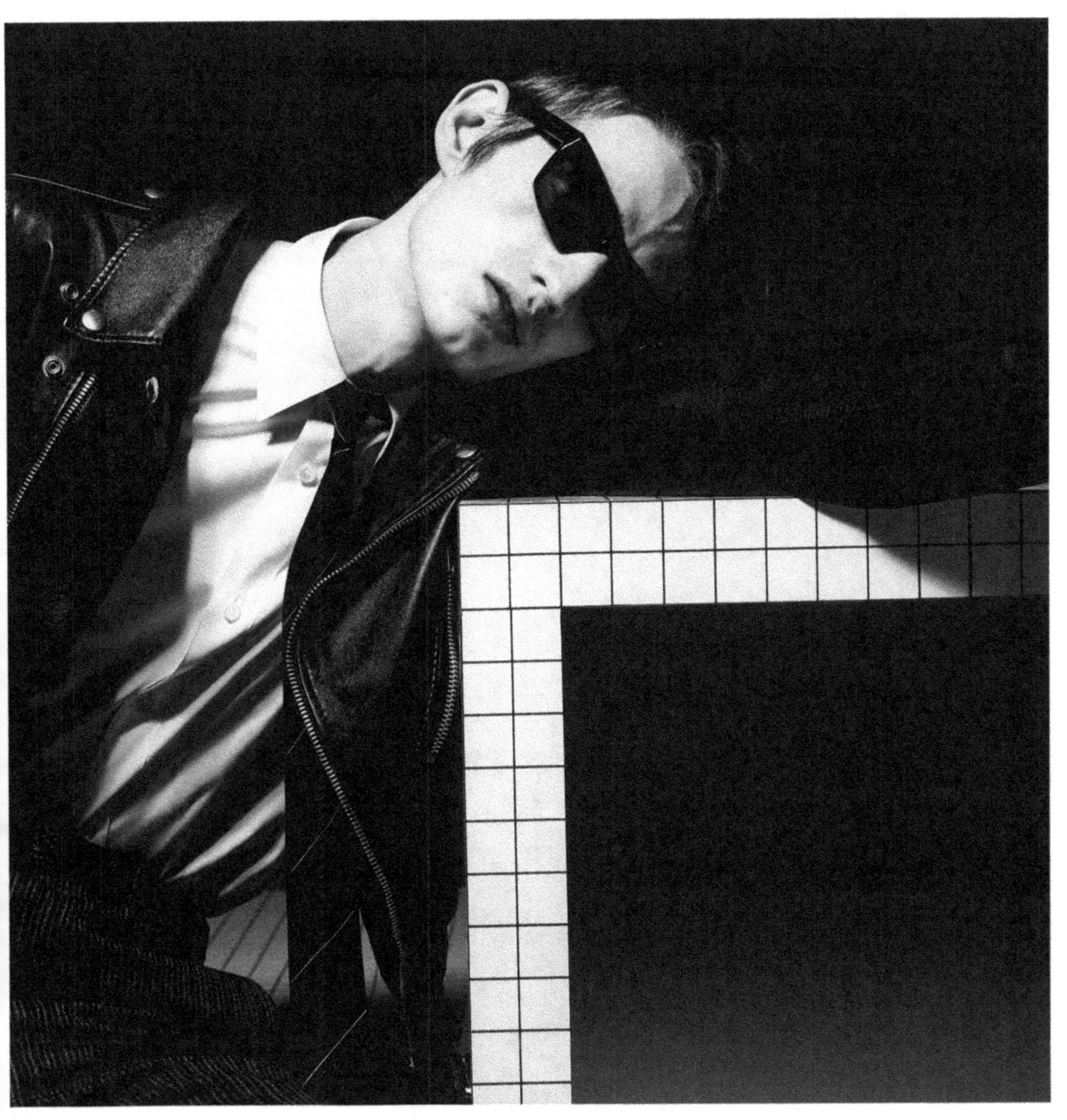

CELINE

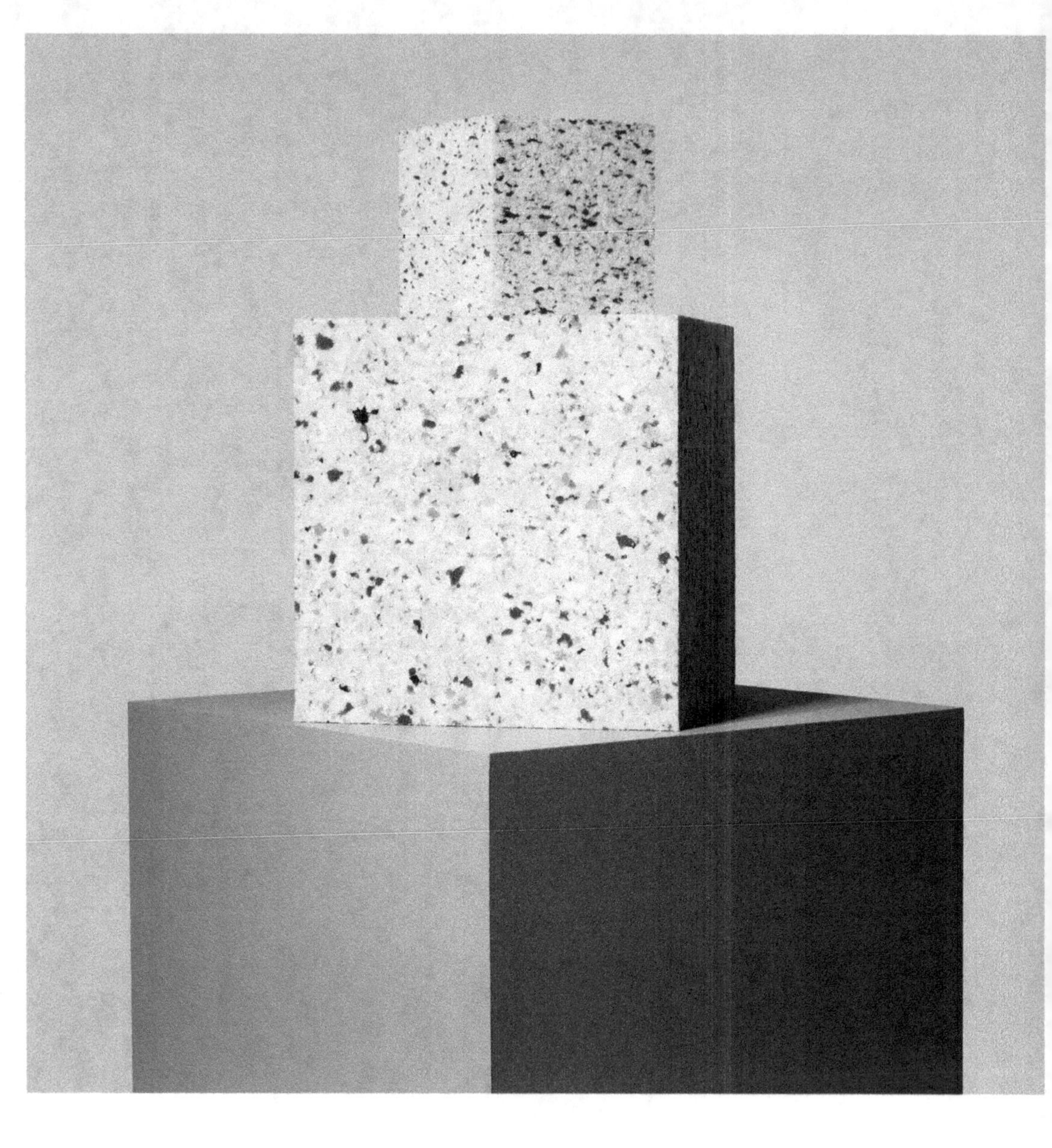

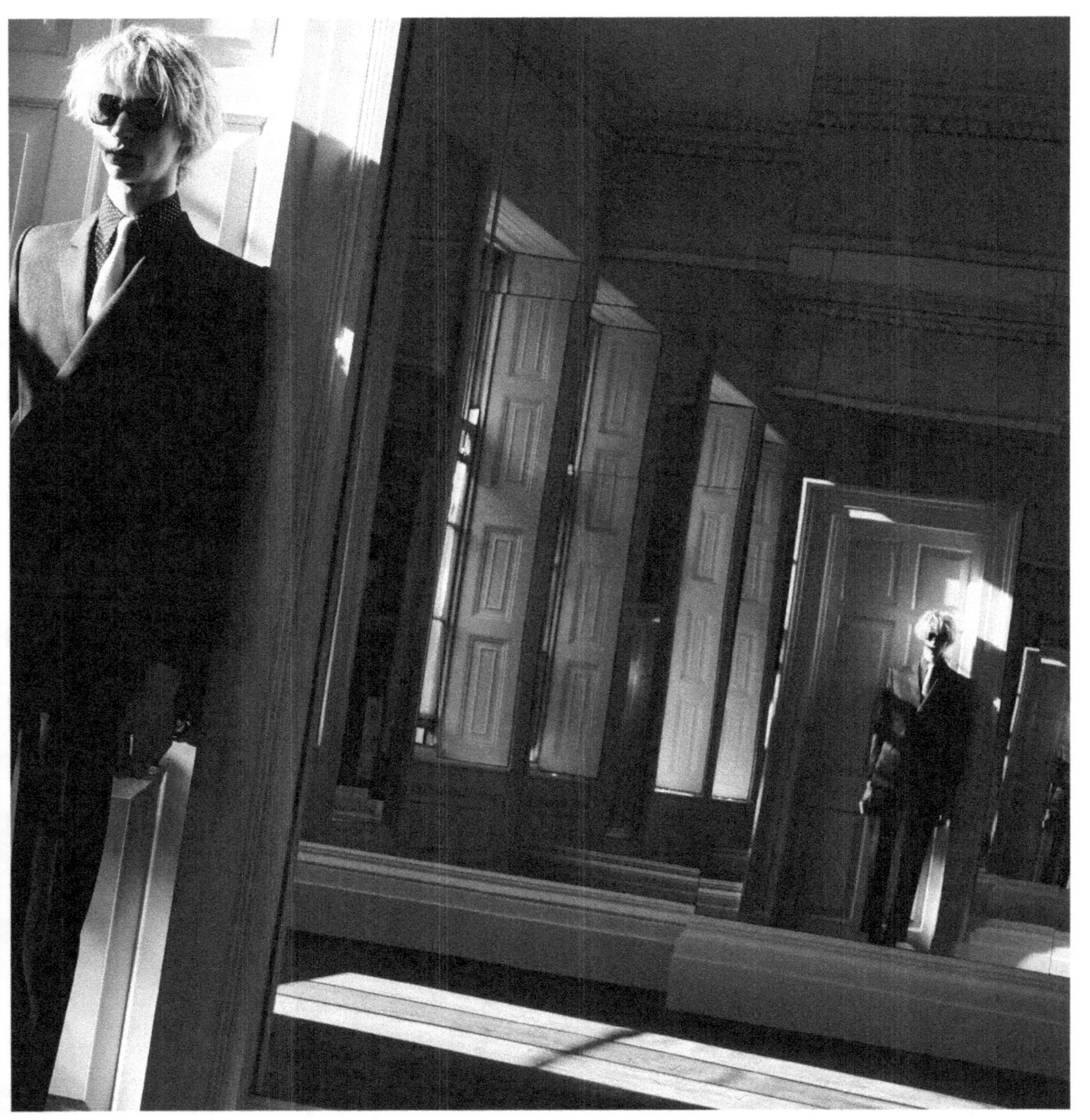

CELINE

GOLD STAR

Gold Star, otherwise known as Marlon Rabenreither, examines the highs, lows and in-betweens of life on his new album Uppers & Downers, *praised by critics for its classic '70s sound, insightful storytelling and understated pop sensibility.*

Drawing from his own life and conversations with friends, Rabenreither sings of the deeply personal and observational. His song "Dani's In Love," for instance, details a dark period in which his girlfriend "literally saved" his life. Throughout the album, the singer's beloved Los Angeles serves as its connective tissue.

Following a slot at the Pitchfork Avant-Garde Festival, shows with Phoebe Bridgers and a European tour, Gold Star is, as Clash *magazine (UK) puts it, "continually striding forward." Here, he discusses his influences, his musical parents, and why he'd like to pick Paul Simon's brain.*

———————

Where you from? I'm from Los Angeles.

When did you start making music? I've been doing it for a long

What felt like your first break? I don't think there was a first break. I think everything is always dependent on the people who support you and believe in you, whether it's fans or the people you work with. I think it's a long sequence of first breaks, and there are things yet to come as well.

> ## "I TEND TO JUST ADDRESS MY OWN LITTLE WORLD REALLY. MY OWN THOUGHTS, AND REAL STORIES— STORIES ABOUT A NEIGH- BORHOOD, FOR EXAMPLE. SOMETHING JUST HONEST AND SIMPLE."
>
> **— MARLON RABENREITHER**

time, since I was a teenager. But I've only been writing songs seriously for five years or so.

Who did you listen to growing up? Everything—the Beatles, Velvet Underground. Those are big ones, but all kinds of stuff.

How did you get started? My parents were musicians. They are pretty creative, and I think it was just always around. It just kind of made sense.

What life events have impacted you and your music the most? My friendships, and the kind of stories that I see, and the ongoing things. I think it's just all the cities I've been to, the people I've met and everything I got from that. I think that all influences me a great deal.

What is the story behind the name "Gold Star"? It was a Phil Spector recording studio in Hollywood, and

GOLD STAR
Marlon Rabenreither, who releases and performs music as Gold Star, is an Austrian-born singer, songwriter and guitarist raised and based in LA. Formerly a member of psych rock outfit The Sister Ruby Band, Rabenreither began his solo project in 2013. He has released three albums as Gold Star: *Dark Days* (2015), *Big Blue* (2017), and *Uppers & Downers* (2018).

PITCHFORK AVANT-GARDE FESTIVAL
Pitchfork Avant-Garde is a two-day Paris block party that takes place October 31 and November 1 ahead of the annual Pitchfork Music Festival Paris. The 2018 lineup included Rostam, Hundred Waters, Priests, Tennyson, Big Thief, Jamila Woods, Julie Byrne and Nick Hakim.

PHOEBE BRIDGERS
Phoebe Bridgers (b. 1994) is an American musician from Los Angeles. A graduate of Los Angeles County High School for the Arts, Bridgers released her 7" *Killer* on Ryan Adams' record label PAX AM in 2015. Her songs have been featured on TV shows *Switched At Birth*, *Castle* and *13 Reasons Why*. In 2017 Phoebe Bridgers signed to record label Dead Oceans.

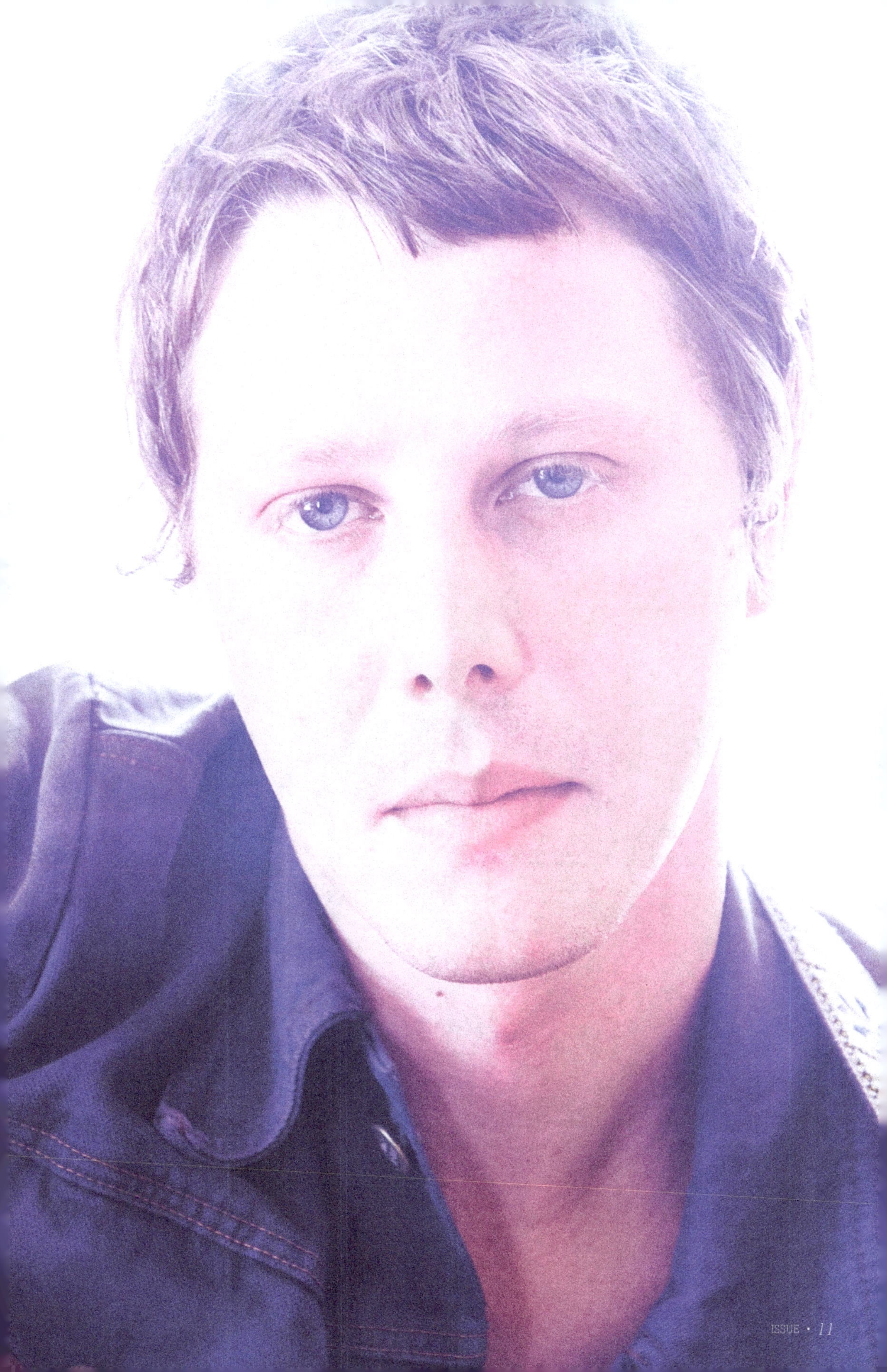

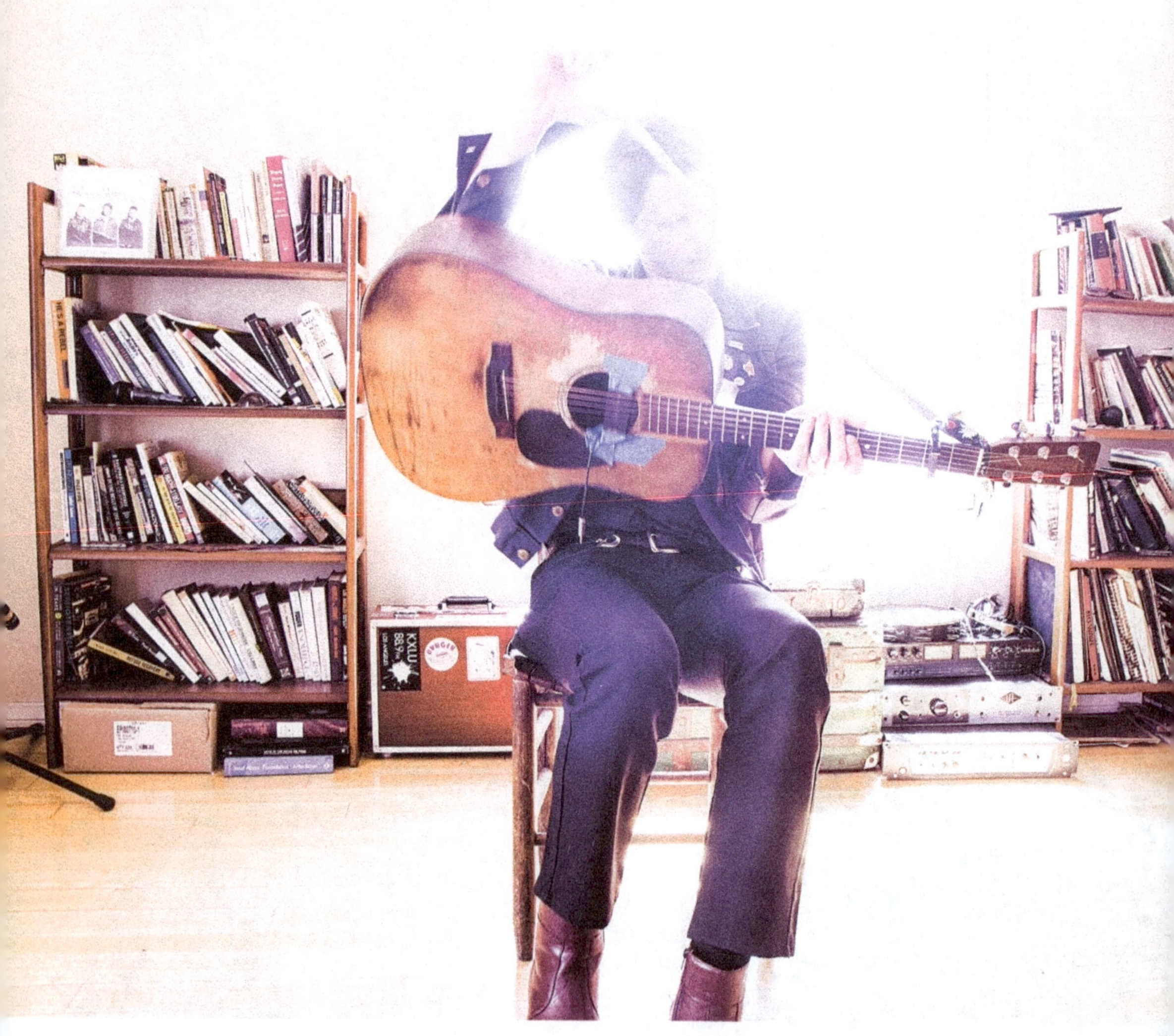

Brian Wilson worked out of there. I was interested in it and how it's from Hollywood, as I am, and it means a lot of things. I think it's open to interpretation.

Tell me a bit about your latest album *Uppers and Downers.* It's twelve songs, and I think they are all distinctly different. The deal was that there would be some very slow somber songs, as well as some upbeat rock and roll songs. I wanted to have a good contrast between these moods and, ideally, everything in between. Just basically the highs and lows of life, and to reflect that through these twelve distinct songs.

What are some things that are important to you, that you like

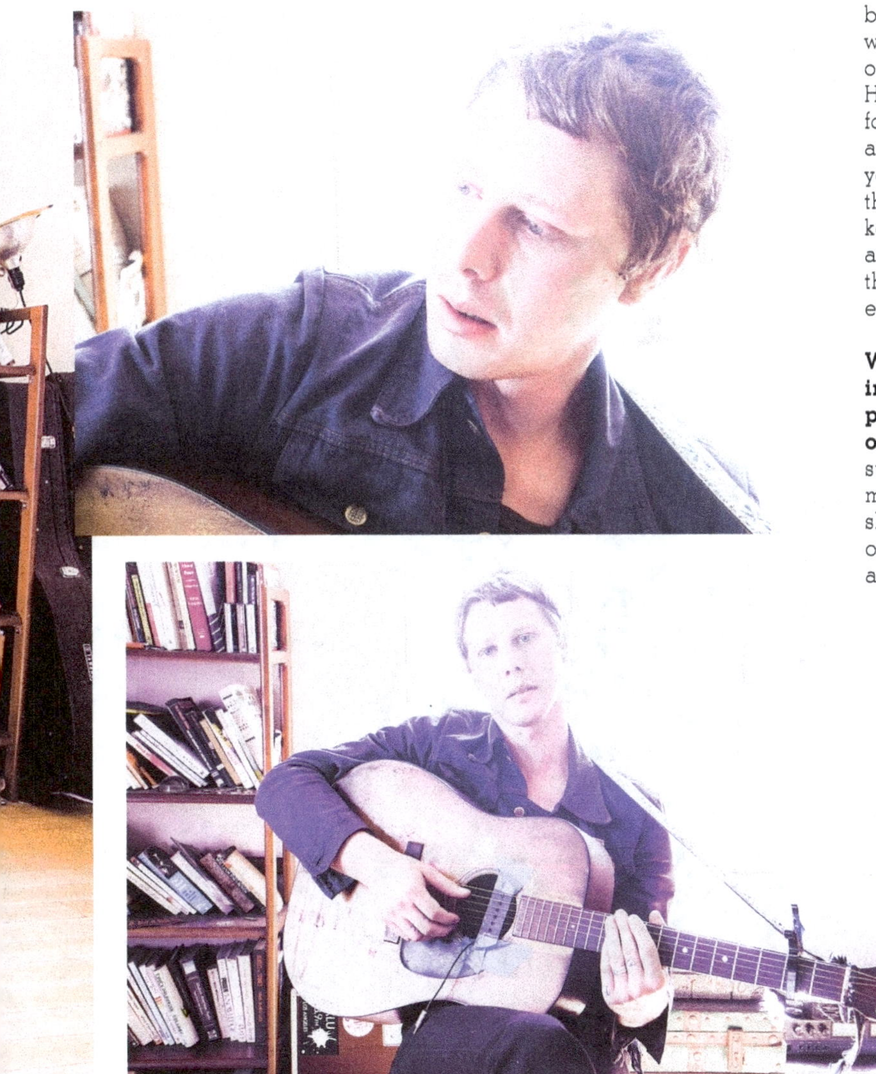

brain. Just to see what his thoughts on songwriting are. He's been doing it for such a long time, and it's like, how do you continuously do that? How do you keep growing as an artist? All those things I'd be interested in knowing.

What are your interests and passions outside of music? I like supporting other music and going to shows. And I'm fond of books. So those are the big two.

to address through music? I think I tend to just address my own little world really. My own thoughts and real stories— whether they are my experiences or my friends. Just to tell stories in that sense, even if they are really small interactions. Stories about a neighborhood, for example. Something just honest and simple in a way. I think that is something I try to address.

Who would you most like to collaborate with and why? That is an interesting question. I'd love to pick somebody like Paul Simon's

TIFFANY BOONE

Originally from Baltimore, Tiffany Boone is a graduate of California Institute of the Arts and the lead female actor on Showtime's highly acclaimed series The Chi. *In her role as Jerrika, Boone plays a girl from the "right" side of the tracks who encourages her boyfriend to outgrow his roots in hopes of opening a restaurant together. A familiar face to fans of the TV series* The Following *and the 2013 film* Beautiful Creatures, *Boone brings a no-nonsense force to the screen with what she terms "black girl magic."*

Birthplace: Baltimore, Maryland.

Ambitions: Make great art. Build a family. Start an art therapy school for children.

Favorite food: Steak and potatoes.

Your passion: All things black.

How did you get involved in this line of work? Who knows? I did impressions for my family and never stopped.

What will your mom say when she sees this? "My beautiful daughter."

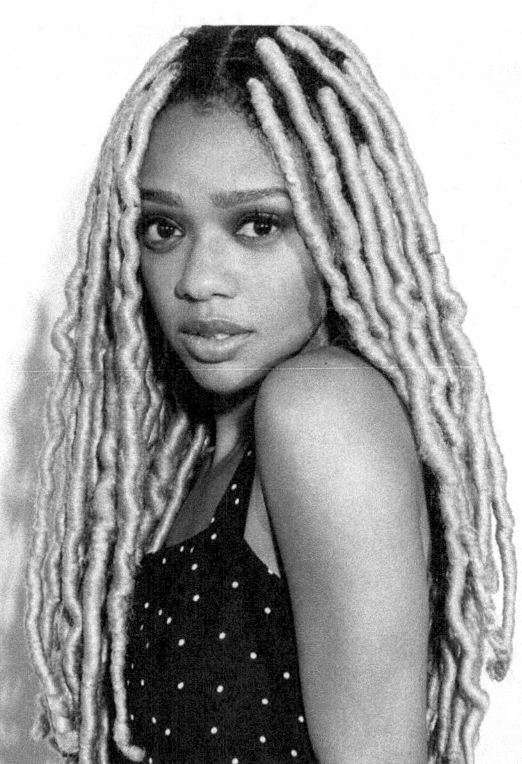

What was your first break? *The Following.*

What have you been in? *Grey's Anatomy, Complications, Beautiful Creatures, The Chi,* and some other stuff.

How do you feel about this career? It's hard, but it's getting better.

How did you decide to become an actor? I didn't decide. It decided.

How would you describe your specialty or type? Black girl magic.

Who's your favorite actor you look up to? Viola Davis.

What would your ideal job be? Art therapist.

Do you consider yourself to be lucky? I consider myself to be blessed.

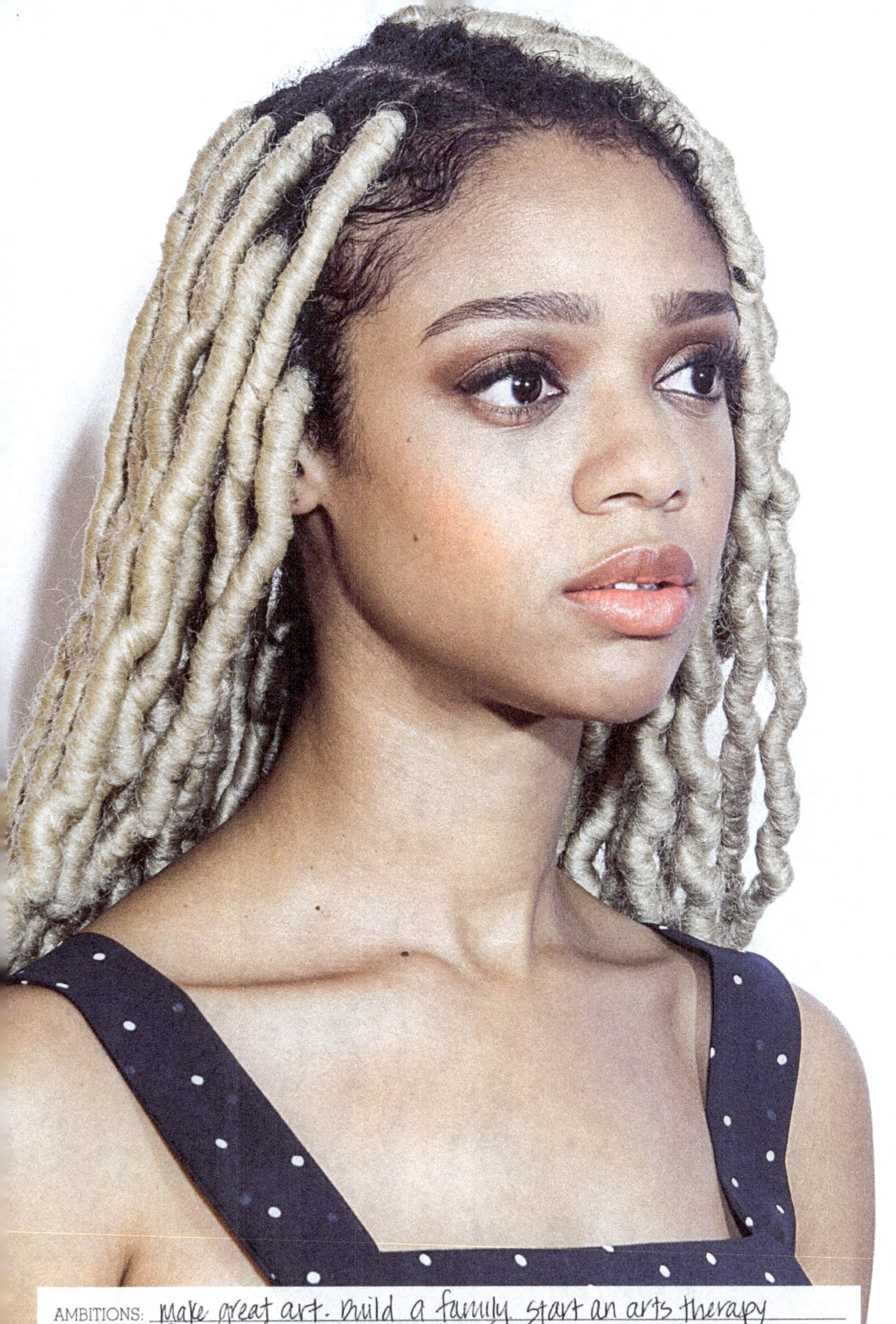

AMBITIONS: make great art. build a family. start an arts therapy school for children

YOUR PASSION: All things black.

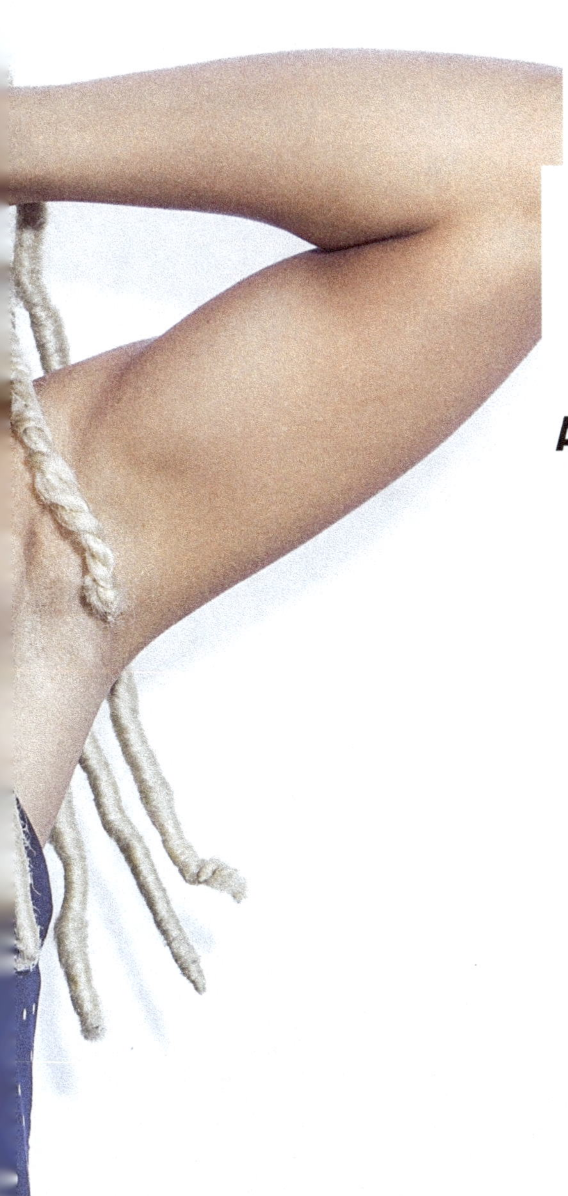

What advantages do you have? I actually take it as an advantage that I'm a black girl in a world where a lot of people might not think that is an advantage. The harder things are, the more joy we find in things.

Would you rather have a car or diploma? A diploma.

What do you think about the need for instant gratification? I think it's sad.

What challenges do you feel the world is facing today? Trump.

What are you most grateful for? Family.

What is your favorite way to communicate? Text. Do not call me.

What is your favorite book, film and music right now? I just read *Between The World and Me*—anything by Ta-Nehisi Coates. I'm about to watch *I, Tonya*, and I feel like that's going to be my

> **"I ACTUALLY TAKE IT AS AN ADVANTAGE THAT I'M A BLACK GIRL IN A WORLD WHERE A LOT OF PEOPLE MIGHT NOT THINK THAT IS AN ADVANTAGE. THE HARDER THINGS ARE, THE MORE JOY WE FIND IN THINGS."**
> — TIFFANY BOONE

How do you feel about how interconnected the world is becoming? I think there are some positives to it. We can learn a lot more about each other, but somehow it's pushing us further away.

What does the future look like to you? The future is female.

How do you feel about having children? Two more years, hopefully.

favorite film. And Jay-Z's *4:44* is my favorite music right now.

LOLA KIRKE

Actress and singer-songwriter Lola Kirke began her musical journey in 2016 when she released her self-titled EP. The collection of four songs introduced her country-rock influences and breathy vocals, a shift from her steadily

in East Los Angeles with partner and producer Wyndham Garnett. Kirke spoke with us about exploring the difference between acting and music, her album title, and her undying love of "dad rock."

"WHEN I'M STUCK WRITING A SONG, I REALIZE THAT THE SONG WILL STAY WITH ME UNTIL IT NEEDS TO. IT CAN BE A GREAT FRIEND AND SOMETHING TO RETURN TO EVERY SINGLE NIGHT."

— LOLA KIRKE

growing acting career that includes major roles in the Amazon series Mozart in the Jungle *(2014-18) and films* Mistress America *(2015) and* Gone Girl *(2014). Kirke has since released her debut album,* Heart Head West *(2018), delving into themes of self-esteem, alienation and longing. She recorded the album*

Where are you from? I'm from New York, but I live in Los Angeles. I am also sort of from London.

When did you start making music? In the early '90s, there were these keychains that you could talk into, and it would play yourself back to you. It was amazing. I think I wrote my first song on a Yak Pak when I was five. Then I took a long break and started making music again when I was eighteen with a ukulele.

Who did you listen to growing up? I listened to all sorts of different music. I've always been a dad rock fan. I remember waking up in the back seat of the car when I was a kid to the guitar solo in Led Zeppelin's "Since I've Been Loving You," and being like, "What is this, guys?" They told me what it was, and that was kind of the beginning of my intro-

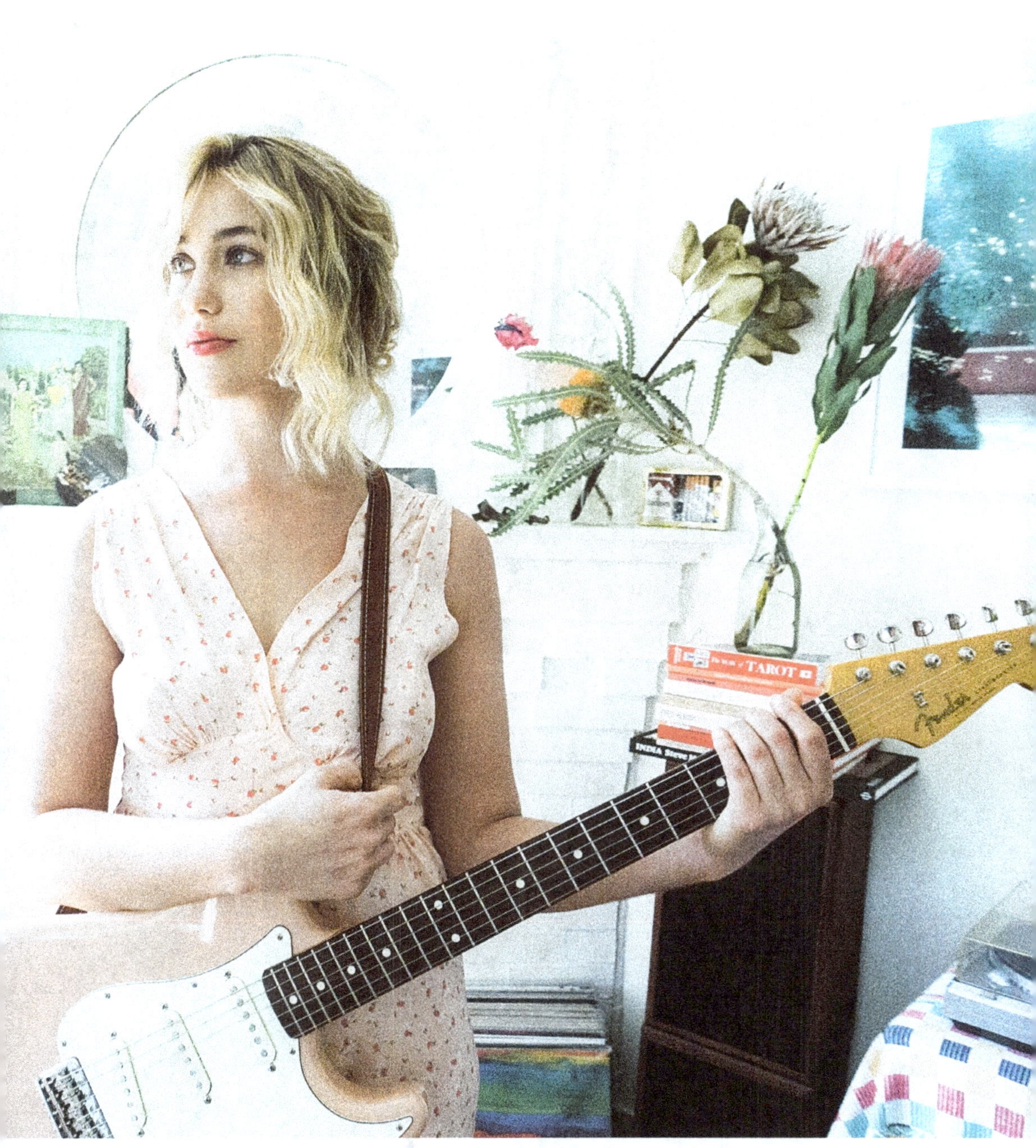

duction to rock'n'roll. The music that inspires me the most now would be if you could take Crosby, Stills, Nash and Young, and draw a family tree that goes down. It would be Gene Clark, Gram Parsons, all of their solo bands. Then it would peter out into all these other bands. That would be the core of my musical taste.

How did you get started? I had an all-girl country band in college. That was the first time I started playing music publicly. Then that petered out, and I was writing songs alone. I would always bring my guitar with me when I would shoot movies because being on location can be incredibly lonely.

When you're a band and you tour with

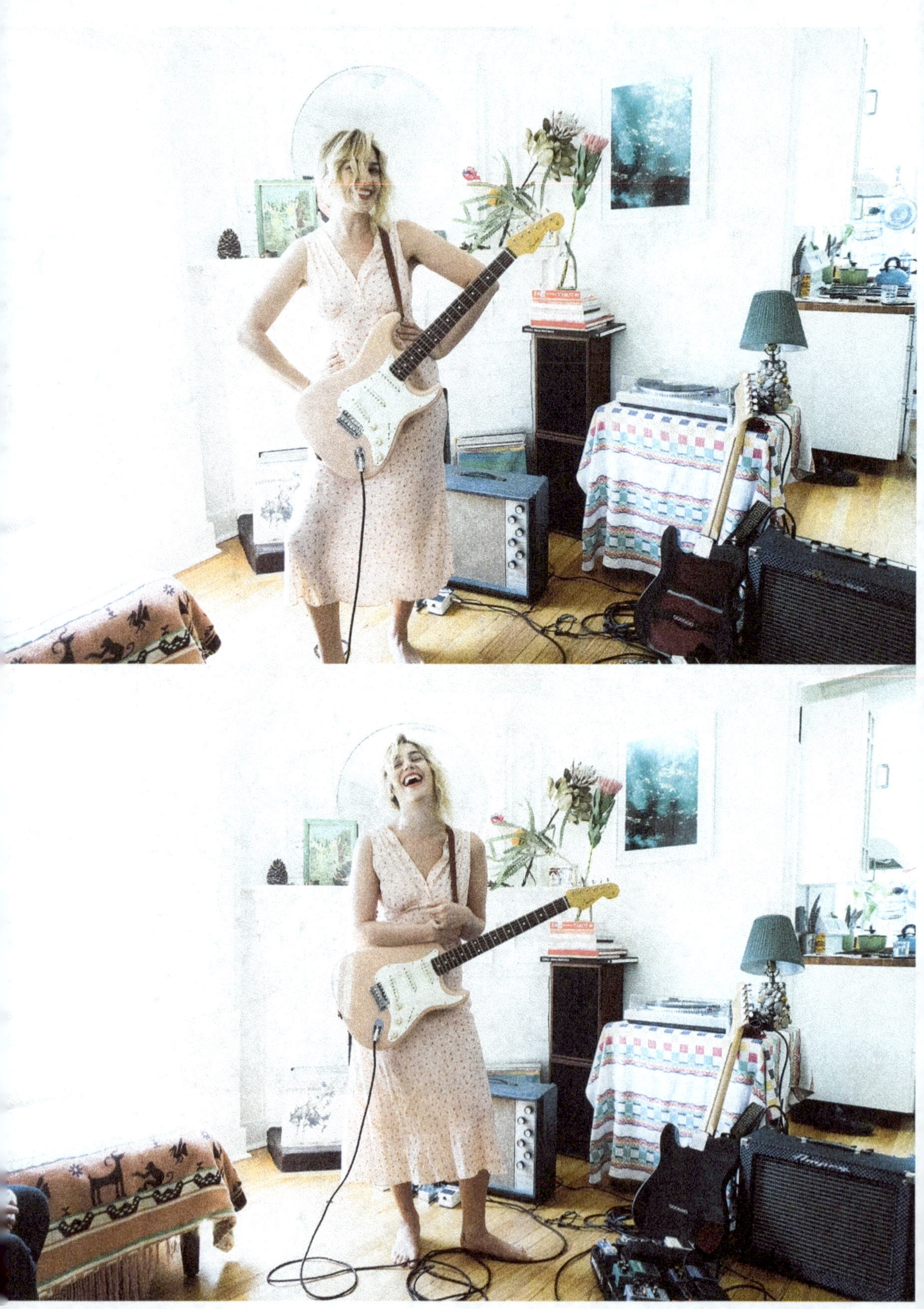

your friends, you're going to a new place every single night. When you're an actor, oftentimes, you're completely alone, and they just plop you into the middle of nowhere because they have really good tax incentives there. It sounds so corny, but my guitar kept me company. I found that songs actually kept me company too. When I'm stuck writing a song, I realize that the song will stay with me until it needs to. It can be a great friend and something to return to every single night.

for very few people, and people that would come would be fans of a character.

They wanted me to be an oboist because I played an oboist on TV for a while. It was exciting that people would show up in that way, but it was also like, "That's not why I'm here." Now people are beginning to pay attention to the music, and it's a really strange feeling. It's affirming in a way I never expected to be affirmed.

How did your debut album come about? It came about pretty

everything live to tape. All of the songs were written in 2017, and they are about a range of things. There's not one specific through line, except things I think about excessively.

What is the meaning of the name *Heart Head West*? It's a version of a line from my song "Out Yonder". If there was a through line on this record, it might be about longing. "Heart head west" was a line about longing—specifically a longing to be where you aren't. The west is such a symbol of

> ## "A LOT OF MY WORK IS KIND OF BORN OF LOW SELF-ESTEEM, AND I DON'T KNOW THAT I WOULD HAVE MUCH TO MAKE IF I WASN'T CONSTANTLY TRYING TO RESOLVE SOMETHING OR AFFIRM SOMETHING FOR MYSELF."
>
> **— LOLA KIRKE**

My partner and the producer of both my record and EP, Wyndham Garnett, was like, "You should make a record," and I was like, "Okay, cool." Then we made a record and it was really fun.

When do you feel you got your first break? Now. My first break as a musician. Right now people are actually paying attention to my music for the first time, separate from certain characters I've played. A lot of times I would play shows in the middle of nowhere

organically. I had made this EP, and then I was touring the EP for a while with a bunch of musicians who were so supportive of me and liked the music. They were like, "You should make a record." And when enough people say that to you, those things that feel like they might be far off or out of reach begin to seem like a possibility.

So, I got together with this group of musicians that I'd been playing with for a while, and we went to this studio in Boyle Heights. We recorded

freedom, both personal and political.

What are some things that are important to you that you like to address through your music? Specifically longing, not just longing for other people, but longing for things that you want for yourself. A lot of my work is kind of born of low self-esteem, and I don't know that I would have much to make if I wasn't constantly trying to resolve something or affirm something for myself.

I hope that other

people can feel seen in their own struggles with self-love through my music. Music is capable of doing that because there are many artists who have made me feel like the deepest, darkest reaches of my soul are in good company.

As a means of expression, how does that compare or contrast to your work as an actor? I have so many questions about what acting really is, but as an actor, I am using myself to become or express a different person. If I do my job at my best, then people will believe that I am another person. As a musician, I am becoming the greatest version of myself. I'm coming into an awareness about that distinction. One is about transforming into other people, and one is about transforming into me.

Who would you most like to collaborate with and why? I already am grateful to collaborate with so many people. My friends are all incredible musicians. From my friend Cornelia Murr to Lilah Larson, who I was just playing with and who is in Sons of an Illustrious Father, and Amo Amo. The list goes on, but those are people I'm already grateful to collaborate with. It would be cool if Emmylou Harris wanted to sing with me.

What are your interests and passions outside of music? People. I am very passionate about acting, reproductive rights, changing the world, being a source of love and light, and seeking out others who want to do the same. And happiness.

What's your favorite book, film, and music right now? I got turned onto this Fleetwood Mac record I had never heard before called *Future Games*, which is really incredible. It's pre-Stevie Nicks and Lindsey Buckingham.

I'm reading *A Dream of Passion* by Lee Stroudsburg right now. A lot of people think of acting as just this thing that people do, and not as an art form. It's been really exciting for me to read about people who are not taking a passive approach towards acting and to develop even more respect for this thing that I already love so much.

I just rewatched *Three Women*. I said that was my favorite film when I was a teenager because I wanted to sound cool. I rewatched it a couple weeks ago, and I was like, "Oh, I didn't get that movie at all." Shelley Duvall, Sissy Spacek and Janice Rule, all of those performances in that movie are incredible. And I love Robert Altman's filmmaking.

is an American singer-songwriter and musician who has released thirty albums over the span of her career and won fourteen Grammys. She has worked with numerous artists including Bob Dylan, Gram Parsons, Linda Ronstadt, and Dolly Parton.

THREE WOMEN
Written and directed by Robert Altman, *Three Women* (1977) is an American avant-garde drama film starring Shelley Duvall, Sissy Spacek and Janice Rule. It depicts the relationship between a woman and her roommate in a mysterious California desert town.

> ## "AS AN ACTOR, I AM USING MYSELF TO BECOME OR EXPRESS A DIFFERENT PERSON... AS A MUSICIAN, I AM BECOMING THE GREATEST VERSION OF MYSELF."
>
> — LOLA KIRKE

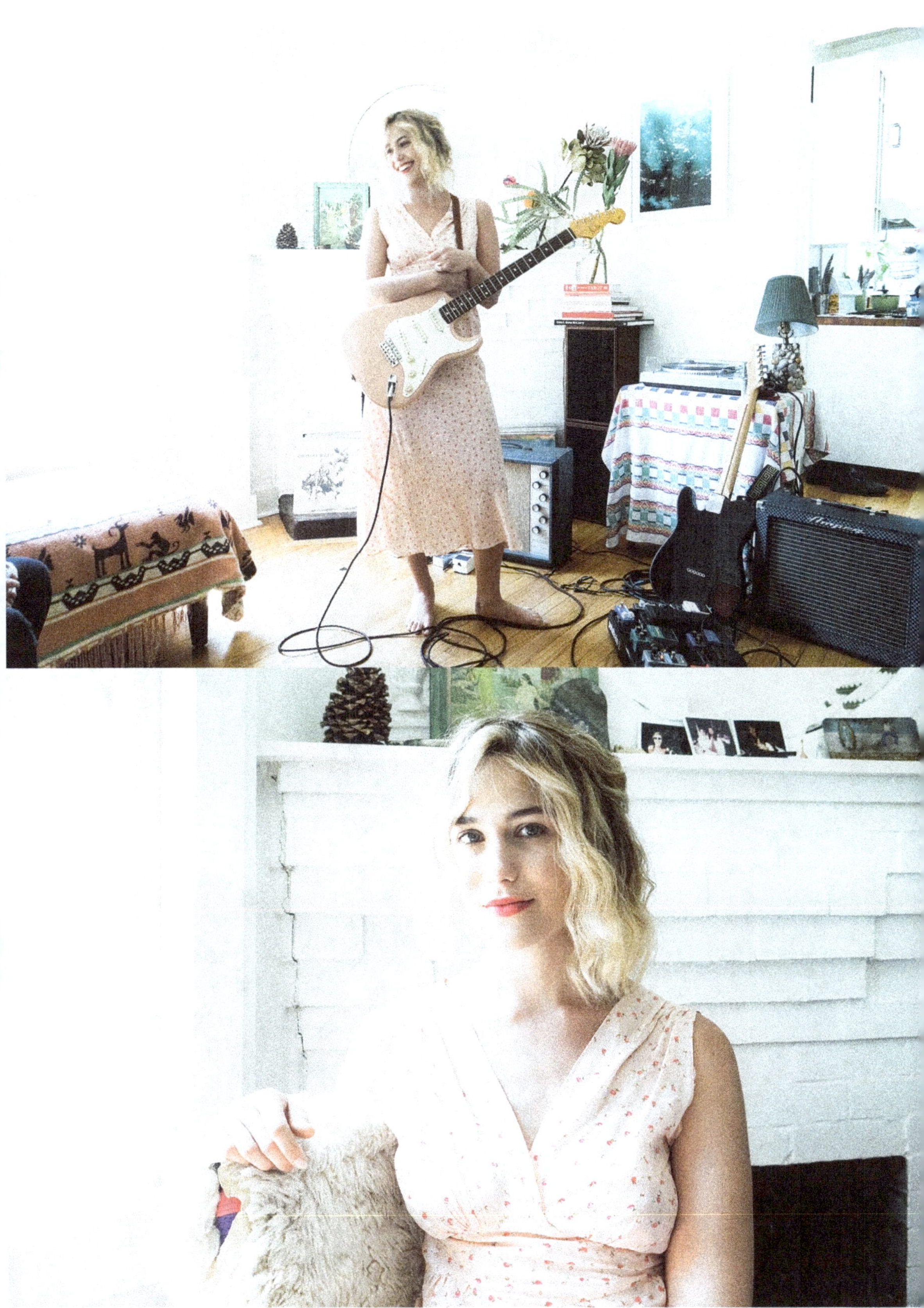

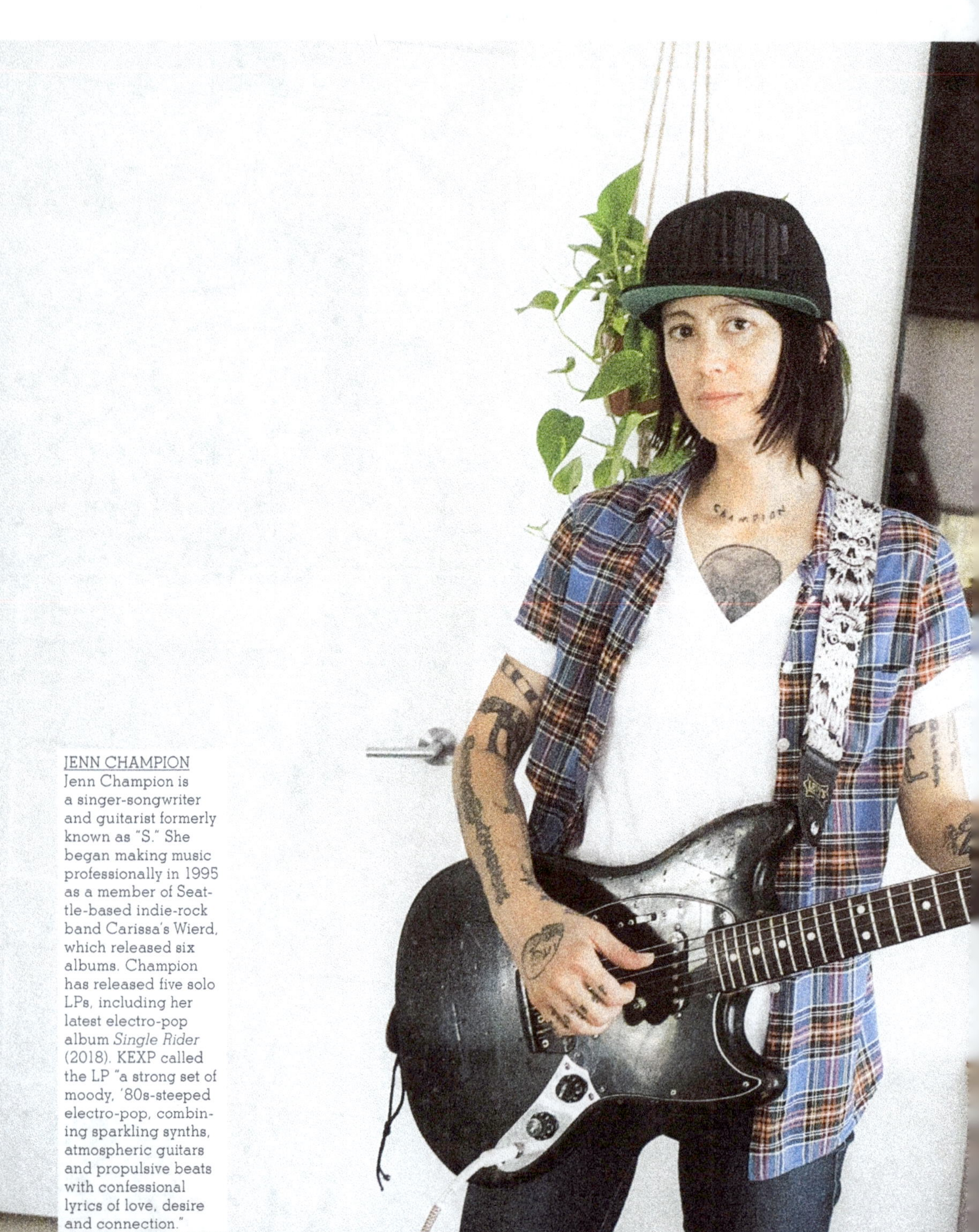

JENN CHAMPION
Jenn Champion is a singer-songwriter and guitarist formerly known as "S." She began making music professionally in 1995 as a member of Seattle-based indie-rock band Carissa's Wierd, which released six albums. Champion has released five solo LPs, including her latest electro-pop album *Single Rider* (2018). KEXP called the LP "a strong set of moody, '80s-steeped electro-pop, combining sparkling synths, atmospheric guitars and propulsive beats with confessional lyrics of love, desire and connection."

JENN CHAMPION

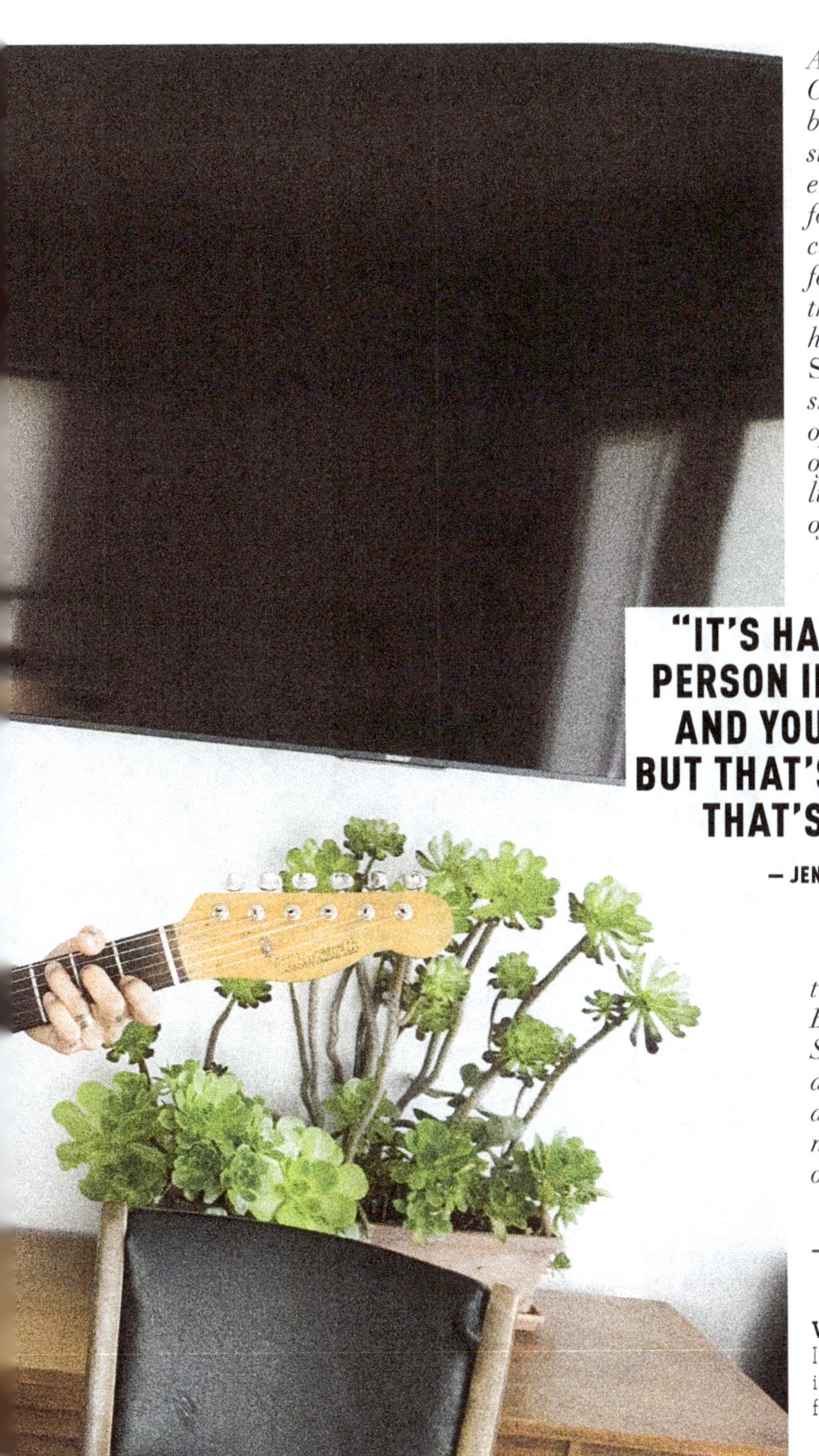

After her band Carissa's Wierd broke up in 2003, singer-songwriter Jenn Champion focused on her solo career, releasing four albums under the moniker "S". On her latest album, Single Rider *(2018), she employs the same open-hearted lyrics of her past work, delivering a collection of synth-filled dance*

"IT'S HARD TO BE A PERSON IN THE WORLD AND YOU STRUGGLE, BUT THAT'S PART OF IT— THAT'S THE DEAL."

— JENN CHAMPION

tracks produced by Bryan Fennell (aka SYML). She speaks about failure, being a "goth kid" and her new-found love of outrun music.

———

Where are you from?
I am currently living in Los Angeles, but I'm from Seattle.

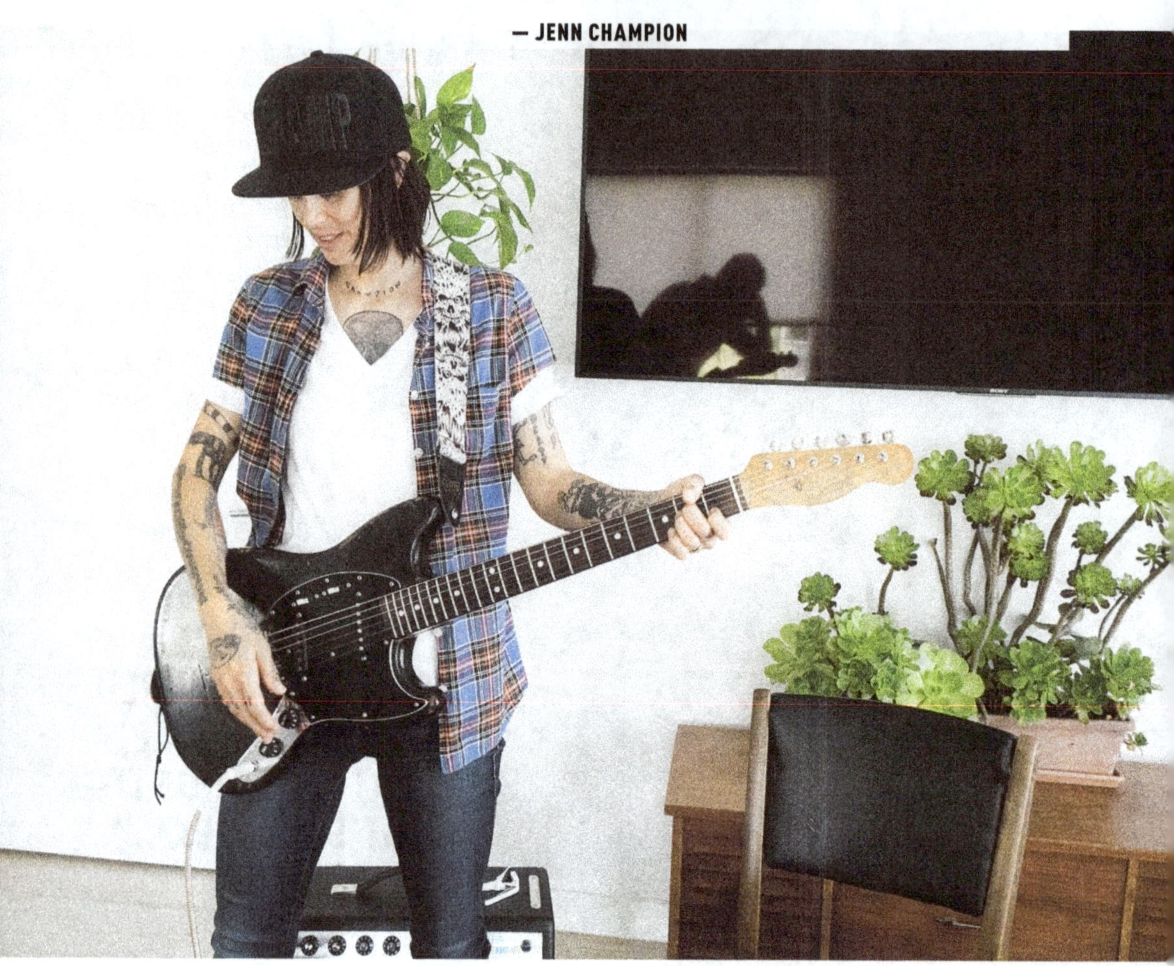

When did you start making music? Probably as a teenager—I've played music since I was a little kid.

Who did you listen to growing up? Middle school was George Michael and Madonna, but they became closet faves in high school. I was like, "People can't know I listen to Madonna." There was also Jane's Addiction and The Cure. I was kind of a goth kid.

So how did you actually get started? I had some friends that played music or played guitar, and they were like, "Hey, can you play this too?" Then all of sudden we were in a band together.

When do you feel you got you first break? Probably being able to play a show in some sense—somebody letting me get up in front of people and play music.

So, tell me a bit about your debut LP as Jenn Champion. It's kind of a record meant to be danced to—even chair dancing, bed dancing, on-the-bus dancing. I love dancing. I was going to use all these synthesizers and some drum tracks. Luckily I had help from a producer because I was like, "I don't know how to do this very well." I can make a beat on a drum machine, but for making it cooler, that's

when a producer really comes in handy. It goes from a super fun dance record, and by the end you're probably crying because it's also sad.

What would you say the big difference is between your work now versus under the name "S"? It's a more high-fi sound now, and I worked really hard to polish up the songs more than I ever have.

What are some things

**that are important
to you that you like
to address through
your music?** Feelings.
Being able to talk
about being sad or
dealing with failure.
It's hard to be a person
in the world, and you
struggle, but that's part
of it. That's the deal.

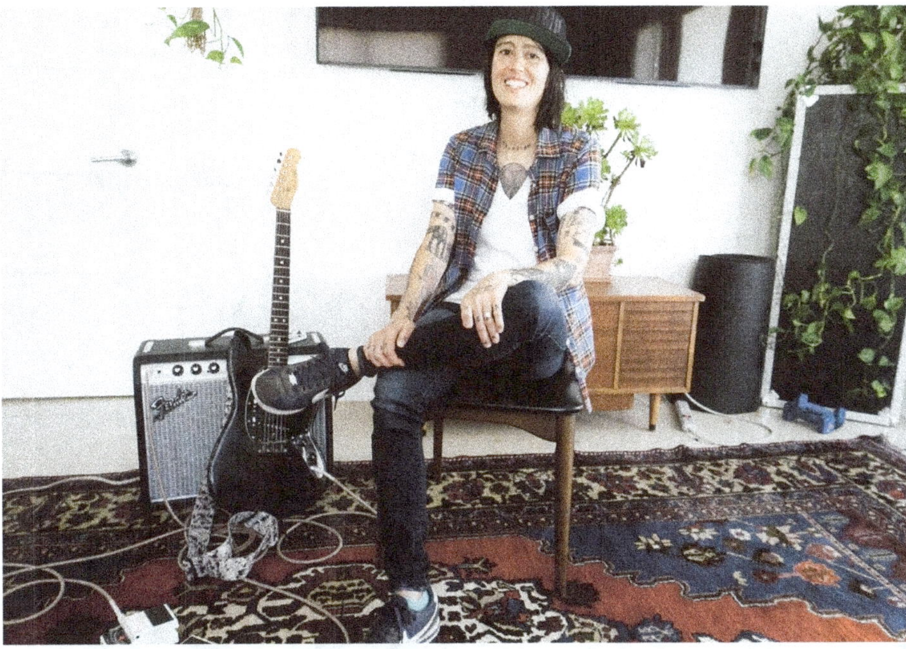

There's a lot of failure,
and there's a lot of
struggling. I guess to
say, "I feel it too," and
hopefully bring some
solidarity to other folks
in the same situation.

**Who would you most
like to collaborate
with and why?** What
comes to mind off the
top of my head is Cardi
B because I really en-
joyed her album, and
trap music is something
I don't know very much
about—I haven't taken
it apart and tried to figure out how it's done.
Things like that interest
me, and she seems like

a wonderful person to
hang out with.
**What are your inter-
ests and passions
outside of music?** I
love dancing. My goal
this year is to learn
how to dance for real.
I have two dogs. I
enjoy lots of art—just
being in the arts, being
around people that do
art, looking at art, see-
ing what other people
are making and talking
to other people about
making stuff.

**What's your favorite
book, film and music
right now?** Book: I
know it's a real faux
pas, but it's been a
while since I've picked
up a book.

I definitely watch
a lot of television. I
watch a lot of movies. I
just watched the show
Barry, starring that guy
from *Saturday Night
Live*. I did see the
Whitney documentary.

You could tell some
parts were missing,
but I cried through the
whole thing.

I'm really into
outrun music right now.
It's kind of '80s, synthy
and mostly instrumen-
tal. I think it stems from
this video game from
the 80s that had this
synth soundtrack, but
I found this song that I
really liked, and then
I was like, "I gotta look
it up. I gotta figure out
this artist." Then I dove
into this whole genre.
There's a band called
Miami Nights 1984.
That's probably my
favorite one. There's
the band College who
you might know from
having a song on the
Drive soundtrack. I en-
joyed that movie. Cliff
Martinez does some
scoring—who I think
is quite amazing at it.
I wish I could do that
kind of thing.

ESTHER POVITSKY

Esther Povitsky has come a long way since her days as a comedy student in Chicago. She co-created and stars in Freeform's Alone Together *(2018) and was recently named one of Variety's "10 Comics to Watch." Along with guest-starring in shows for*

Where are you from? I grew up in Skokie, Illinois and lived there until I was twenty-one. I went to college, but then I moved here, meaning LA.

Favorite food? Spaghetti with red sauce never gets old.

Turn-offs: People who play games or are too charming. Extra charm is always a problematic sign.

What will your mom say when she sees this? "You couldn't blow dry your hair or iron your shirt?"

What was your first break? There's no such

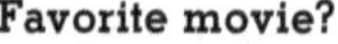

> ## "THERE'S NO SUCH THING AS A BREAK ANYMORE. THIS IS 2018: YOU HAVE TO DO A MILLION THINGS TO WORK UP TO HALF A BREAK."
>
> **— ESTHER POVITSKY**

Netflix and Hulu, Povitsky also hosted a sex talk show for women titled Cocktales with Esther *in 2015 and regularly performs stand-up across Los Angeles. She tells us what a career-altering break looks like in 2018, her beliefs about luck and her deep gratitude for her dog.*

Favorite movie? *Bridesmaids* and anything with Brittany Murphy in it.

Artist you would most like to work with: Lady Gaga, Kristen Wiig.

Your idea of heaven: Dogs, oat milk lattes, really comfy sneakers.

Turn-ons: Smarts, niceness, big noses!

thing as a break anymore. This is 2018: you have to do a million things to work up to half a break. Right now I have my show, *Alone Together*, and we're filming season two. I also have my podcast, *Glowing Up*. I'm also a stand-up comedian, but none of those are a break.

What have you been

ESTHER POVITSKY
Esther Povitsky is a writer, actor and comedian who co-created and stars in Freeform's *Alone Together* (2018). She has previously guest starred on The CW's *Crazy Ex-Girlfriend* (2015), Netflix's *Love* (2016) and Hulu's *Difficult People* (2015). Before moving to Los Angeles, Povitsky studied comedy at Chicago's Second City.

ALONE TOGETHER
Alone Together is a comedy series starring Esther Povitsky and Benji Aflalo and produced by The Lonely Island's Andy Samberg, Akiva Schaffer and Jorma Taccone. The film follows two platonic millennial friends navigating life, love and status in Los Angeles.

GLOWING UP
Glowing Up is a podcast series featuring comedian Esther Povitsky and writer Caroline Goldfarb that delves into the worlds of beauty, health and diet.

THE SUBTLE ART OF NOT GIVING A FUCK
The Subtle Art of Not Giving a Fuck is the second book by blogger and author Mark Manson. The book is a provocative reaction to the self-help industry and "a culture of mindless positivity."

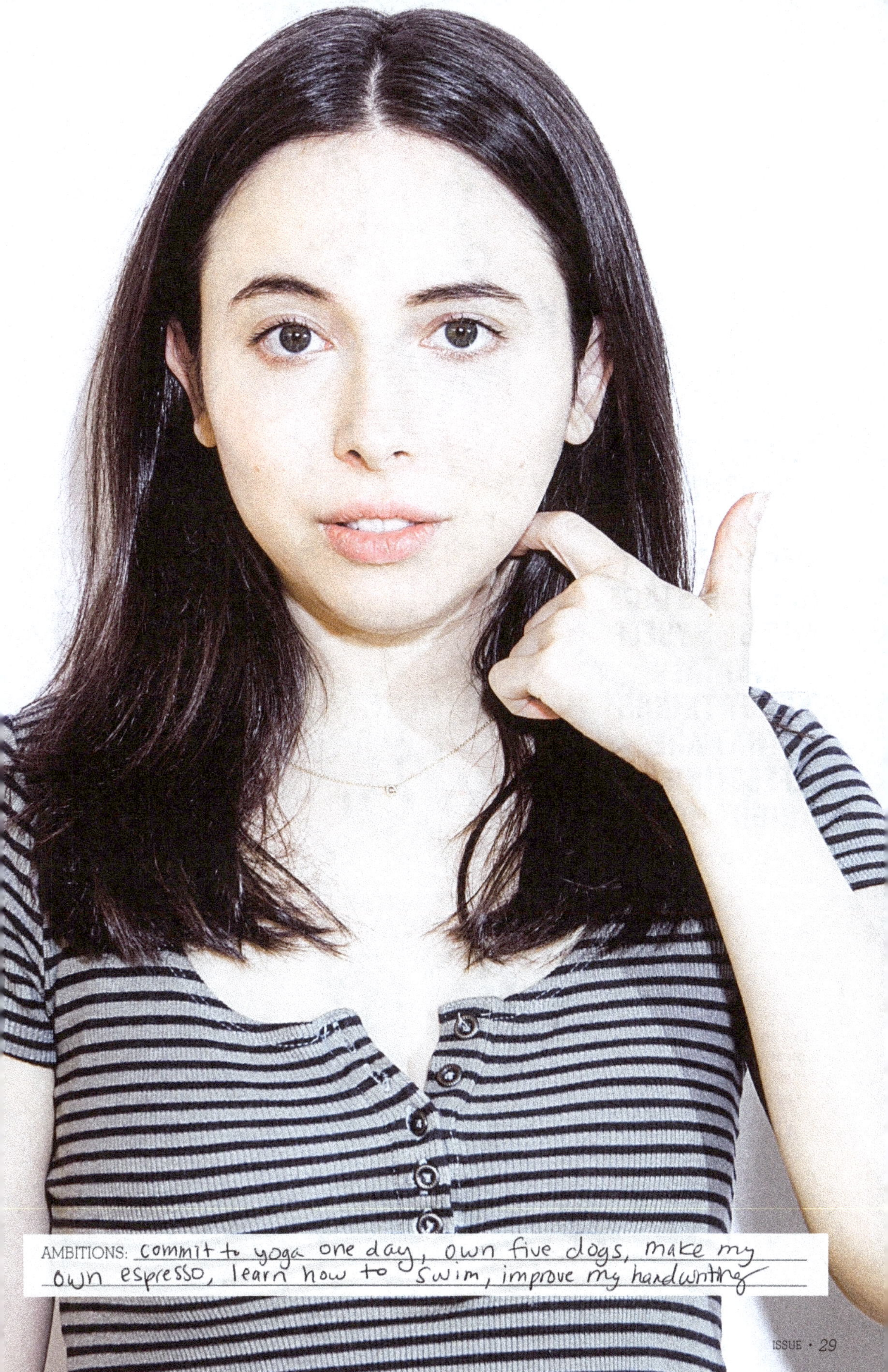

AMBITIONS: commit to yoga one day, own five dogs, make my
own espresso, learn how to swim, improve my handwriting

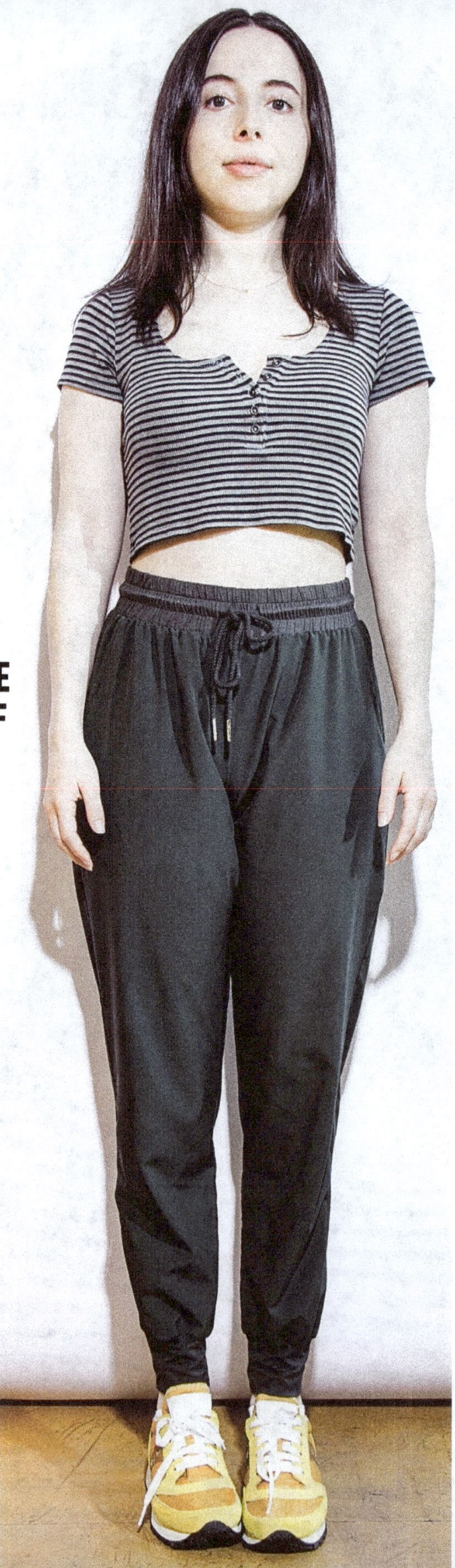

in? I'm on a show called *Crazy Ex-Girlfriend*. I play Maya, who's basically just me if I had a job as… a paralegal? I never know what my job is on that show. Sometimes I think I'm an office assistant.

I also have my show *Alone Together*, about me and my best friend living in LA and being misfits. We're in a platonic male-female

"MY FAVORITE PART IS MY STAND-UP BECAUSE I GET TO GO ON STAGE AND BE MYSELF AND TALK ABOUT THINGS THAT ARE AFFECTING ME RIGHT NOW."

— ESTHER POVITSKY

friendship, and we're never getting together. That's kind of the law of the show.

How do you feel about this career? It's fun and cool. My favorite part is my stand-up because I get to go on stage and be myself and talk about things that are affecting me right now. That's just very fun to do. So I feel fine about this career. I mean, sometimes it's hard to not lay in bed all day, but I think everybody feels that way.

How did you decide to become an actor? I decided I would be a stand-up comedian when I was twenty-one. I dropped out of college and moved to LA to pursue stand-up, and then through that I realized I wanted to write TV and stuff for myself to act in. It just kind of happened. When you're in LA, it's like you become an actor by just being here. Drinking all that pressed juice just makes you an actor.

How would you describe your specialty or type? I don't have a specialty or type. I'm just myself and that's that.

What actor do you look up to? I really like Rachel McAdams. I'll never forget her iconic performances in *Mean Girls* and *The Notebook*. They happened so close together and were such a big part of my formative years. Of course I love Tiffany Haddish because she's my friend, but I'm also really proud of her, and she's funny.

What would your ideal job be? Working on a farm with a million puppies. Everyone loves puppies. I know it's fucking basic, but sometimes it's okay to be basic. It's a big deal in our culture for a reason, and it's because we are all a little bit basic.

Do you consider yourself to be lucky? I don't believe in luck because my dad is a compulsive gambler, so he's taught me that there is no such thing as luck.

What advantages do you have? People say I'm pretty, but I don't know or see that because I don't identify as that. But I'm starting to be like, "Ok, I guess I must be kind of cute."

Would you rather have a car or diploma? A car. I wasn't allowed to have a car because we couldn't afford it when I was in high school. I wanted a car so bad, and when I finally got a car in LA it was just the best. I still have dreams about how happy I am that I have a car and what it was like when I didn't have a car. I never even look at my diploma.

How do you feel about how interconnected the world is becoming? I feel really good because it lets me connect with my parents more, and I love that I can reach people far away. I recently did a tour of Australia, and it was so cool that I had fans in a place so unimaginably far away.

What does the future look like to you? The future looks like an oat milk latte and maybe some kind of breakfast food that has avocado in it. I'm basic. It all goes back to the basics.

How do you feel about having children? I don't know how I feel about having children, but my parents have very mixed feelings about me having children, which is stressful.

say it all the time because we all want to be grateful, but we're not present and it's hard to do. Every time I see her and cuddle her, I think about how she's my dream come true and how I'm so happy she's in my life.

What is your favorite way to communicate? I don't like texting because it hurts my

able with is the best.

What is your favorite book, film and music right now? Music will always be female pop. Right now I'm revisiting Katy Perry's *Teenage Dream* album. I'm having a renaissance with it. For film, I love *Sunset Boulevard*. I've re-watched that a lot. For books, I'm reading *The Subtle Art of Not*

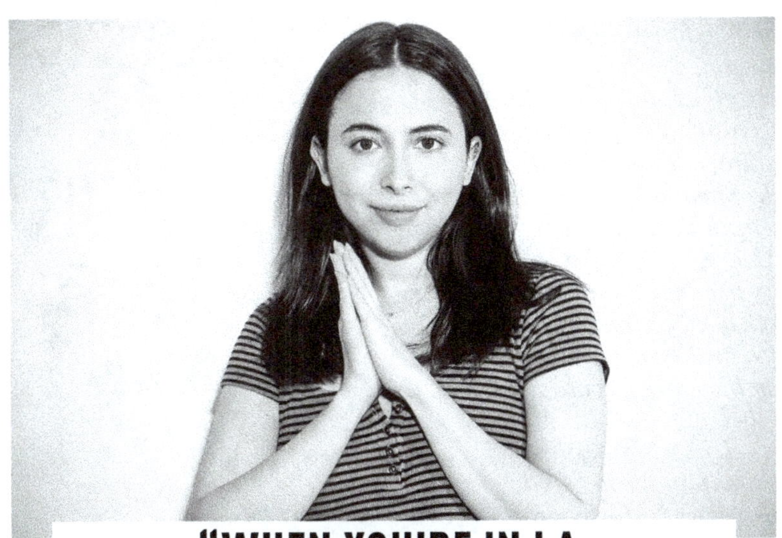

What challenges do you feel the world is facing today? The world is facing so many challenges that I couldn't stand here and list them. Factory farming is awful and so are a lot of other horrible things that are happening.

What are you most grateful for? I'm so grateful for my dog. I

hands. I don't like talking on the phone because I'm friends with a lot of people who love talking, which I love, but sometimes it's too much, and it's hard to get off the phone. My favorite way to communicate is with people who I can just say, "Shut up. I'm going. Bye." Communicating with people that you're really comfort-

Giving a Fuck, and I really like where he's going with things.

ANNA ST. LOUIS

Interview by **Kevin Morby**
Images by **Jan-Willem Dikkers**

Kansas City-raised songwriter Anna St. Louis made a stir in the LA music scene last year with her cassette First Songs *(2017), a folk and country-tinged document of her initial explorations as a songwriter and guitarist. She recently dropped her full-length debut* If Only There Was A River, *co-produced and released by long-time friend Kevin Morby on his Mare Records label.*

Himself an established songwriter and performer, Morby remembers a young St. Louis fronting a punk band in their home town—an unexpected beginning for someone who, according to Morby, creates a gentle world "where the heart leads straight to the soul and everything is cloaked in beautiful mystery."

With If Only There Was A River *steadily gaining fans like NPR's* All Songs Considered *(which premiered the video for first single*

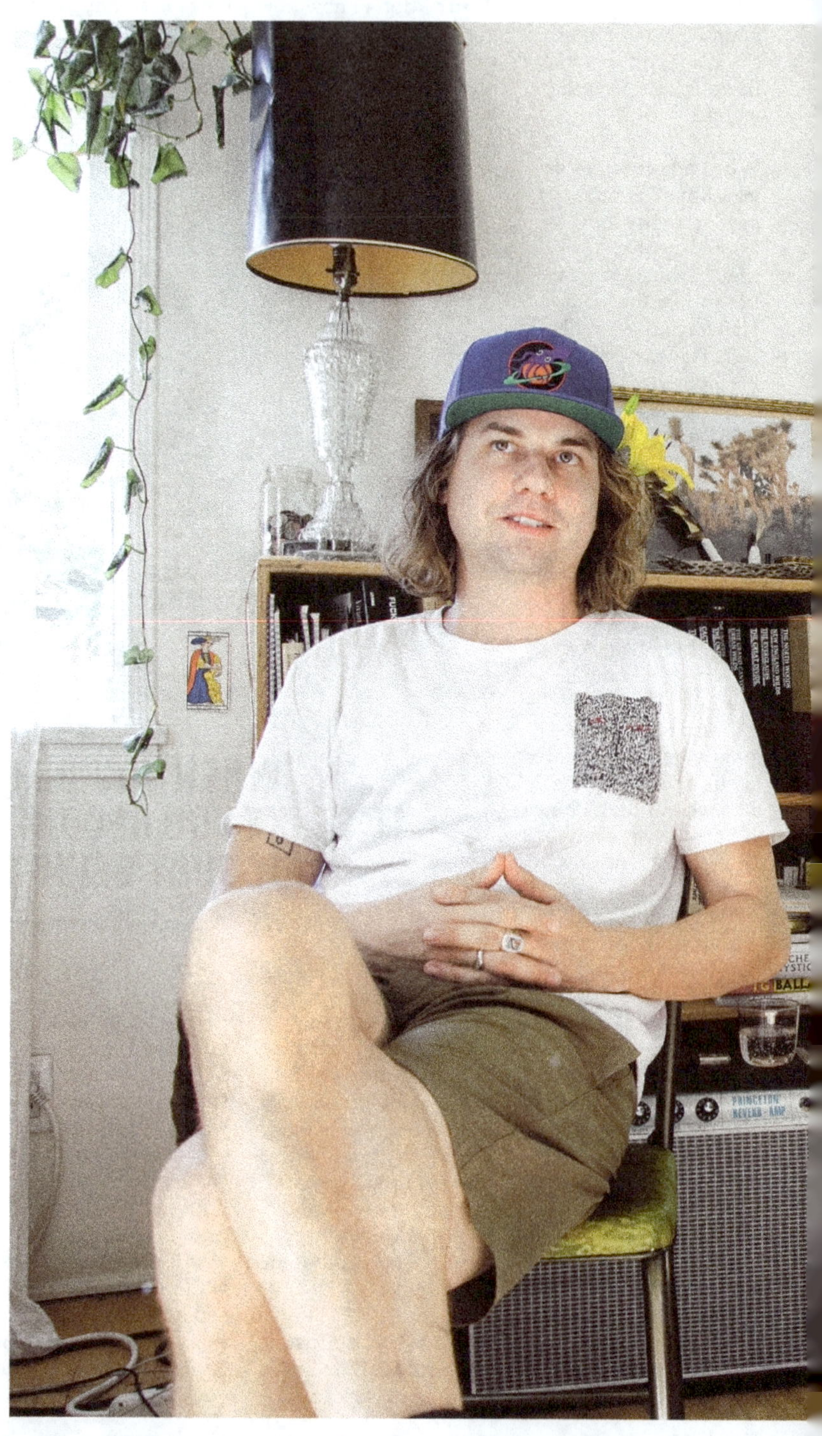

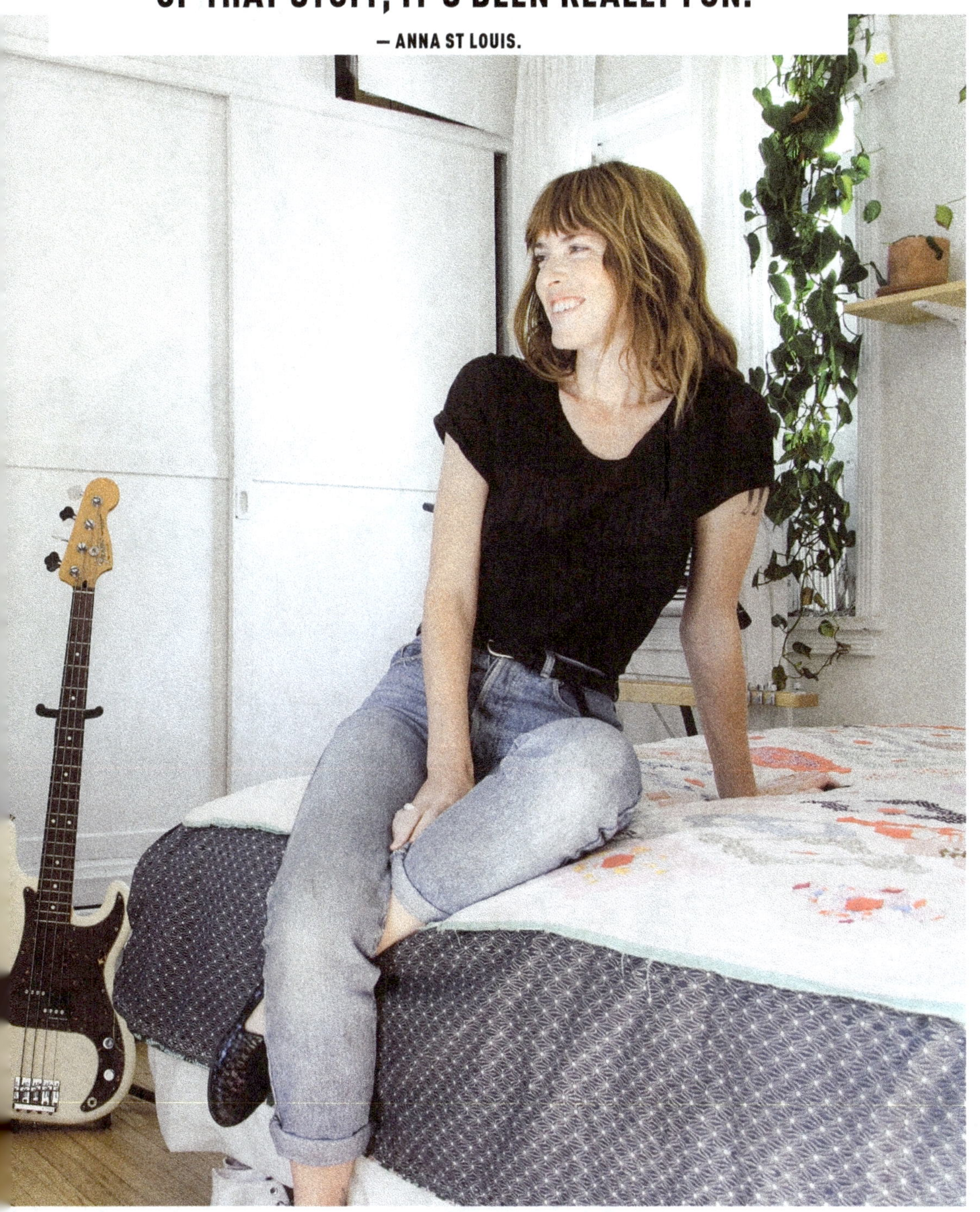

> "WHEN THE RECORD WAS COMING OUT I WAS GETTING A LITTLE FREAKED OUT. YOU CAN ALWAYS LOOK BACK AND THINK, 'I COULD HAVE DONE THIS DIFFERENTLY OR BETTER.' THEN ONCE I LET GO OF THAT STUFF, IT'S BEEN REALLY FUN."
>
> — ANNA ST LOUIS.

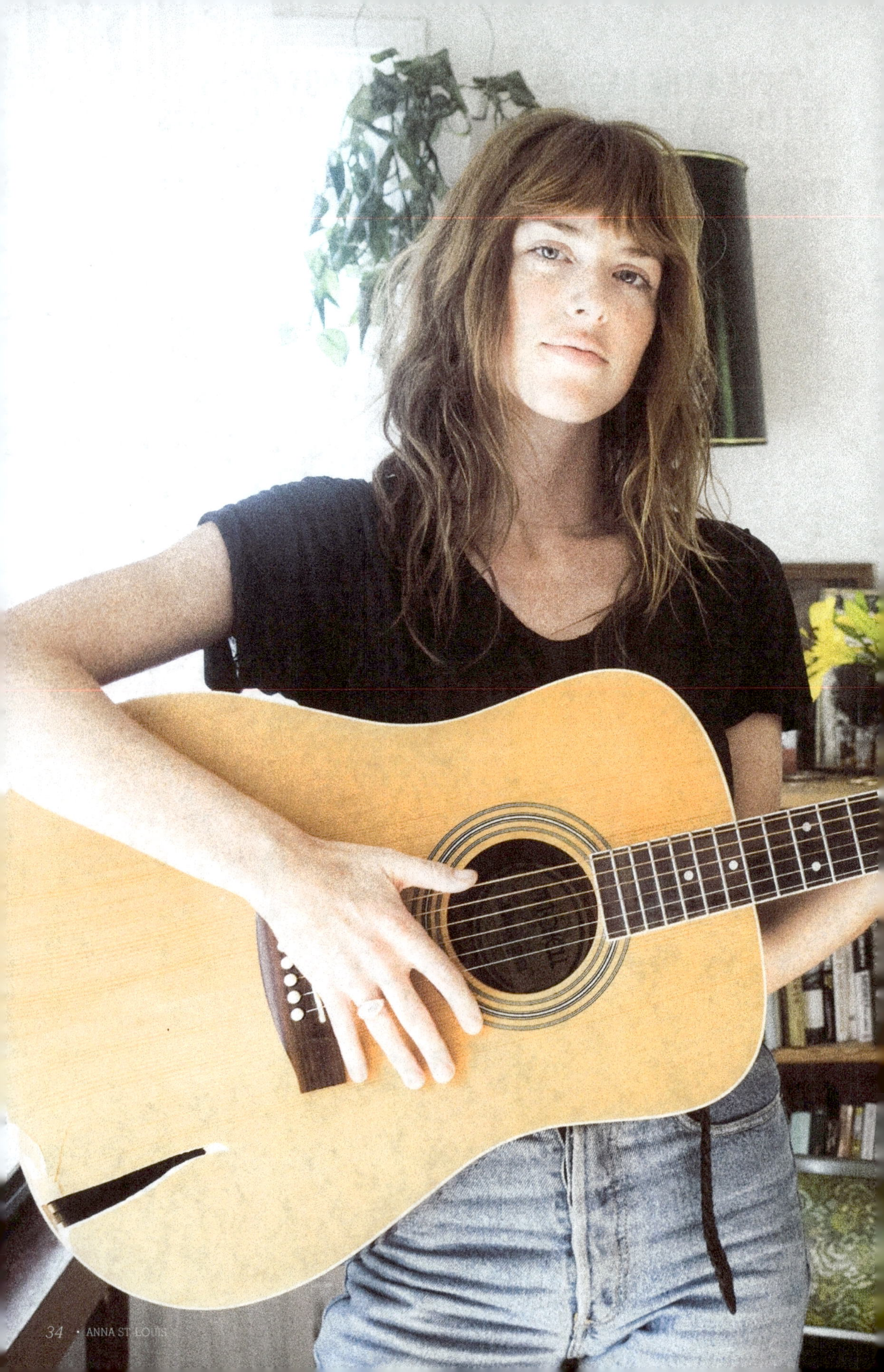

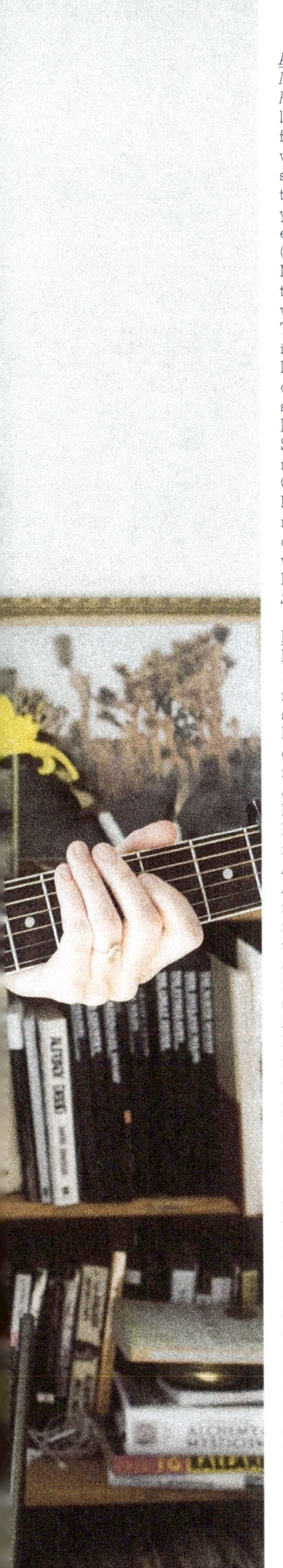

ANNA ST. LOUIS
If Only There Was A River is the first full-length studio album from Anna St. Louis, who began writing songs after moving to Los Angeles five years ago. She enlisted Kyle Thomas (King Tuff) and Kevin Morby to produce the album, which was engineered by Thomas in his home in Mount Washington, Los Angeles. The collection of eleven songs also features Justin Sullivan (Night Shop) on drums and multi-instrumentalist Oliver Hill (Pavo Pavo). Her previous release, a cassette called *First Songs*, was featured by NPR, *Pitchfork*, and *Stereogum*.

KEVIN MORBY
Kevin Morby (b. 1988) is an American musician, singer and songwriter. Formerly known as the bass guitarist of the folk rock band Woods and frontman of The Babies, Morby later-began a solo career, releasing *Harlem River* (2013) and *Still Life* (2014) to positive reviews. In 2016 he released *Singing Saw* to widespread critical acclaim. The following year, his fourth studio album, *City Music*, was released. During live performances, Morby is accompanied by his backing band: Meg Duffy (guitar), Cyrus Gengras (bass) and Nick Kinsey (drums).

BROOKE AND MIKE TULEY
Brooke Tuley and her husband Mike are musicians from Kansas City, Missouri. Along with Anna St. Louis they formed the garage band Bloodbirds, which was active between 2012-15. The band self-released three tapes before their debut LP *Psychic Sur-*

"Understand") and substantial tours for both artists, Morby and St Louis found time to chat about growing up together in the Midwest, listening to their own records and why they're both still daunted by performing for family.

———

Kevin Morby: Anna St. Louis, contrary to popular belief, is your real last name.
Anna St. Louis: It's true, yeah. I was born with it.
KM: But it's a little confusing because you come from Kansas City.
ASL: That's true. You know that because—
KM: I also come from Kansas City. I grew up there with Anna. What is the origin of the last name "St. Louis?"
ASL: That's a great

question. We actually don't know because my great, great grandfather disowned his family and moved. He would never talk about where he moved from, and that's why he moved to Kansas City. He started working on the railroad. Then the following three generations were railroad workers. Anyway, the name is probably French-Canadian or French.
KM: Right, French. St.

> ## "WHEN YOU BREAK IT DOWN, THE ORIGIN OF THE WORRY IS THAT YOUR ALBUM IS YOUR PERMANENT RECORD. IT'S OUT THERE AND IT'S A COMPLETE DOCUMENTA-TION OF ALL THE CHOICES YOU MADE AT THAT TIME IN YOUR LIFE."
>
> **— KEVIN MORBY**

Louis: There's a lot of French architecture in that city.
ASL: Yeah, I guess so.
KM: There is.
ASL: There is an arch, right.

KM: Anna, we grew up together in Kansas City.
ASL: Yes.
KM: As the viewers may not know, the first time I ever saw you perform music; you were in a punk band.
ASL: Mm-hmm.

KM: How did you get started? 'Cause you just sang—you just sang in a punk band called…
ASL: I don't remember their name.
KM: Okay, we won't go there, but you were in a punk band and you just sang.
ASL: Right.

KM: What was your first instrument? When did that come into play?
ASL: Yeah, at first, I just sang. Now looking back, I don't know how I did that. That's the most intimidating thing. I would just jump in and get into it.
KM: I know. You were really good at it too.
ASL: Thanks. I have no idea how I did that.
KS: That is a tough thing to do. To not have the security of your instruments. It's such a safety net for me.
ASL: Totally. I didn't start playing an instrument until I started playing the bass. I don't know. I think I was twenty-four or twenty-three. Yeah, it's around there.

KM: Then from the bass, the natural step up to the guitar. You had a Fender Bullet, I remember.
ASL: No, it's a Fender Lead. I still have it. It usually hangs right there, but it's at my sister's house.
KM: Didn't your sister give you the guitar?
ASL: She got it in high school. My granddad took her to a pawnshop after school one day, and they got it. Then it just sat around for a long time, and then

I started carrying it around for years. I had it before I even played it. I eventually learned it many years later.

KM: When would you say you wrote your first song that you thought you would be comfortable showing to people?
ASL: I don't know. I started writing songs and guitar once I lived in LA, so only in the past five years. I think when I was first learning guitar and experimenting with writing, I was

sending a lot of the songs to our friends Mike and Brooke (Tuley). I think I slowly worked my way into sharing it with people.

KM: You did a lot of it in this room. You started recording songs in this room.
ASL: Some of them, but it was before I lived here.
KM: Right! Because you went to Iowa to record.
ASL: Yeah.

KM: That is great.

What's next?
ASL: About my career?
KM: Yes. Well, you just went on your first tour as a solo artist. How did you like that?
ASL: It was so fun. It was really one of the best experiences of my life. I had such a good time. I think I lucked out, It was a really great crew, I was playing with really cool musicians, and it was a beautiful time of the year. Also, just to be able to play every night and in front of new

> ## "I THINK THERE IS MORE PRESSURE PLAYING IN LA, OR WHATEVER CITY YOU LIVE IN. BECAUSE THEN YOU KNOW A LOT OF PEOPLE. I THINK PLAYING IN FRONT OF YOUR FAMILY AND CLOSE FRIENDS IS THE HARDEST THING."
>
> **— ANNA ST LOUIS**

people was really fun.

KM: Before that, you were just playing a lot of shows around LA.
ASL: Yeah.
KM: To me, I love the anonymity of going on tour. Obviously, people know who you are and they come to see you, but you don't know who they are most of the time. That's what I like the most about tours – not having to perform for anybody like your family, or your friends, or anything. Those are

gery in 2013, followed by *MMXIII* in 2015.

<u>TED LUCAS</u>
Ted Lucas was a fixture in the Detroit rock scene of the '60s and '70s His first group, The Spike Drivers, is considered one of the earliest psych bands. Following that band's collapse, Lucas paid bills doing session work with Motown Records. In 1972 he recorded a demo for Warner Brothers Records which would become *Ted Lucas*, released in two private editions in 1975. The album was released with artwork by the legendary Stanley Mouse, originally created for Jimi Hendrix.

<u>WAXAHATCHEE</u>
Waxahatchee is an American indie music project, formed in 2010 by American singer-songwriter Katie Crutchfield, previously a member of P.S. Eliot. The band is named after Waxahatchee Creek in Alabama. Originally an acoustic solo project, her recordings tend to now involve a backing band, and the music is increasingly performed in this way. Crutchfield, as Waxahatchee, has released four albums to date; *American Weekend* (2012), *Cerulean* Salt (2013), *Ivy Tripp* (2015) and *Out in the Storm* (2017).

the times that I get the most nervous.

KM: How does playing locally compare to going on tour? What's the big difference for you?

ASL: I feel a lot more confident, just more excited.

KM: Also with family, they will let you know. Recently, I played in Nebraska and that's where my parents grew up. Literally, it was a reunion of friends that they hadn't seen since high school. They invited them to the

when you have a show in front of those people, it's a super high reward, and when you have a bad show, you feel like shit. The good thing about family and friends is they always tell you it's good no matter what.

ASL: It feels really good. Last week, when it was coming out, I was getting a little freaked out. I think it's really easy as you start to gain new skills and learn things about what you're doing. You can look back and be like,

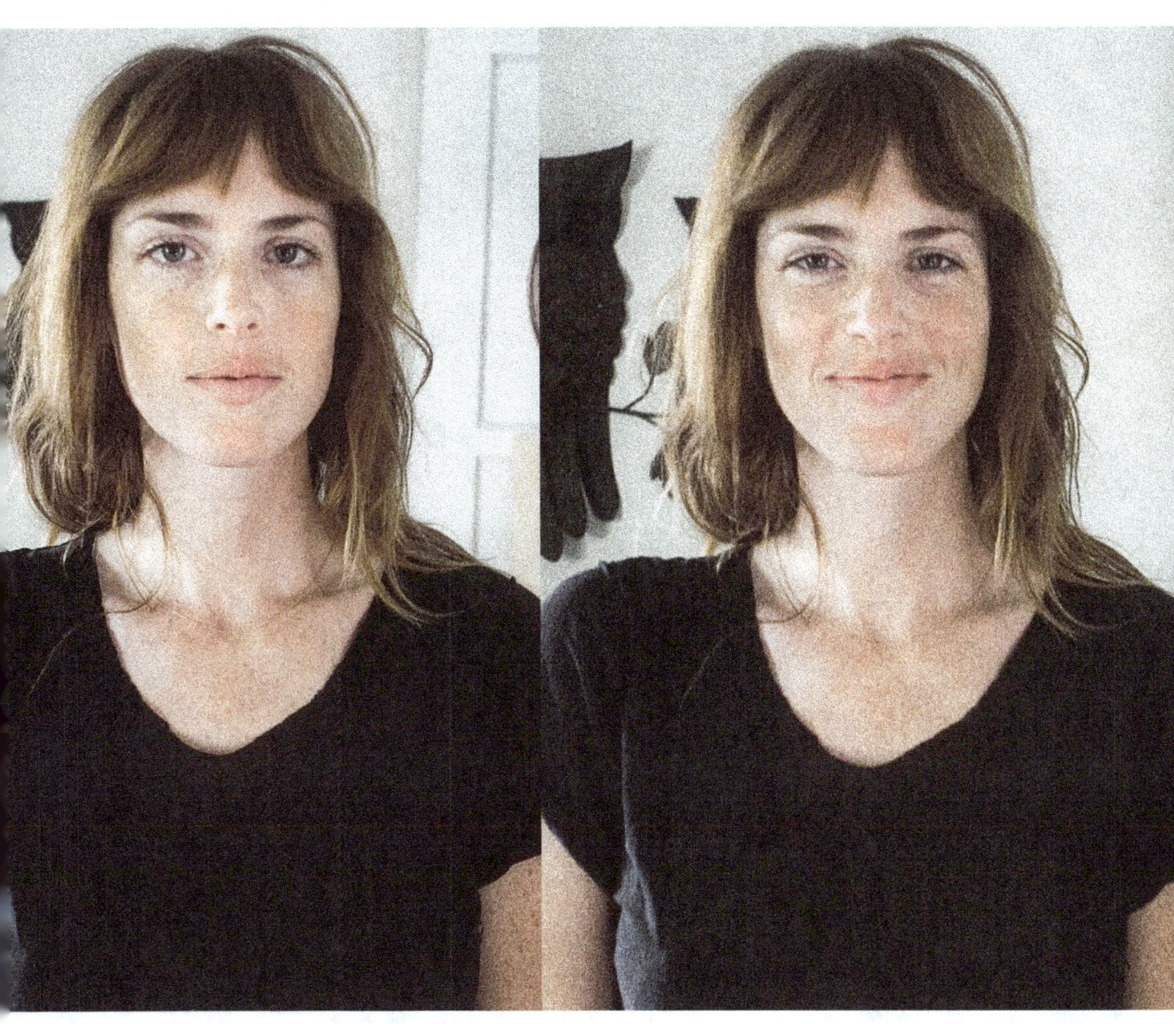

KM: I love my family dearly, and I love my friends dearly, but it brings up a certain type of nerves.

ASL: Yeah. My first show was just people I knew and family, which was really scary.

show, which is nice. I like providing that for my parents, to be kinda like the fire that they get around and talk, but it's a lot to take on sometimes.

KM: I also feel that

ASL: Yeah, and then they still love you afterward too, hopefully.

KM: Your first record just came out. How does it feel to have an album out in the world for everyone else to listen to?

"I could have done this differently or better." I was doing a lot of that, and then I was like, "That's nonsense. Just have fun with it." Then once I let go of that stuff, it's been really fun.

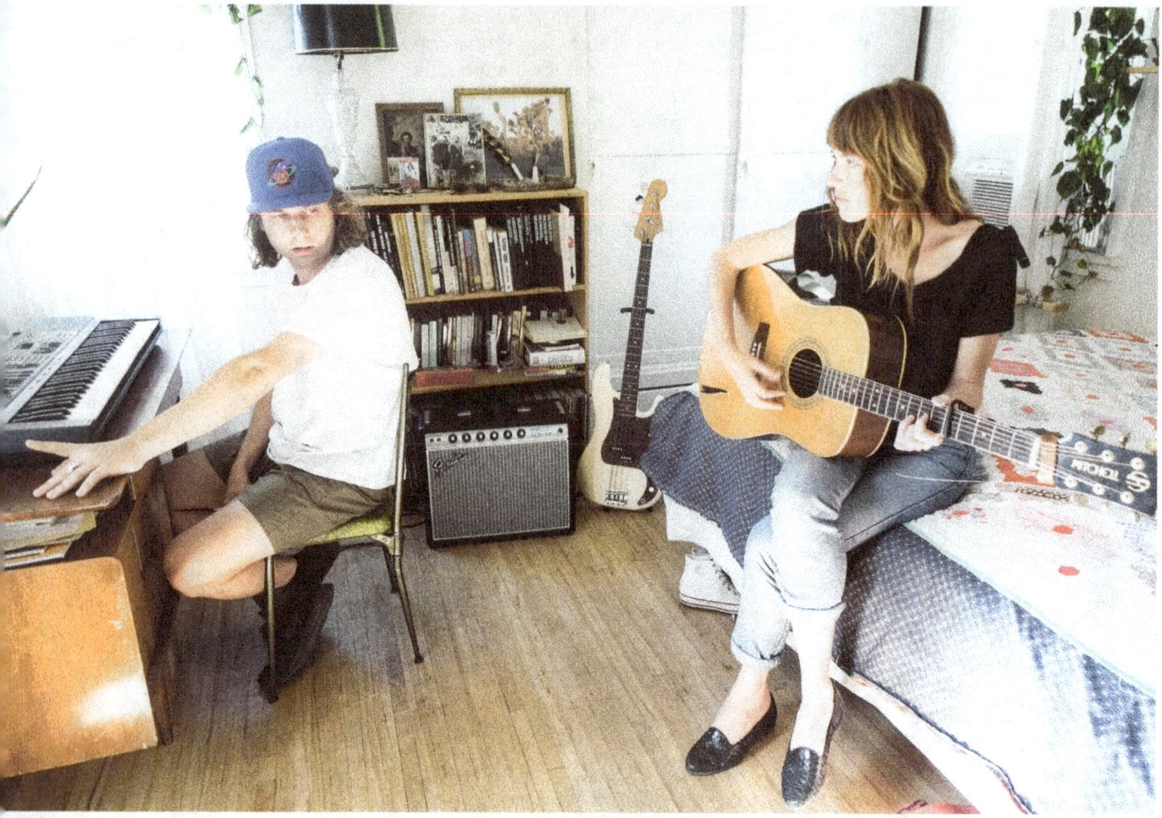

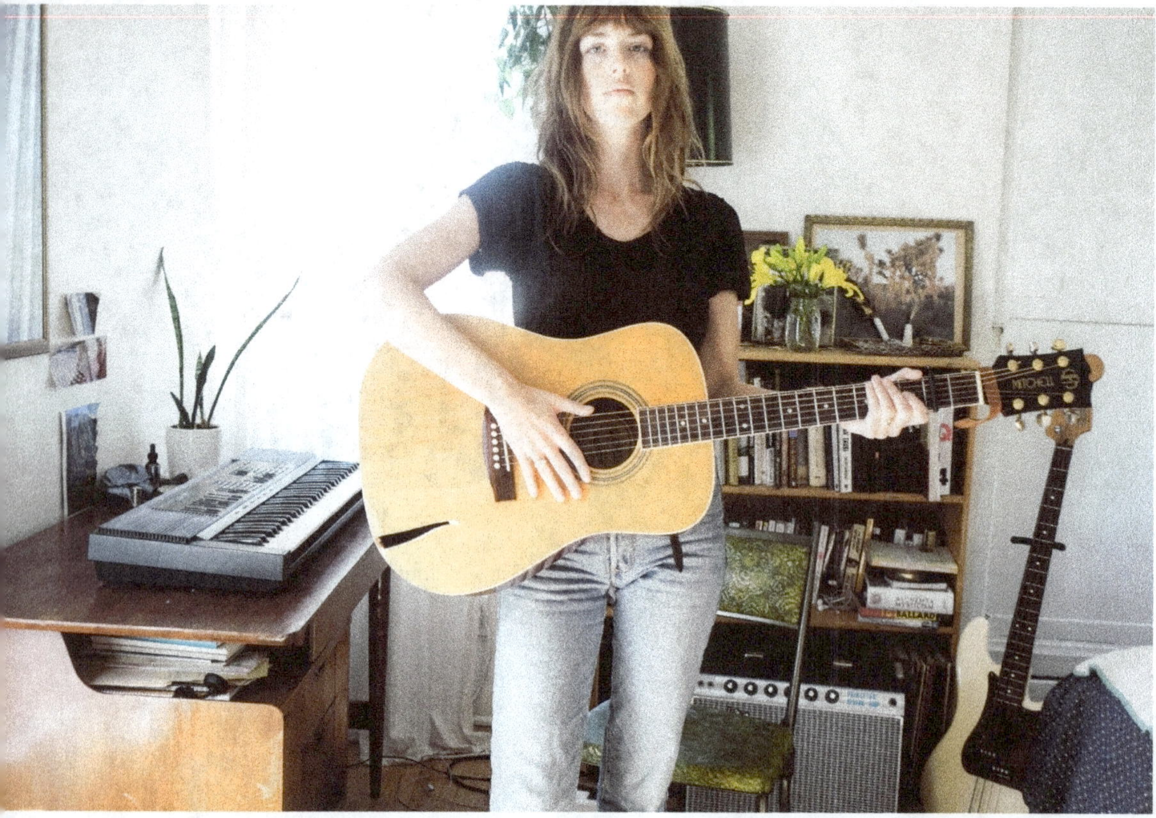

KM: I know what you mean. Every record, there is always something that you would have changed a little bit, and it's usually something that just you would notice. But I like it in the fact that when you break it down, the origin of the worry is that it's your permanent record. It's out there, and it's a complete documentation of all the choices you made at that time in your life. It's a snapshot of that.
ASL: Yeah, and just who you are and the information you have.

KM: And you're like, "Well, there's no

ing it's out there, it is a totally done thing.
KM: It's like a package.
ASL: And listening to it on Spotify, it had a different sound.
KS: Yeah, totally. I know exactly what you mean. It has become real, I guess it's like going to the movie theater and seeing a movie that you made yourself.
ASL: Yeah.

KM: I don't know if I have any more questions. Let's do a rapid-fire question.
ASL: Oh, my God! I hate those.
KM: What's the last book you read?

of *A Star Is Born*?
ASL: I liked it.
KM: Nice. I know some people who say it's horrible, and they walked out. I know some people who really own up to loving it. I know some people who say it's bad, but they could talk about it all day.
ASL: I'm always down to just escape into a movie, and it was good for me for that.
KM: To me, it has the air of the Jonny Cash movie, *Walk the Line*, or something like that. I'm going to see it.

KM: Two more. What is the last television series that you watched?

was great. Great performance.

KM: There you go. Good talking to you.
ASL: Great work here.
KM: How was that? Was it horrible?

changing it." I have a thing when I release a record. I listen to the mix. I listen to it so much leading up to the release day. Then the moment it is available for everyone else, I no longer have any interest in it. It's like giving something away.
ASL: Yeah, I definitely did that with the tape. It's funny. With the album, I did listen to it because I streamed it the day it was out.
KM: It's always a nice feeling to do something like that.
ASL: Yeah. It was like, "It actually sounds different in a way." Know-

ASL: Beginning to the end, it's *Lonesome Dove* by Larry McMurtry, given to me by you.

KM: What's the last song you listened to that you didn't play?
ASL: I've been listening to Ted Lucas, and the song is called "Baby Where You Are." It's so beautiful.

KM: Nice. I think the song is great. What is the last movie you saw?
ASL: *A Star Is Born.*
KM: Wait. Did we talk about that?
ASL: We did, in a group setting, yeah.
KM: What do you think

ASL: The whole thing?
KM: Just the beginning episode.
ASL: I don't want to say what it is.
KM: What is it?
ASL: *Parenthood.*
KM: I've never seen it, but it sounds like a good TV show.
ASL: I got sick a few weeks ago, and I started watching it. Now I've watched three seasons and I'm into it.

KM: The last question is: what's the last show you saw?
ASL: I went to Desert Daze. I saw you perform and Cut Worms and Hand Habits. It

SUNNY SULJIC
x OLAN PRENATT

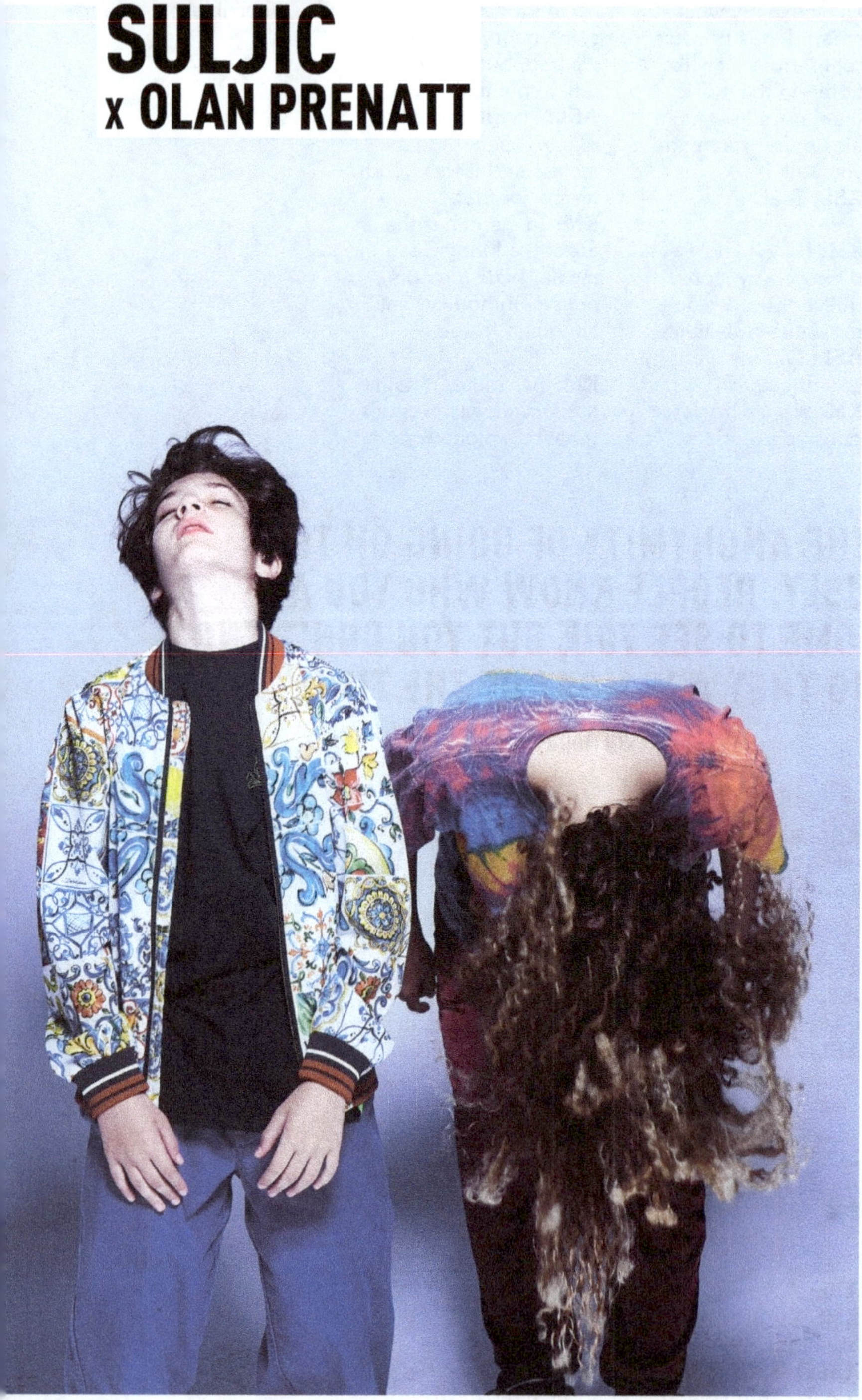

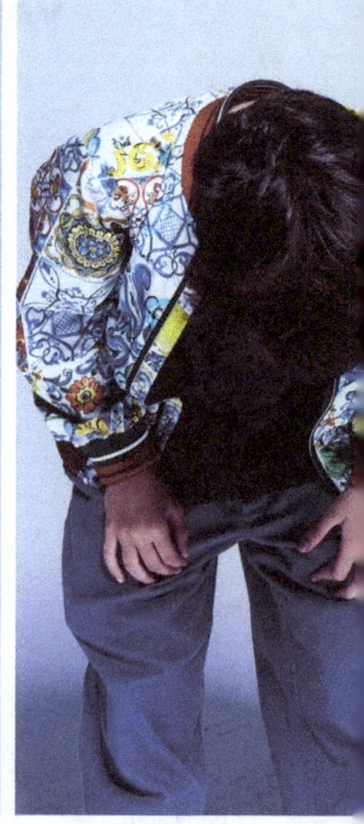

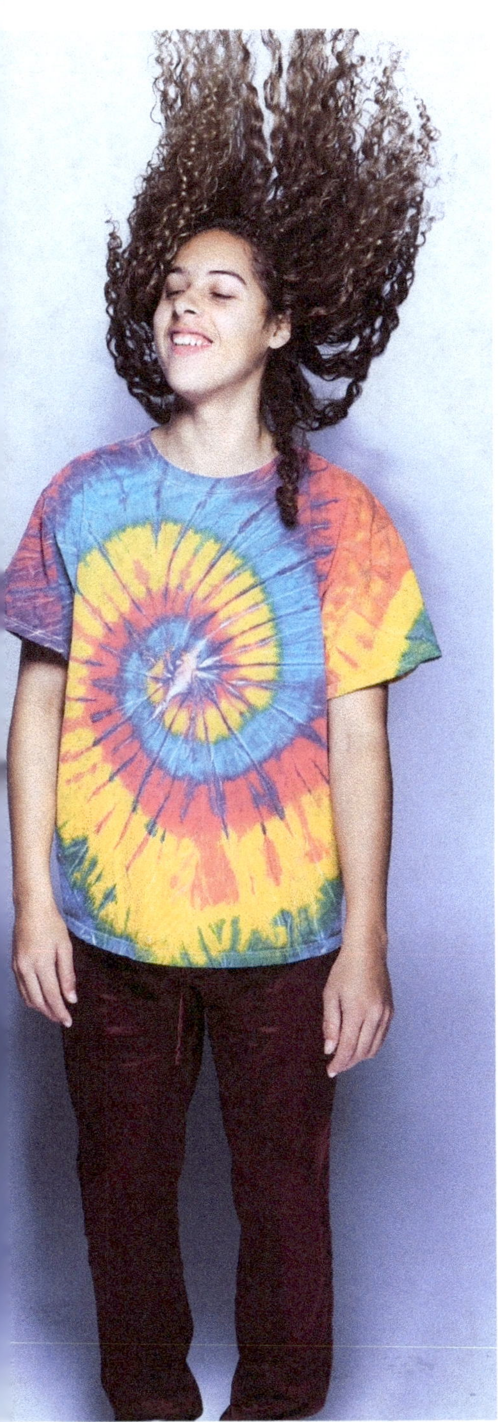

MID90s

Images by

Jan-Willem Dikkers

Jonah Hill's directorial debut, Mid90s, *is garnering praise from critics and the public alike for its portrayal of a group of young skateboarders in '90s era Los Angeles and the "unfussily authentic" coming-of-age story woven throughout. Actor Sunny Suljic, who appeared in the 2017 film* The Killing of a Sacred Deer, *stars as the main character Stevie, a thirteen-year-old who lives with his aggressive older brother Ian [Lucas Hedges] and single mother Dabney. He escapes his turbulent home life by hanging out with a new group of friends he meets at a local skate shop—Ruben, Ray, Fourth Grade and Fuckshit—plunging him into a world of excitement and danger.*

Olan Prenatt, who plays Fuckshit in the film, chats with Suljic about the parallels between Suljic and his character Stevie, his love of Jonah Hill and growing up on set.

Olan Prenatt: Hey, what's up? What's your name? My name's Sunny Suljic.
Sunny Suljic: Oh, Jamal Smith.

OP: Sick! Okay!
SS: Nah, my name is Sunny Suljic and I play Stevie in *Mid90's*. So...
OP: I'm going to start out with your thoughts on reading the script. What came to your mind?
SS: My first thought on the script was it was just so professional and so authentic. It really had a strong impact on me. The words: all the "likes" and "umms", it felt so natural and authentic and I was just blown away

OP: Where are you from?
SS: Originally I'm from Atlanta, Georgia, but five years ago I moved to Los Angeles.

OL: How did you get started?
SS: Well, I was probably around seven or eight. I always wanted to be an actor from around five or six, around that time I thought it was pretty cool. I'd see younger kids in films and was pretty inspired so I thought maybe I could do that as well. My mom is very supportive—she was like, "Alright, let's do it!" I met with some people, they told me to go to Los Angeles to this program called IMTA [International Modeling and Talent Association] where a

bunch of managers and agents looking for people go—a specific place to get casted by managers and agents, and I found the right one and am here now.

OL: How did they find you for this film?
SS: I was skating in my local skate park. Well, I'll start off at the actual beginning. The co-producer

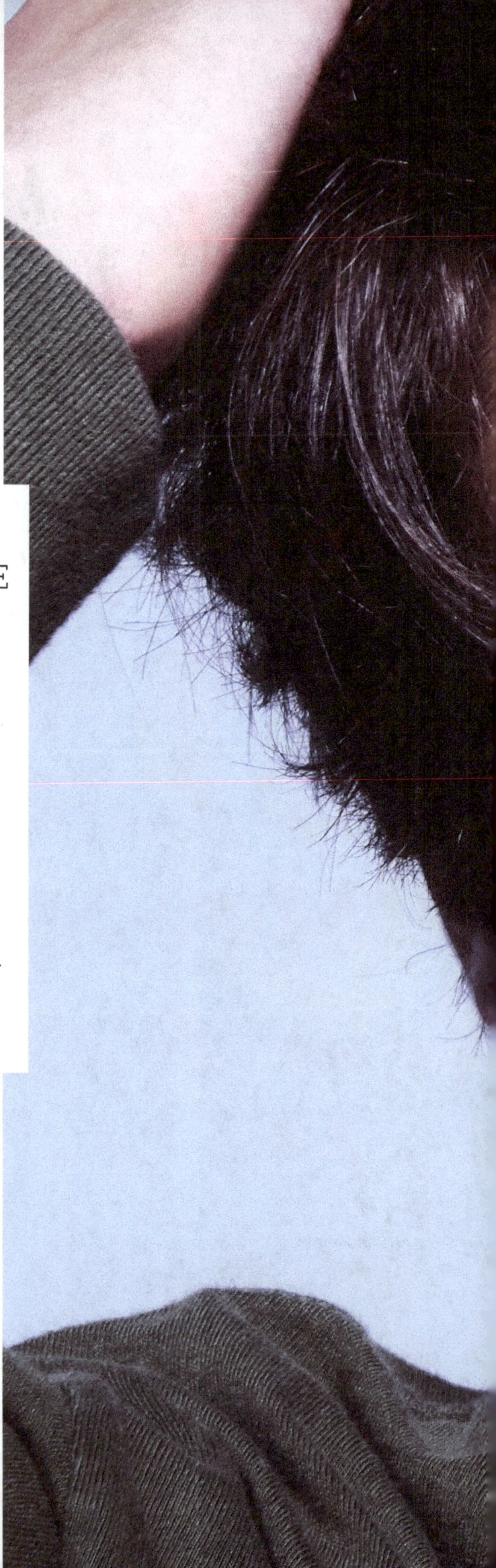

"THEY CAME TO THE SKATE PARK, AND WE JUST STARTED TALKING. IT WAS A NORMAL CONVERSATION, BUT I WAS LIKE, "OH MY GOD THIS IS JONAH HILL THAT I'M TAKING TO.""

— SUNNY SULJIC

on the film Mikey Alfred—I had no clue that Jonah was making a film or that he would even be co-producing—I'd seen him at the skate park before. We'd made a video, and I guess he found me at an audition this one time. Jonah was just trying to cast a bunch of skaters and teach them how to act rath-

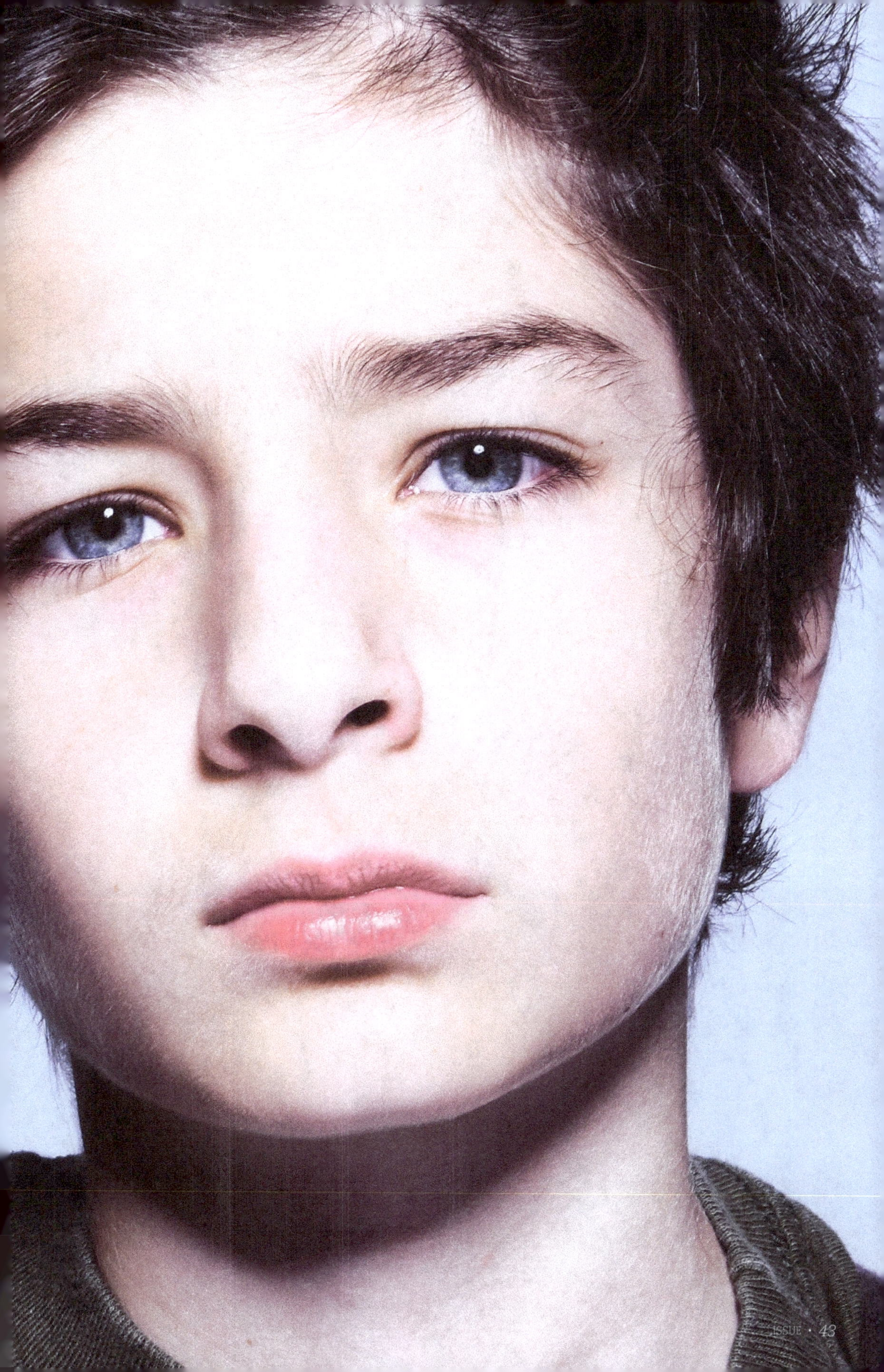

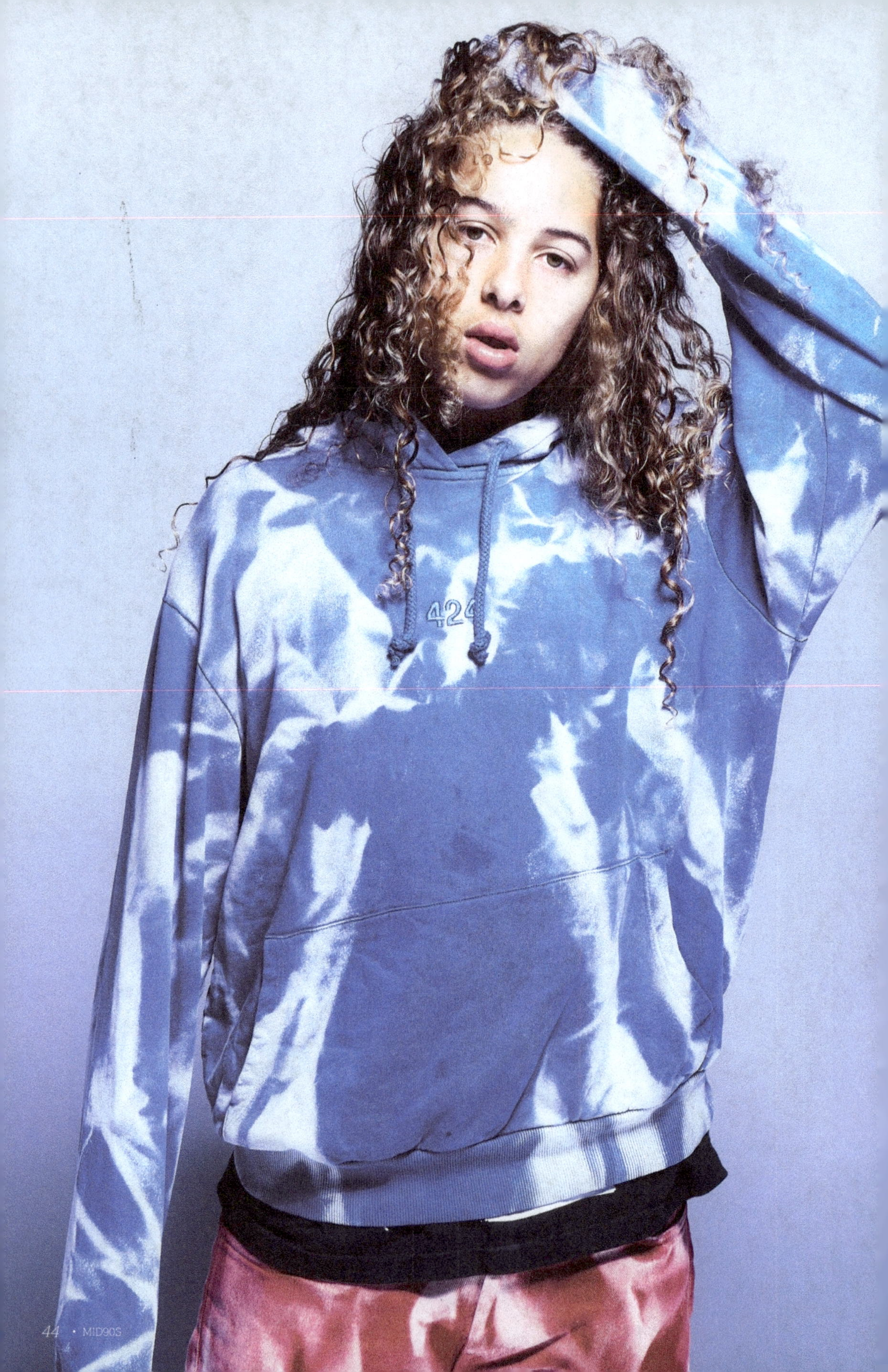

er than vice versa.

Mikey came across me and said to Jonah, "There's this kid, and I've also seen him at an audition." So they came to the skate park, and we just started talking. It was a normal conversation, but I was like, "Oh my god this is Jonah Hill that I'm taking to." He asked me if I had any acting experience. I told him I was in *The Killing of the Sacred Deer*, and he was like, "No way." He was pretty good friends with Yorgos, the director of that film, and Yorgos put in a really good word for me. Jonah cast me after a couple auditions. It was a very long process actually.

OL: What made you want to do this project?
SS: Well two things: Jonah was involved with it, and it involved skating. Literally two things that I love. I love Jonah Hill. It sounds weird saying his full name. I loved Jonah at the time and still do. But I loved him more as an actor, and now he is just just a really good friend of mine.

OL: In what ways do you most identify with Stevie?
SS: Probably the way I love skating, the way I appreciate it. The slogan phrase "Fall, get back up"— that's the same thing with skating. The drive and the commitment Stevie has. That's one thing that I can relate

> **"IT MAKES SENSE BECAUSE OF HOW AUTHENTIC AND RELATABLE THIS MOVIE IS TO EVERY SINGLE HUMAN. I FEEL LIKE EVERYBODY'S EITHER BEEN THROUGH THIS PART OF THEIR LIFE OR IS LIVING THIS PART OF THEIR LIFE."**
>
> — OLAN PRENATT

to. Definitely not personal experiences—like in the film his personality is not too outgoing. He kind of matures over the time, but he's a shy kid. I'm definitely the opposite. I'm 100% an outgoing person.

OP: So when you were going into the role and creating the character in your head, who were you creating?
SS: Jonah had already created a backstory, and lot of scenes that didn't make it into the film. I didn't really have to think about it because of previous things that happened before we started shooting. Jonah would just explain, and then we would do a bunch of scenes and talk about it for a while. I already knew a lot about the character, and we'd do a lot of rehearsing.

OL: Was the film the same or different from what you first imagined when reading the script?
SS: I think I understood it. In the script there were normal conversations, and they were really realistic, very authentic. It just felt like we were all hanging out at a skate shop. I could already imagine it, and I think that's a great thing about writing—if you can make someone imagine what you they are reading then you're a great writer.

So, at the start I could already

imagine the scenes, and from that point on I think the only thing that I didn't expect was how well-portrayed the skating was actually going to be. Because when you think of a skate movie, it's going to probably be a really cheesy movie. If portrayed wrongly, it doesn't turn out right. So I think when we started shooting, and I was seeing some clips I was just shocked. I mean, it was insane.

OL: During the course of the film, Stevie does some growing up. Do you feel that this film has matured you?
SS: Yes. I learned some history of the '90s, and I matured a little bit over the process because Jonah taught me a lot of his personal experiences, and Lucas [Hedges] and Katherine [Waterson] are all professional actors.

OP: Who is your favorite character in *Mid90s*?
SS: Well there are a bunch of universal characters. No, every time I watch it I have a different favorite character. But, I think it's Fourth Grade, who Ryder McLaughlin played.
OP: I initially thought Fourth Grade was cool as hell, but after watching it a few times I noticed that in the last scene, where he is playing his tape, how much Ryder really got into

that character. The next time I watched the movie it made me stuck on Ryder.

If you could choose only one aesthetic from the '90s, and everything else be not in your reach, what would it be?
SS: I definitely think the clothing.
OP: Clothing over music?
SS: Yes 100% clothing over music because the music naturally evolves. But with clothing now, there are no innovations. It's not anything original. They just repeat some of the clothing from the '80s or '90s, the'70s or '60s.
OP: It's all recycled.
SS: In the '90s when you hear rap or you see the clothes, it's like there is something new. It's like, "Whoa, baggy pants, that's crazy. Whoa, RnB, it's crazy." Music just evolved, and with clothing, it's all the same.

OP: Did you view Ian (Stevie's aggressive older brother) as, not on script, but in your head? Your emotions seemed so three-dimensional.
SS: In all the scenes I didn't see Lucas [Hedges] as a boy at all. I completely saw through the character. I was tearing up, bro. Because if you make a movie with Lucas and he has to beat you up—ugh! He's the nicest person I've ever met. He's super genuine. He won't ever say any-

native Olan Prenatt portrays the character "Fuckshit" in Jonah Hill's *Mid90s*. Poised to become one of skateboarding's leading ambassadors, Prenatt rides for Illegal Civilization, a prominent LA-based skate crew and creative collective that has collaborated with rappers Tyler the Creator and The Game, as well as streetwear giant Converse.

<u>LUCAS HEDGES</u>
Lucas Hedges is an American actor and son of writer-director Peter Hedges. He studied theater at the University of North Carolina School of the Arts and began his acting career by playing supporting roles in Wes Anderson's comedy-drama *Moonrise Kingdom* (2012) and the crime biopic *Kill the Messenger* (2014). He made his breakthrough in 2016 playing a sardonic teenage orphan in Kenneth Lonergan's drama *Manchester by the Sea*, which earned him a nomination for the Academy Award for Best Supporting Actor.

<u>THE KILLING OF A SACRED DEER</u>
The Killing of a Sacred Deer is a 2017 psychological thriller film directed by Yorgos Lanthimos, from a screenplay by Lanthimos and Efthymis Filippou. It stars Colin Farrell, Nicole Kidman, Barry Keoghan, Raffey Cassidy, Sunny Suljic, Alicia Silverstone and Bill Camp. The story is based on the ancient Greek play *Iphigenia at Aulis* by Euripides.

> **"THE ONLY THING THAT I DIDN'T EXPECT WAS HOW WELL-POR-TRAYED THE SKATING WAS ACTUALLY GOING TO BE. BECAUSE WHEN YOU THINK OF A SKATE MOVIE, IT'S GOING TO PROBABLY BE A REAL-LY CHEESY MOVIE. SO I THINK WHEN WE START-ED SHOOT-ING, AND I WAS SEEING SOME CLIPS I WAS JUST SHOCKED. I MEAN, IT WAS INSANE."**
> — SUNNY SULJIC

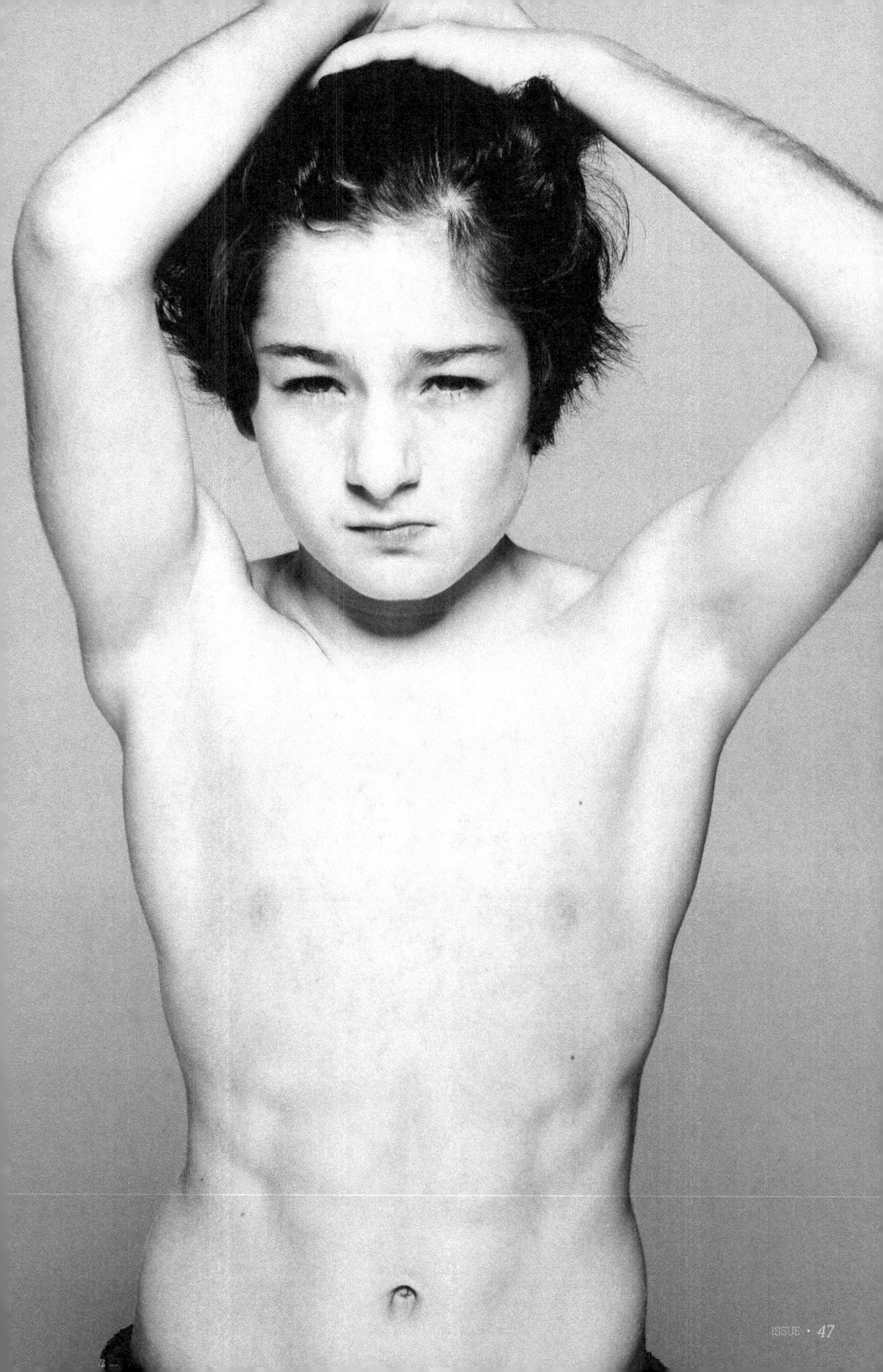
ISSUE · 47

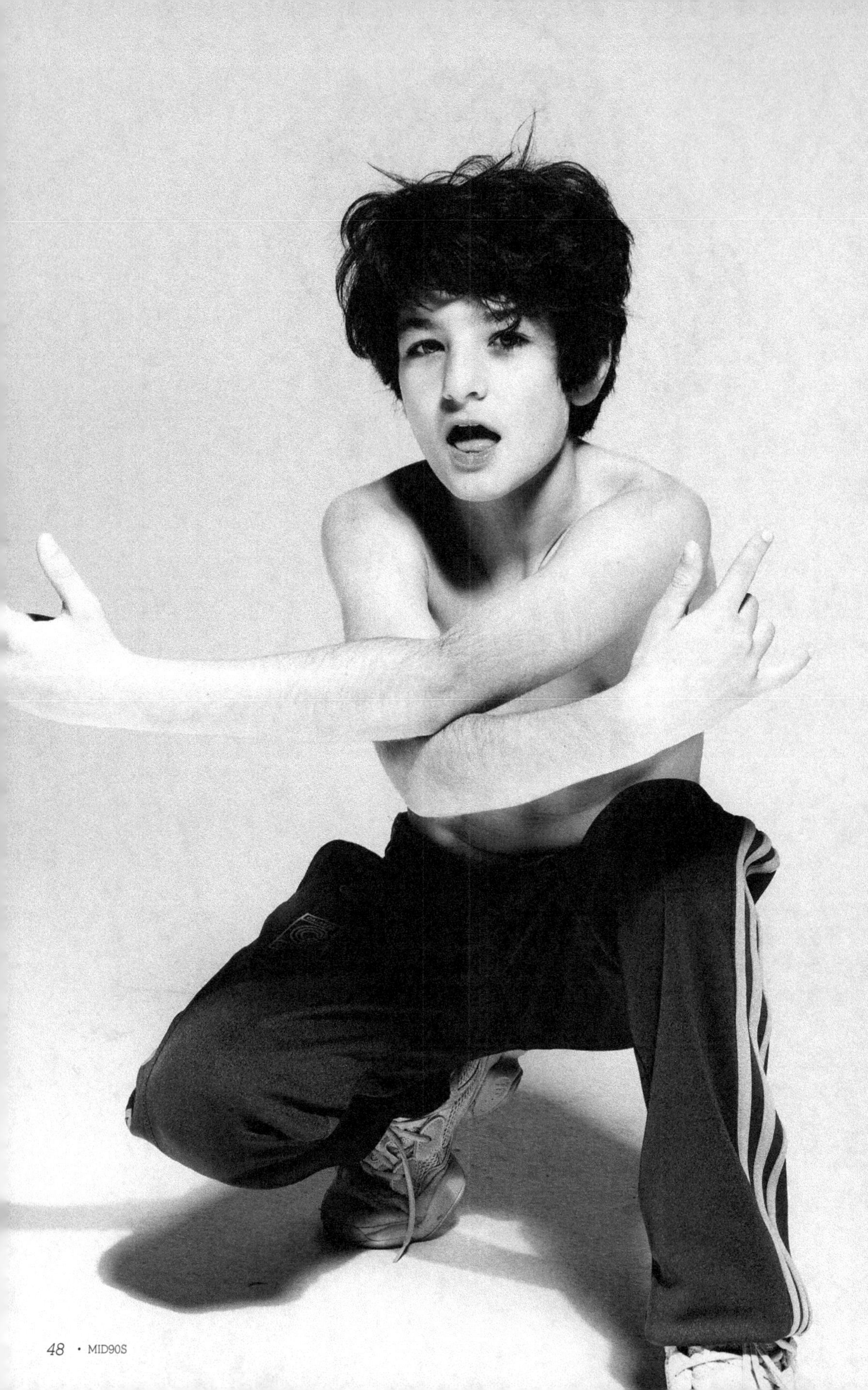

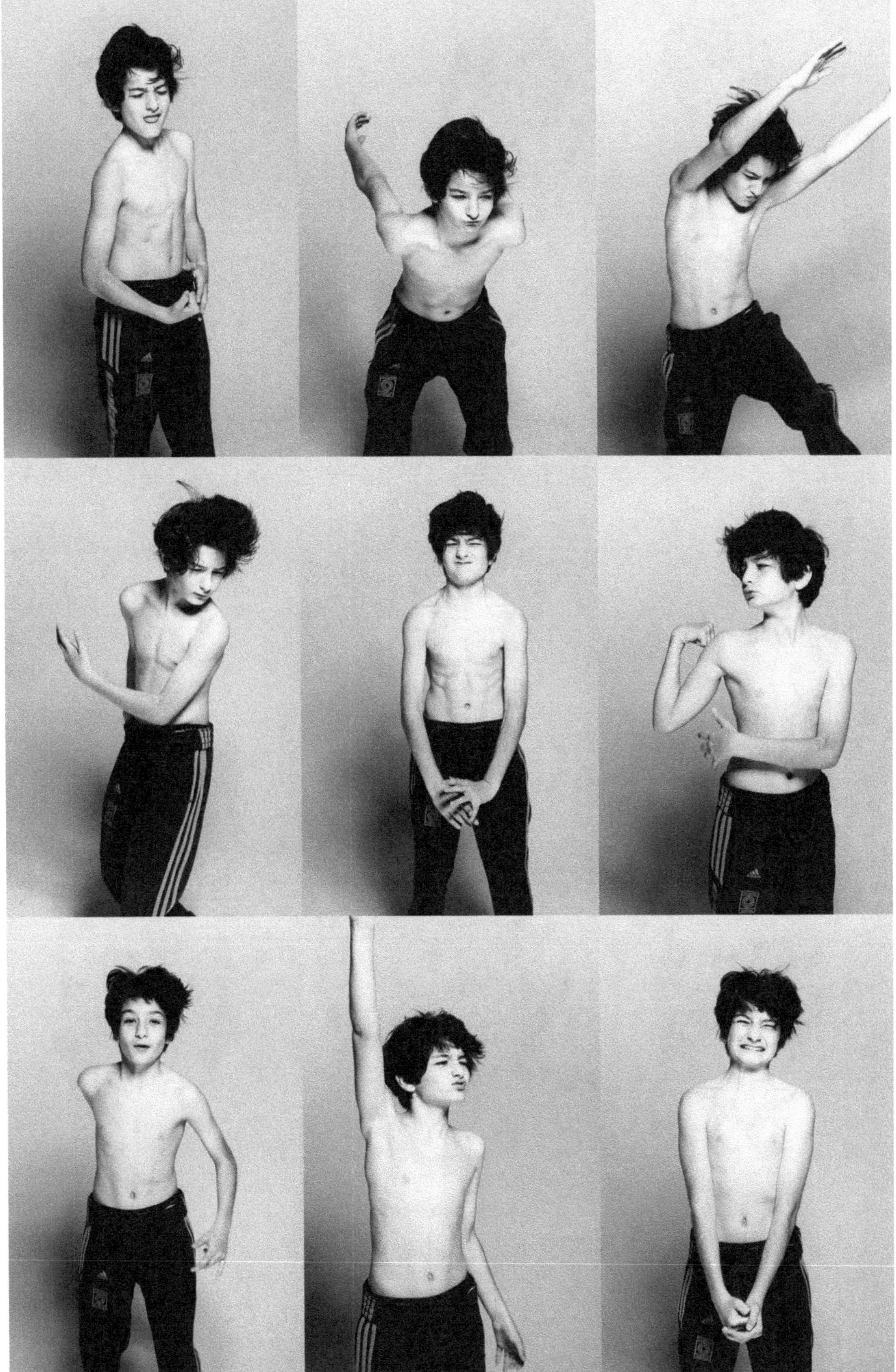

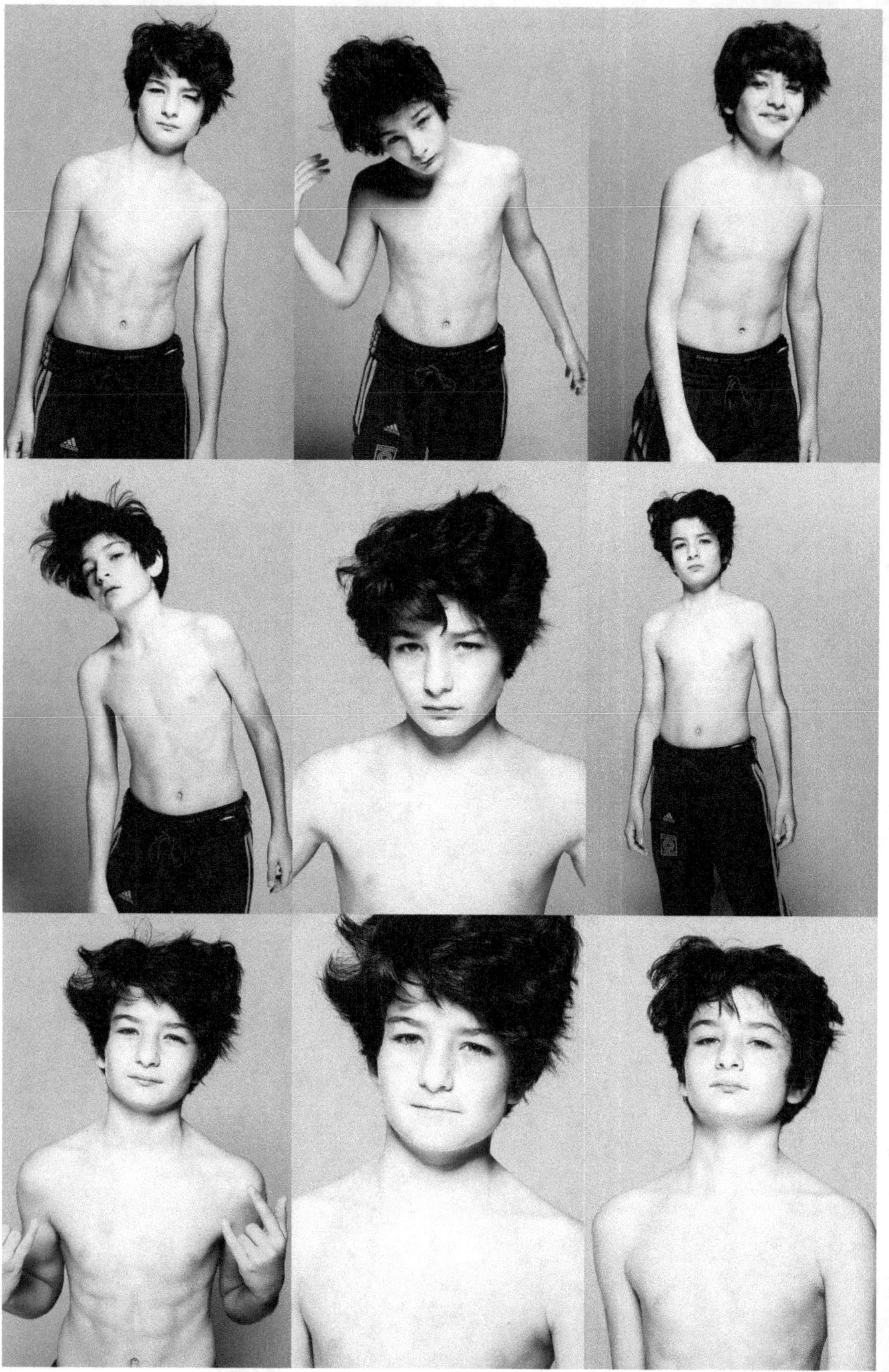

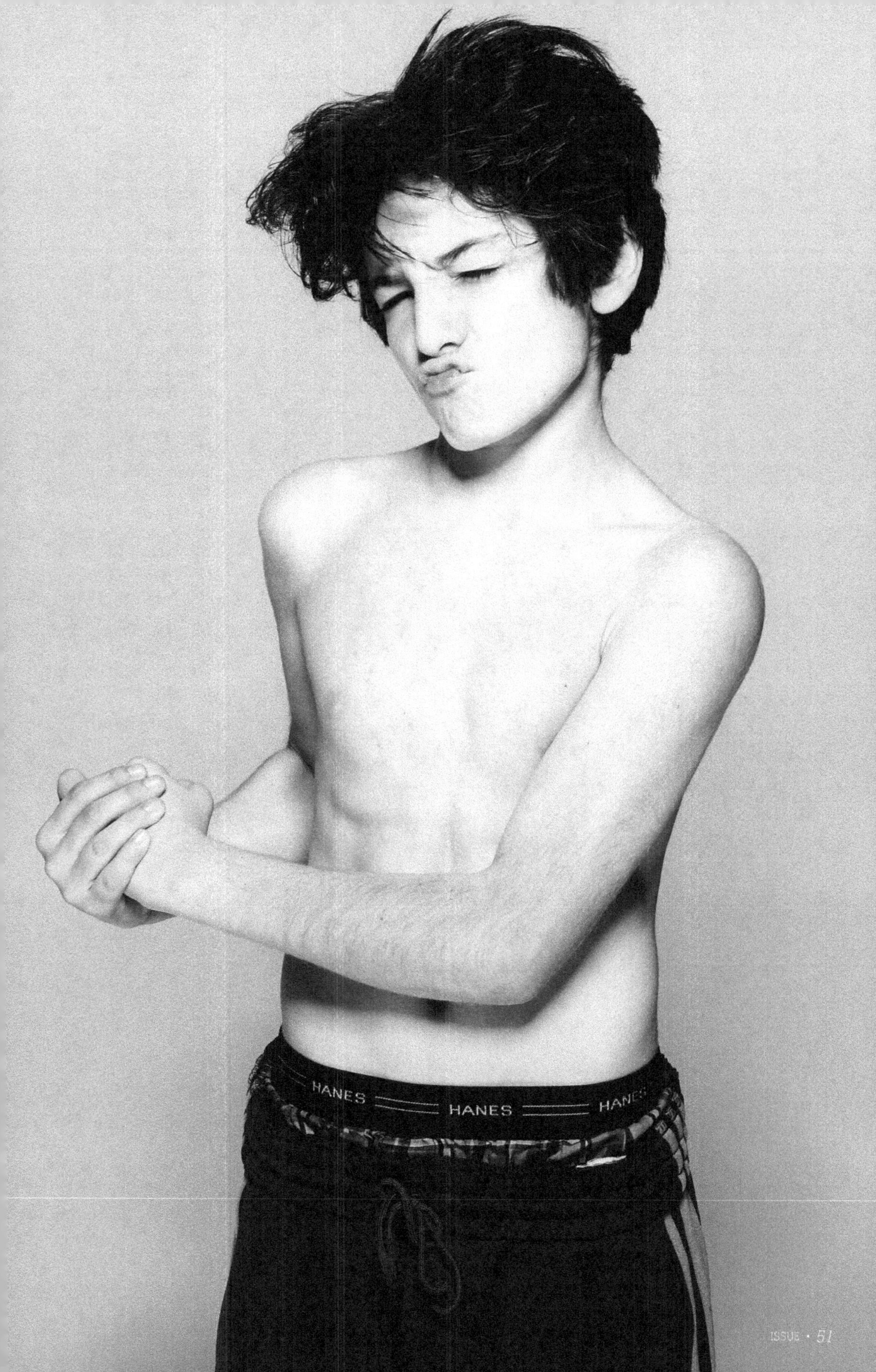
HANES
HANES
HANES

thing insulting to you. I'd start shooting, and he would start doing the push-ups and acting all tough, and I would just laugh bro, because that's not him. But he did such a good job getting into character.
OP: I never knew. I met him on set, but he was in character the whole time, and I didn't know it. Then when I saw him later I

word, it messes you up. You think of it as acting and start getting out of character.

OP: What do you think people will get out of the film?
SS: I think teenagers will look at it and think, "Oh, this is what we're doing right now. This is cool." Then young

could make people cry. Like, grown men just cry.
OP: It makes sense because of how authentic and relatable this movie is to every single human. I feel like everybody's either been through this part of their life or is living this part of their life.
SS: I think that is

to impress them or that you have to do a little more to make them laugh or anything like that, that's the minute that you know you just don't feel comfortable with that person. You can't fully express yourself and that really stuck with me.

OP: What is your favorite film?
SS: *Good Will Hunting. Deadpool 2.*
OP: Sick.
SS: *The Conjuring. Groundhog Day. The Truman Show.*
OP: Okay that's five right there, you're good.
SS: *Incredibles, Incredibles 2.*
OP: Sick. I'll cut you off.
SS: *The Shining.* Did I say *The Shining?*
OP: No you didn't say that.

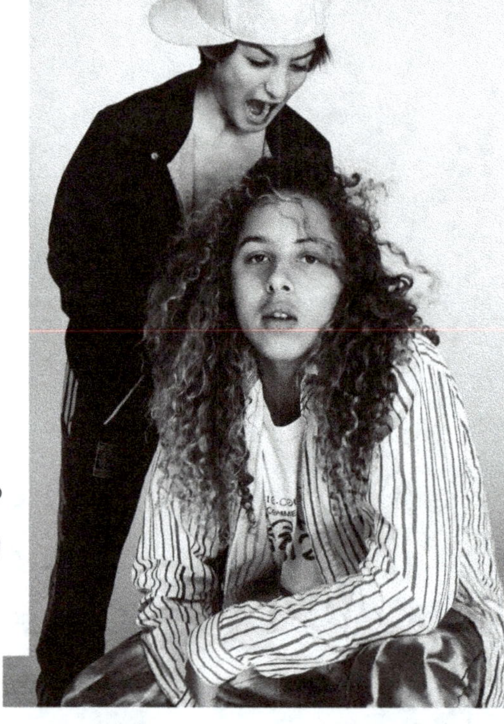

> **"THE DRIVE AND THE COMMITMENT STEVIE HAS. THAT'S ONE THING THAT I CAN RELATE TO, BUT HE'S A SHY KID. I'M DEFINITELY THE OPPOSITE. I'M 100% AN OUTGOING PERSON."**
> — SUNNY SULJIC

was like, "Whoa, you were in character that whole time."
SS: Yes, exactly. He's good.

OP: Did you learn any lessons making the film?
SS: I think understanding the scenes better. That's the most important thing because if you don't understand even one

adults will think, "Oh, I wish I was in the '90s or a cool period." But I think most adults will really reflect on it. A lot of adults will think, "Oh, I know friends like that." A lot of people opened up for the Q&As. Some were super emotional. It's so tight that Jonah

what they are going to take away from it.

OP: What did you learn from your character's experience?
SS: I would say, if you're already friends with that person then you don't really have to go out of your way to be with them. If you feel like you have

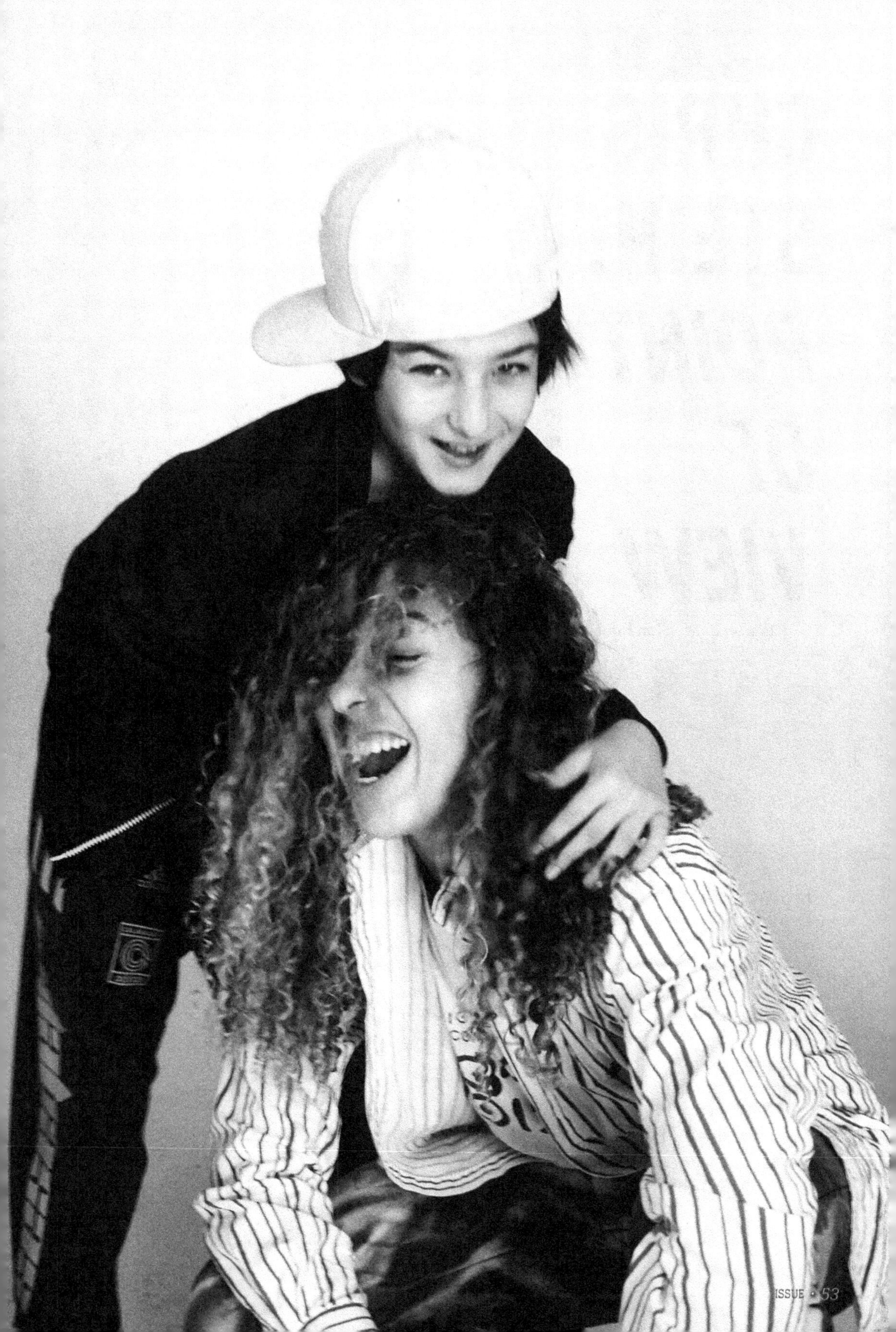

ISSUE · 53

CHRIS STEIN: *POINT OF VIEW*

In conversation with **Jon Ronson**

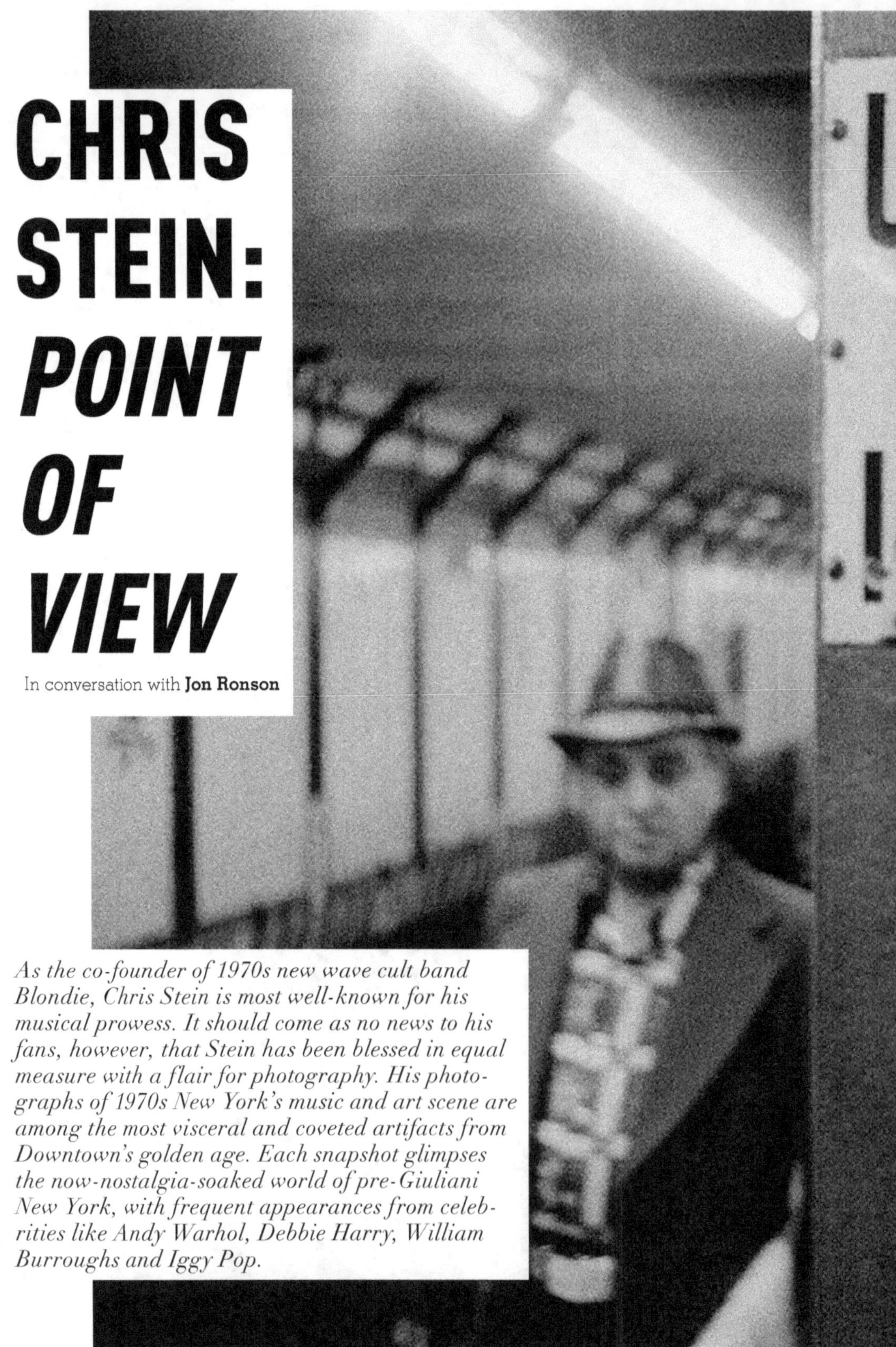

As the co-founder of 1970s new wave cult band Blondie, Chris Stein is most well-known for his musical prowess. It should come as no news to his fans, however, that Stein has been blessed in equal measure with a flair for photography. His photographs of 1970s New York's music and art scene are among the most visceral and coveted artifacts from Downtown's golden age. Each snapshot glimpses the now-nostalgia-soaked world of pre-Giuliani New York, with frequent appearances from celebrities like Andy Warhol, Debbie Harry, William Burroughs and Iggy Pop.

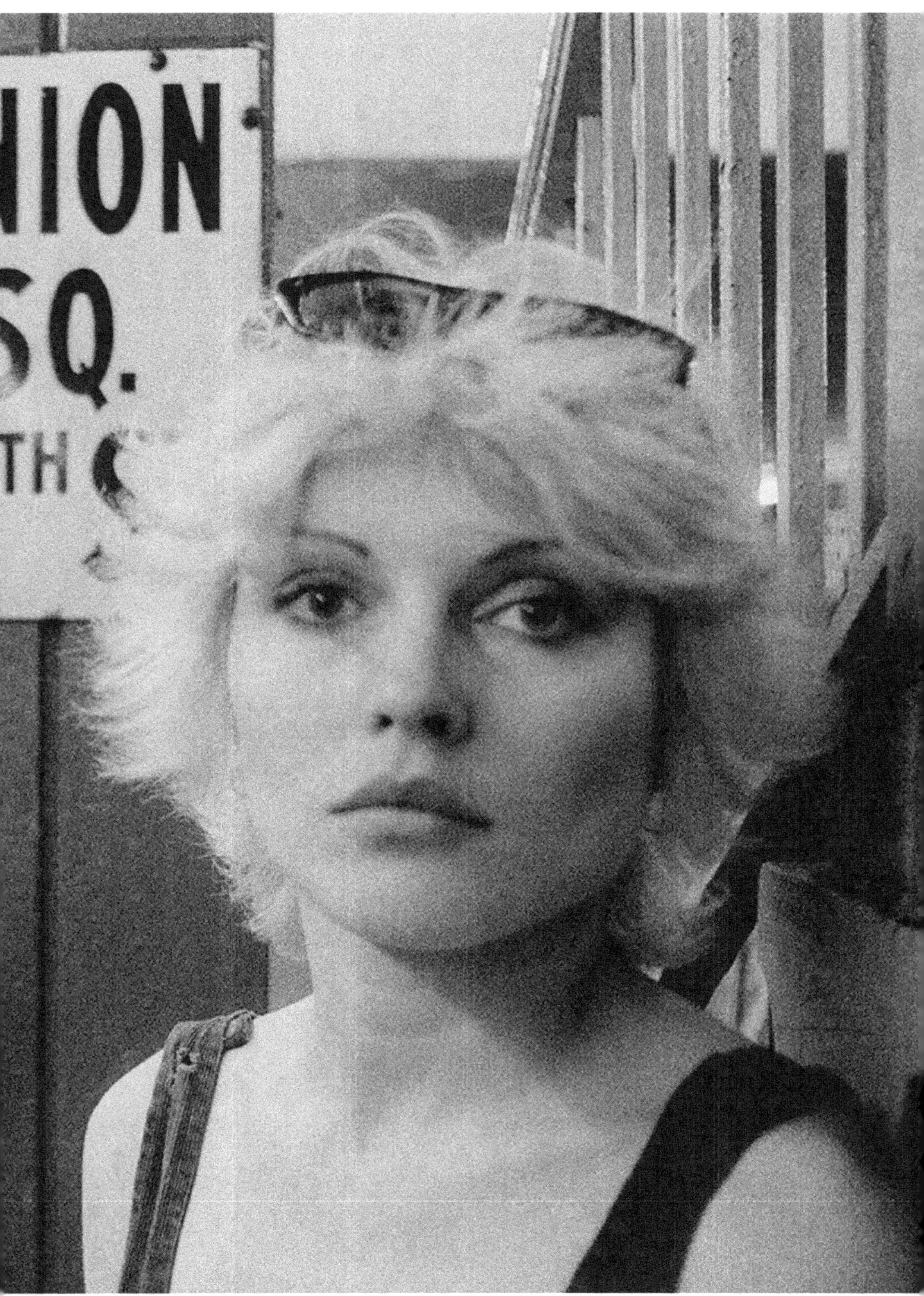
NION
SQ.
TH

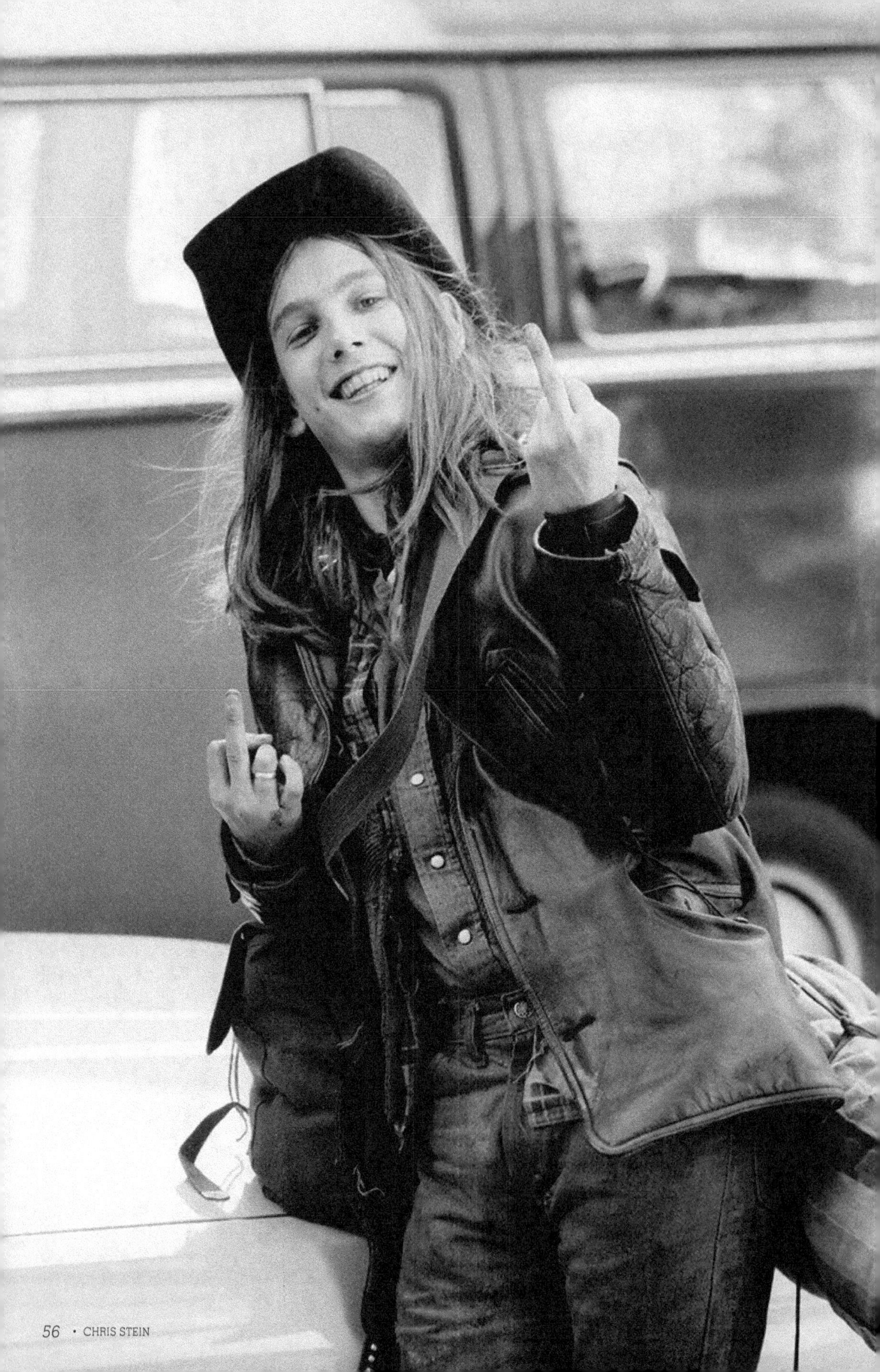

CHRIS STEIN
Chris Stein is a musician, photographer, songwriter and the co-founder and lead guitarist of new wave band Blondie. Originally from Brooklyn, Stein wrote and co-wrote many Blondie hits and was an integral part of the early '70s New York punk scene, capturing thousands of photographs of its atmosphere and key figures. He has published a number of photo books including *Negative: Me, Blondie and the Advent of Punk* (2014) and this year's *Point of View: Me, New York City and the Punk Scene* (2018).

JON RONSON
Jon Ronson is a Welsh journalist, author, documentary filmmaker, screenwriter and radio presenter. Ronson's books include the bestseller *The Men Who Stare at Goats* (2004), the basis of 2009's feature film, as well as *The Psychopath* (2011) and *So You've Been Publicly Shamed* (2015). He is also known for his award-nominated BBC Radio 4 program *Jon Ronson On...* as well as other radio contributions, including *This American Life*. Ronson has co-written the screenplays for *Frank* (2014) and Netflix's *Okja* (2017) and appeared on various TV programs, as well as hosting his own late night panel, *For the Love of...* (1997-98).

BLONDIE
Blondie is a New York rock band formed by singer Debbie Harris and guitarist Chris Stein in the mid '70s. A pioneer of new wave and punk rock's music evolution, Blondie has released a total of eleven albums, including

Stein's newest photobook Point of View: Me, New York City, and the Punk Scene *(2018) comes four years after his last photo exposé,* Chris Stein / Negative: Me, Blondie, and the Advent of Punk *(2014). True to its name,* Point of View *offers a deeply personal perspective on his early roots in New York's punk music and art scene. Each page is brimming with everyday life—from Stein's apartment to New York's gritty streetscapes to the Ramones performing at Arturo Vega's loft—and is sprinkled with candid photographs of '70s icons.*

Bestselling author and journalist Jon Ronson penned the forward to Point of View. *Having grown up in Wales during the 1970s epoch of punk, Ronson recalls watching the New York scene from afar with the sort of reminisce that marks a true fan of the era. Here Ronson rejoins Stein, covering topics of identity, historical turning points and the shifting landscape that is New York City.*

> **"ALL MY FRIENDS WERE OUTSIDERS. EVEN BEFORE I GOT INTO THE REAL ARTSY, BEATNIK-EMULATING CROWD, EVERYBODY WAS STILL ON THE FRINGES. THAT WAS THE NORM."**
>
> — CHRIS STEIN

Jon Ronson: Chris, I'm curious what you were like as a teenager and a young man. Because where I grew up in Cardiff, there was nobody cooler than you and Blondie. What was it actually like to be you?

Chris Stein: All my friends were outsiders. Even before I got into the real artsy, beatnik-emulating crowd, everybody was still on the fringes. My earliest group of friends were more mainstream and went on to be normal. Then I hooked up with people who were musicians, photographers and artists. I was sixteen or seventeen, and we all smoked a lot of pot. But even that first group was pretty fringe. That was the norm.

JR: There were a few bands who came along before punk was mainstream, and Blondie was one of them. Could you sense that something was in the air? Did it feel like history was being made?

CS: I was always in this kind of *Zelig* position. The first time I ever smoked pot

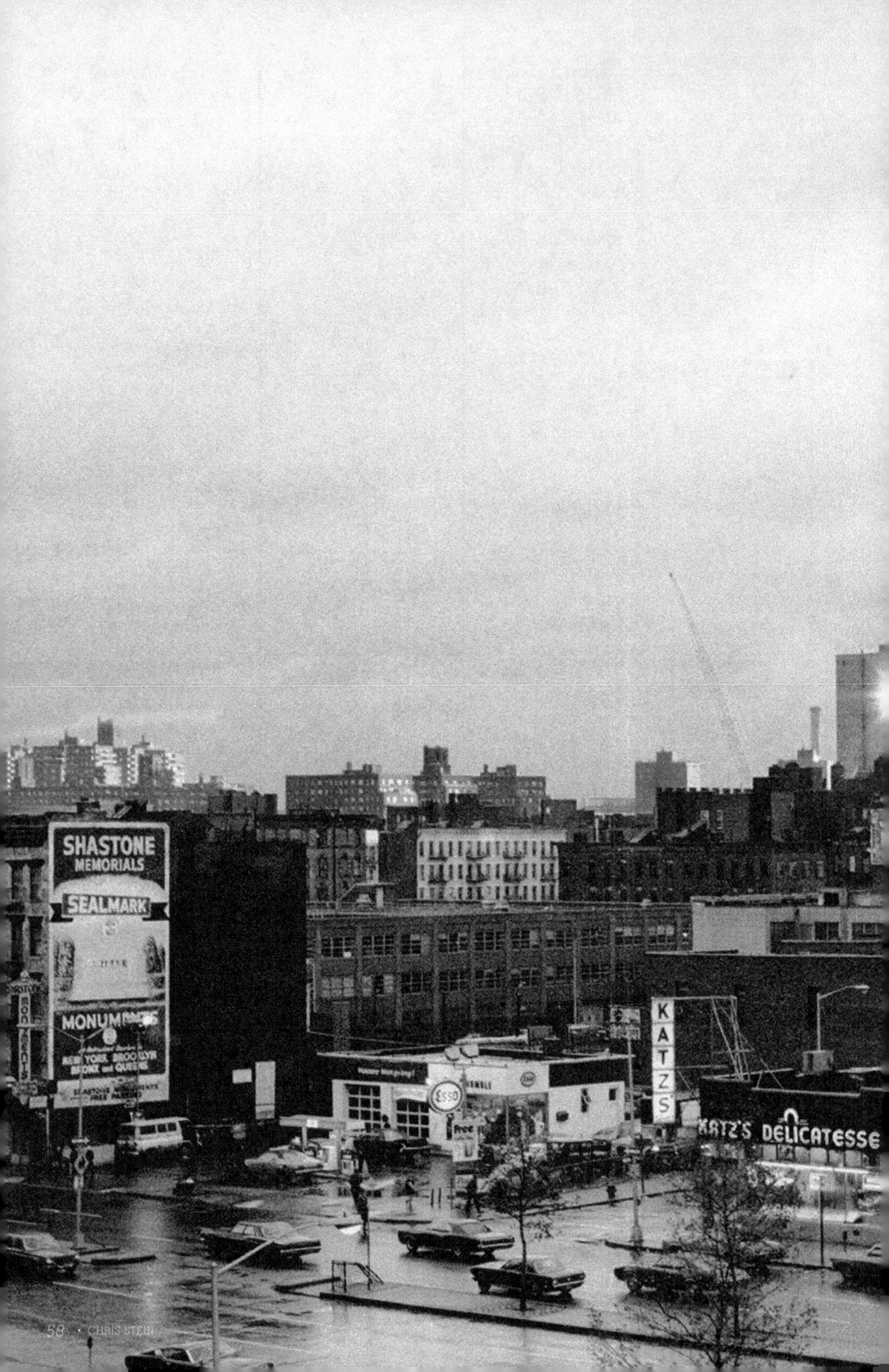

SHASTONE
MEMORIALS
SEALMARK
MONUMENTS
NEW YORK, BROOKLYN
BRONX and QUEENS
ESSO
KATZ
KATZ'S DELICATESSE

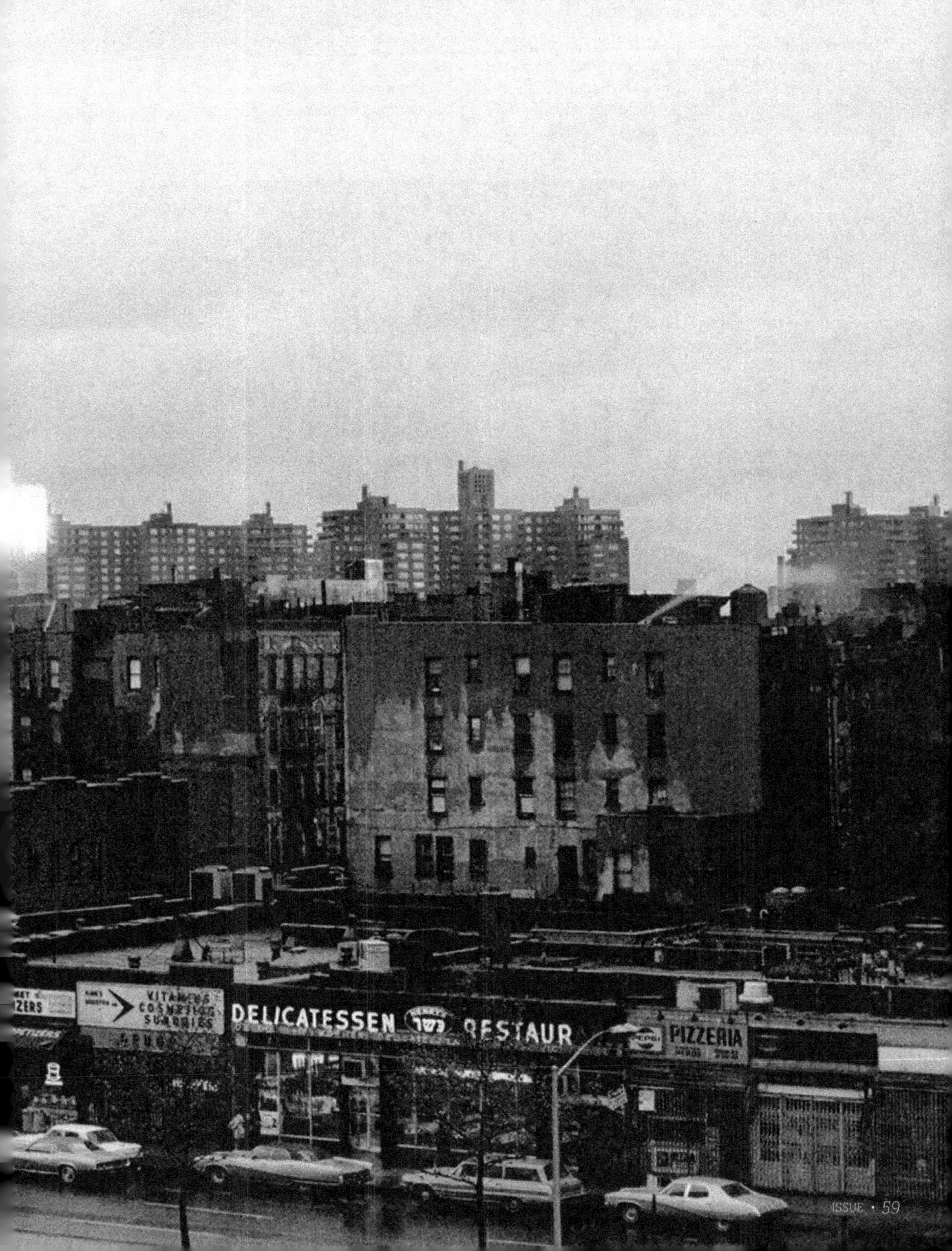

VITAMINS
COSMETICS
SUNDRIES
DELICATESSEN RESTAUR
PIZZERIA
PEPSI

was at the Newport Folk Festival in 1966, a year after Dylan went electric. I almost went in 1965 but didn't make it until the next year when I was sixteen. By that time, everybody had accepted all the electric bands, and The Lovin' Spoonful, Paul Butterfield and all those guys played.

I used to hang around the MacDougal Street milieu, which was the center of the youth scene before the East Village. I jammed at the Night Owl with my friends, and then we played with the guys who went on to become The Left Banke.

JR: How did you see yourself back then? Did you see yourself as a musician or a photographer?

CS: I identified as a musician, mostly. I spent more time playing with my friends in bands, so more energy went into music than photography. I was always carrying cameras around though.
There wasn't any kind of popular music school back then the way there is now. There was just Juilliard, which I wasn't cut out for. So I went to the School of Visual Arts which was kind of the equivalent.

JR: I've always thought of photographers as on the outside looking in, observing things rather than being

part of it, which sometimes means you don't feel you fit in. Do you remember feeling confident or feeling awkward? Were you comfortable in your skin?

CS: No, I was always a nerd and had to push myself to go into social situations. All my friends identified

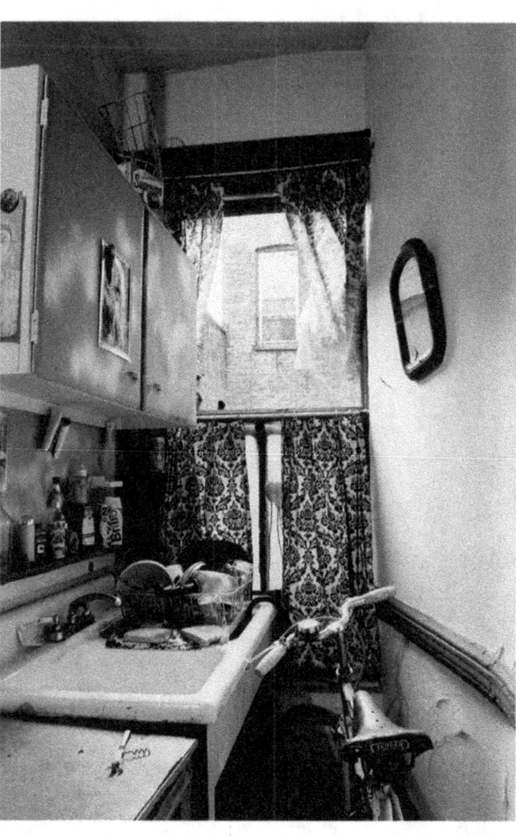

with David Hemmings and *Blow-Up*, but that kind of confidence is few and far between. Maybe some of those aristocratic British photographers were confident, but I think for the most part it was something else.

JR: Did it ever get sketchy? You were

dealing with some famously shy people, like Andy Warhol. Did photography ever become a burden, where people thought you were being intrusive?

CS: By the time I was going to CBGB, everybody was friends and there were a bunch of photogra-

phers around. So that was a given. Then as the band became successful, it was a kind of doorway for my photography.
Bowie was really cautious, but I think it was more about controlling his image. I only got a couple shots of him and Debbie.

their self-titled first album in 1976, *Parallel Lines* (1978) and 2017's *Pollinator*. The band holds multiple awards, including two Grammys, and has been inducted into the Grammy Hall of Fame and the Rock and Roll Hall of Fame.

ZELIG
Written, directed and starring Woody Allen, *Zelig* (1983) is an American mockumentary set in the 1920-30s about a man who adopts the personalities and mannerisms of those with whom he is interacts. Co-starring Mia Farrow, the film incorporates cameo commentaries from Susan Sontag, Saul Bellow and Irving Howe.

NEWPORT FOLK FESTIVAL
The Newport Folk Festival is an annual folk music festival held in Newport, Rhode Island. The festival began in 1959 as the counterpart of the Newport Jazz Festival and is considered one of the first modern music festivals, remaining an important site for the expansion of the folk genre.

THE LOVIN' SPOONFUL
The Lovin' Spoonful is a US rock band known for a number of 1960s hits including "Do You Believe In Magic" and "Summer in the City." Founded by musicians John Sebastian and Zal Yanovsky, the band has had a rotating cast including Cass Elliot and Denny Doherty of the Mamas & the Papas. The Lovin' Spoonful has released seven studio albums and was inducted to the Rock and Roll Hall of Fame in 2000.

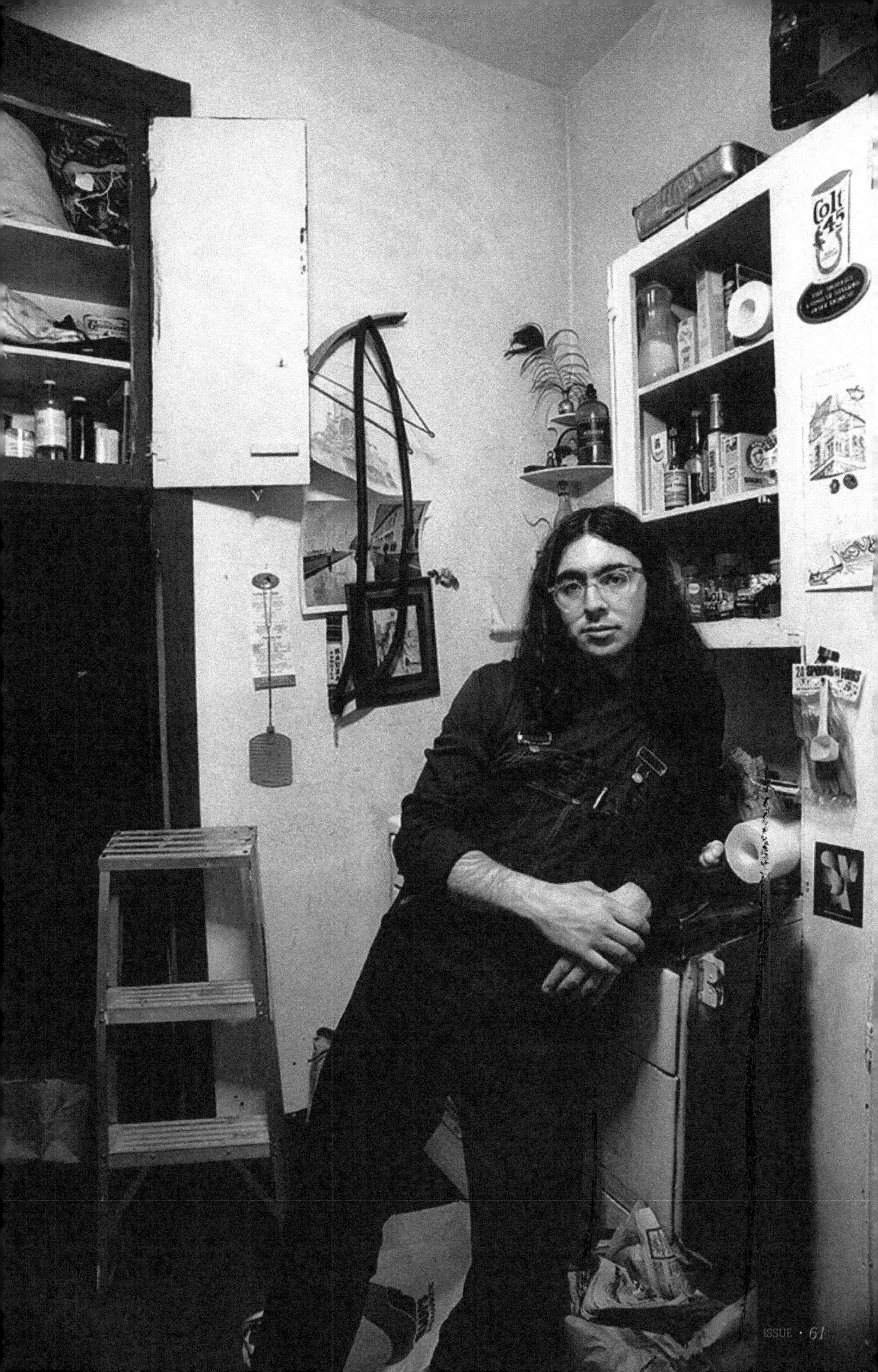

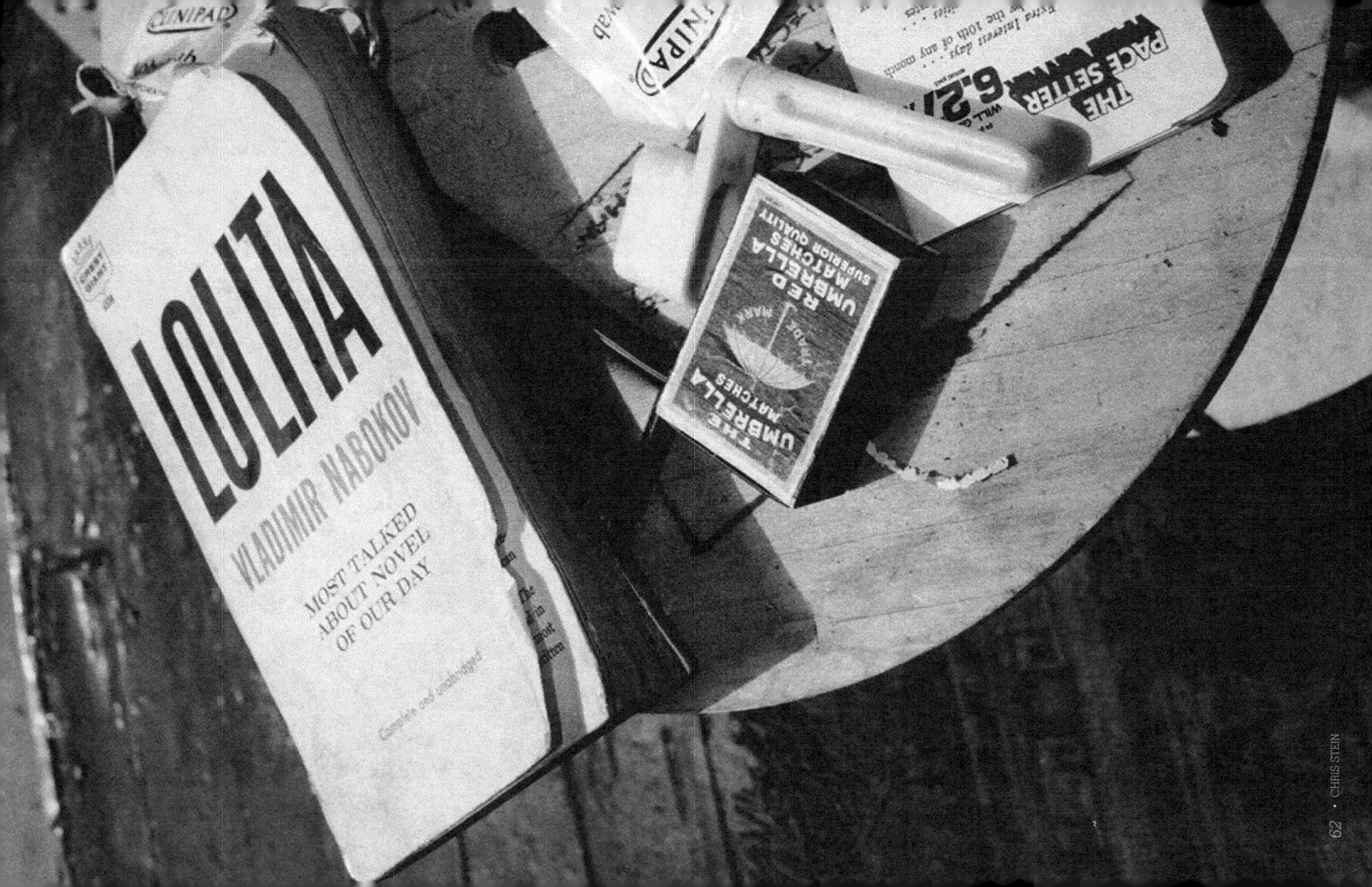

LOLITA
VLADIMIR NABOKOV
MOST TALKED
ABOUT NOVEL
OF OUR DAY
Complete and unabridged
THE UMBRELLA MATCHES
RED UMBRELLA MATCHES
SUPERIOR QUALITY
TRADE MARK
THE PACE SETTER

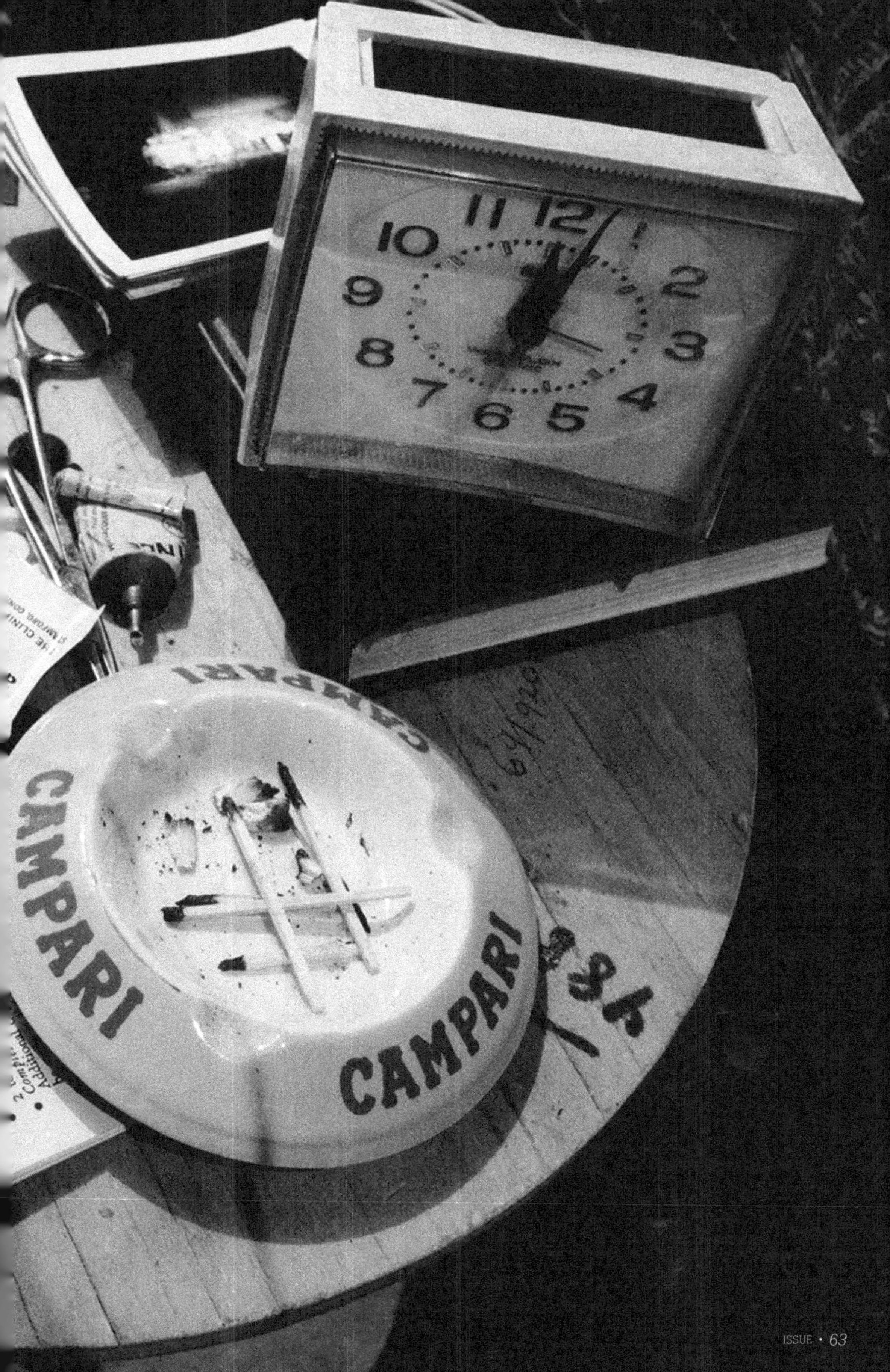

CAMPARI
CAMPARI
CAMPARI

JR: Did he say something to you about it?

CS: I just got the sense that he wasn't sure of my ability. I would have liked to get a couple more posed things. The shots I did with Iggy and Debbie at the same time are more creative than the shots with Bowie.

JR: Did you ever feel shy in those days?

getting in with different crowds.

Then I started wearing makeup, which I liked the reaction to and the freaking people out. I loved going out on the subway and having people look at me like I was a complete weirdo.

JR: Eventually, people must have felt shy and socially awkward around you when

Dick, I couldn't do it." I thought that was funny.

JR: What do you miss most about those days?

CS: I miss my youthful energy. I recently missed playing a bunch of shows because of an irregular heartbeat—really stupid and boring. But I was probably a lot more egotistical

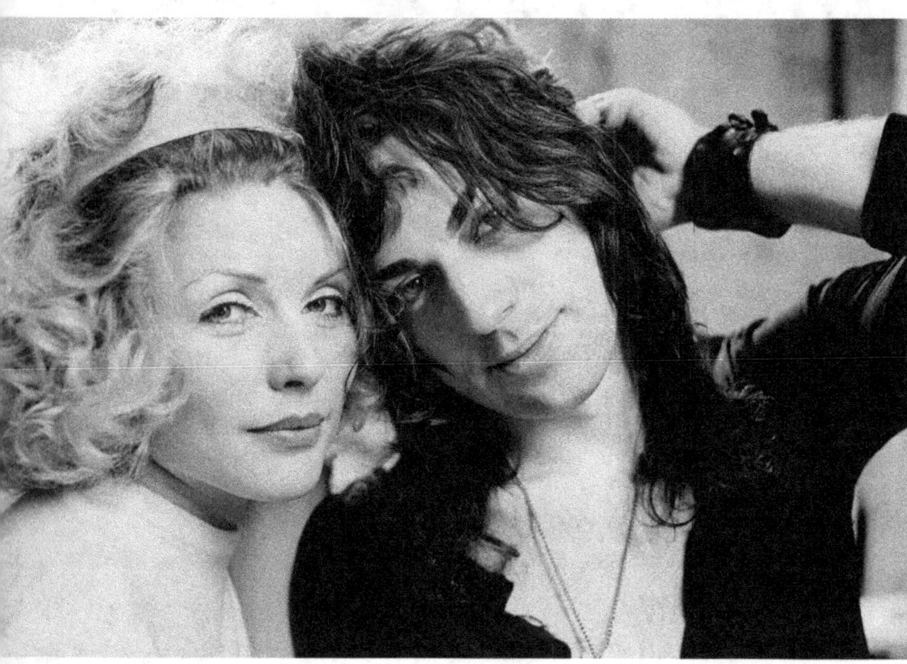

I don't know how I would have handled meeting people like Warhol.

CS: I felt shy initially. When I first started going out to clubs on my own, I would frequently have a flask of bourbon or cheap whiskey to bolster my forward motion as it were. But it passed when I started meeting people and

Blondie became so successful.

CS: I guess. We ate with Anthony Bourdain when he was filming *Parts Unknow*, right before he died, and he said he was in the same place as us a couple of times. And I said, "Why didn't you say hello?" And he said, "Oh, you guys were like Liz and

and crazy back then, and I like where I am at mentally now.

But as far as the environment, there are a lot of aspects of corporate New York that I really don't like now. Soho was so great back then, and now it's a shopping mall. Times Square had an atmosphere, and I liked the funkiness and shittiness of it. That's missing

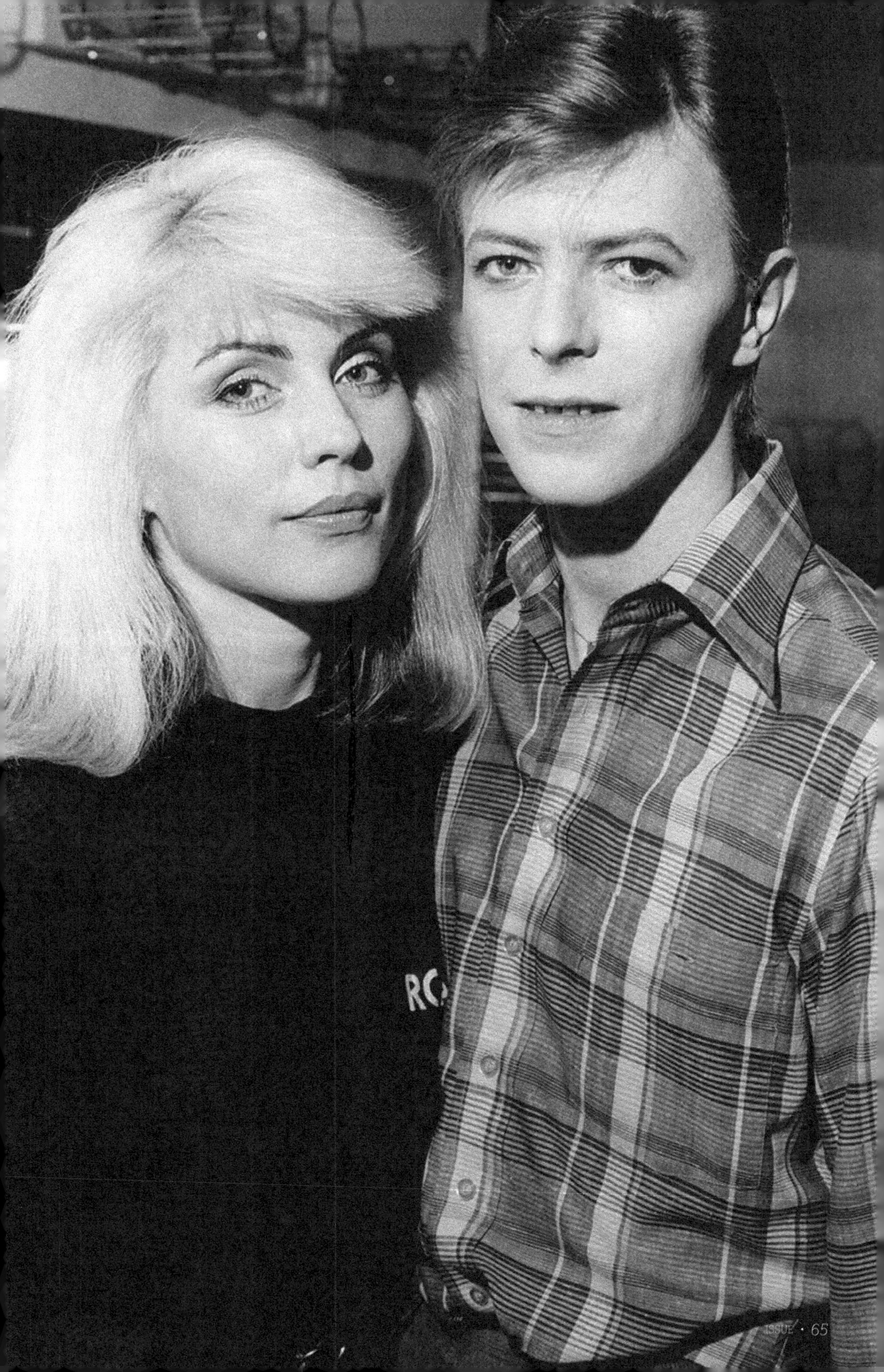

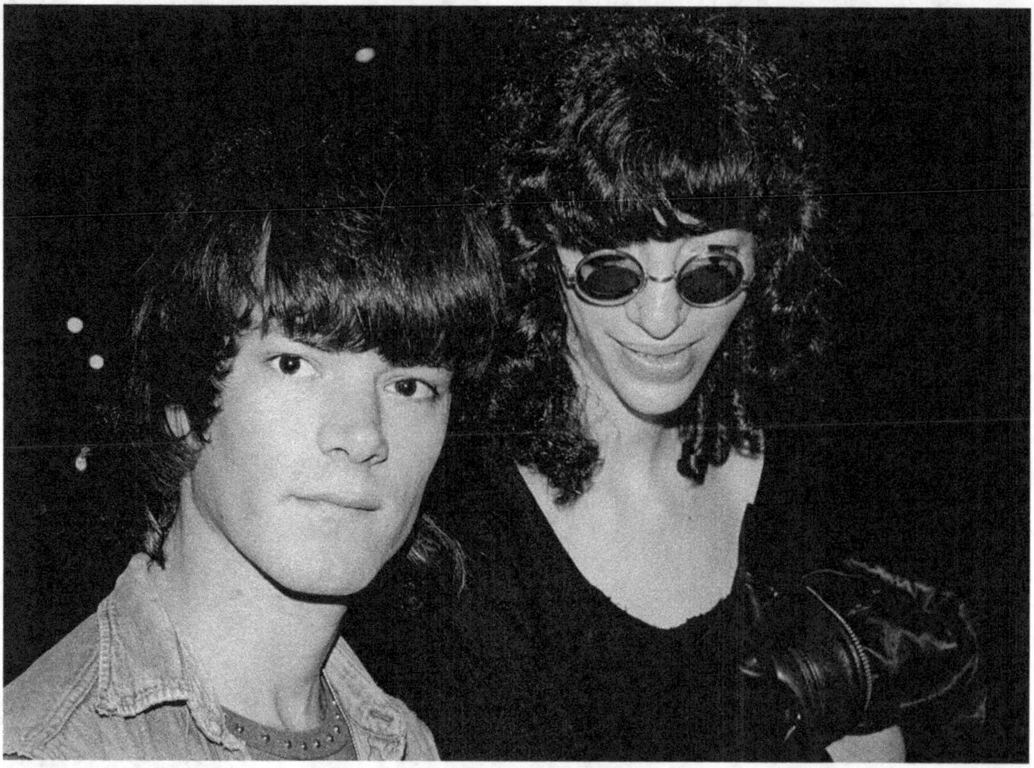

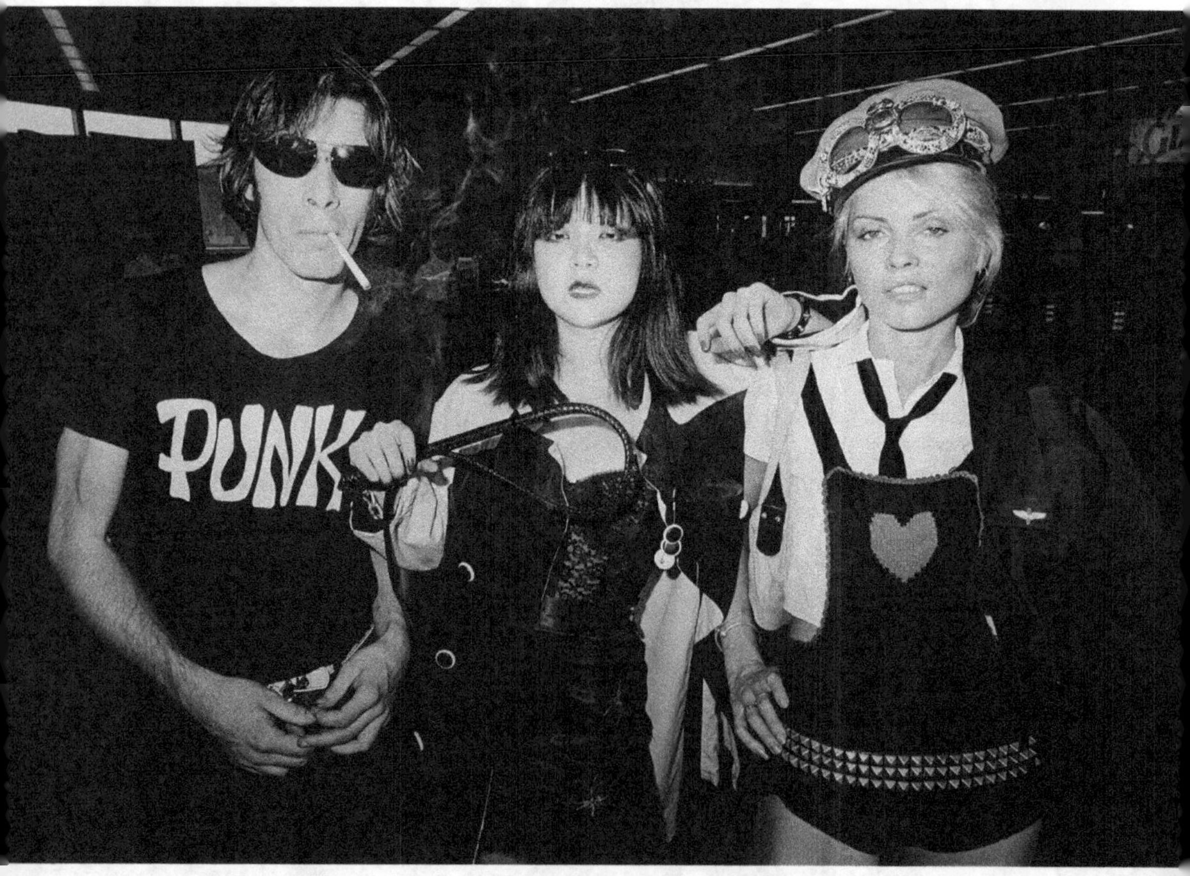

birth of the MPAA film rating system.

<u>RUDY GIULIANI</u>
Rudy Giuliani is an American politician, attorney, former Mayor of New York City and current advisor to President Donald Trump. He succeeded David Dinkins as Mayor of New York City in 1994 until 2001 and is best known for his successful efforts to clean up New York's streets and lower its crime rates.

<u>THE FIFTH ELEMENT</u>
The Fifth Element (1997) is a French sci-fi action film co-written and directed Luc Besson and starring Bruce Willis, Gary Oldman and Milla Jovovich. Set in the 23rd century, the plot follows Willis as a cab driver suddenly tasked with the responsibility of saving planet Earth.

<u>MAX'S KANSAS CITY</u>
Max's Kansas City was a popular New York nightclub and restaurant opened by Mickey Ruskin in 1965. Located at 213 Park Avenue South, Max's was a hub for many famous musicians, poets, artists, politicians and celebrities in the '60s and '70s, until its closing in 1981.

<u>CBGB</u>
CBGB was a New York club and music venue opened in 1973 in Manhattan's East Village. It became famous for hosting punk and new wave bands such as Blondie, Talking Heads and the Ramones. The club closed in 2006 with its final concert featuring Patti Smith.

<u>"LIZ AND DICK"</u>
"Liz and Dick" was the popular nickname for celebrity couple Elizabeth Taylor and Richard Burton. In

now. You know the Scorsese movie *After Hours?*

JR: Yeah, of course.

CS: That's what Soho was like. It's a great encapsulation of the whole atmosphere and how crazy it was. It was like some kind of weird dream. A lot of where we were was very dreamlike. There were little cliques of people who were isolated and unaffected by notoriety, just functioning on their own with their weird little clubs you could go to.

I remember I was at a squat, an abandoned building with a weird, makeshift club in a basement. We had been watching some jazz band there, and we walked right out into the Thompson Square riots which were in full swing.

JR: What do you remember about the riots?

CS: It was crazy, and the police were definitely overreacting. We saw them pull this guy off a bicycle who was just driving by. He had nothing to do with anything, and they just grabbed him and dragged him off his bike. We got out of there pretty fast.

JR: I watched the first episode of season two of *The Deuce* last night, the HBO porn show.

CS: Yeah, it's very dour.

> ## "I'M TEMPTED TO SAY IT'S LESS OF A STRUGGLE NOW FOR PEOPLE TO SUCCEED. IT FEELS LIKE LIL PUMP OR SOMEBODY IS IMMEDIATELY THRUST OUT THERE AND SELLS A MILLION RECORDS OVERNIGHT."
>
> — CHRIS STEIN

JR: At one point I turned to my wife and said, "Every time they turn on the radio in this show, an iconic classic of the time is playing." Like "Roadrunner" or "Don't Worry About the Government." I bet in the mid-'70s, when you turned on the radio most of the time the songs that came out were shit songs that nobody remembers.

JR: I look back on those times and what you've captured and created musically as one of the most exciting, iconic times of my lifetime. The people you met— Basquiat, Warhol— the things that you did as Blondie and the music that you created, culture doesn't get any better than that. Did it feel like that at the time? When I look at your photographs, it feels like you knew you were in the middle of something amazing.

CS: It was always exciting, but I don't know how much focus I had on the future and what was coming at that point.

I'm tempted to say it's less of a struggle now for people to succeed. It feels like Lil Pump or somebody is immediately thrust out there and sells a million records overnight. It's probably not the case, and people are probably still struggling. But we really did have a physical struggle living in very shitty environments and not having any money. That was going on, and maybe that lends itself.

JR: It probably did lend itself. I remember when I lived in Manchester in England, and the rehearsal rooms were really cheap. Bands could afford to rehearse and record, and nobody needed a job. These days if you want to live in Manhattan you have to be pretty rich, and as a consequence I think creativity doesn't happen as much. So when did you see it all change? I guess it was Giuliani where things started to go wrong.

CS: Well, 9/11 was the real big change. Two years after that is when the money started pouring in, which is part of why people are so suspicious about 9/11 because it seemed like it opened the floodgates of corporate interest. Things that had been in the private sector were suddenly taken over.

Otherwise, the change had been gradual from about 1995 onwards. We went right from Dinkins to Giuliani.

JR: I have no idea what Dinkins was like as a mayor.

CS: He was non-existent. He didn't do anything anybody could see, and that was why you could go into grocery stores

downtown and buy drugs pretty easily. It was the height of drug plagues on the Lower East Side at any rate.

JR: When Giuliani became mayor, did you watch it gradually disappear?

CS: It felt like it took about ten years for it to make a dramatic change. I remember the police busting all the bodegas and grocery stores that were selling drugs. That was on its way out. But it seemed more gradual. I mean, ten years really isn't a long time, and maybe it was even less.

JR: One of the things I like so much about your photographs is you're not capturing grime or misery. You're actually capturing a lot of happiness. You can tell that New York hadn't been gentrified, but you're portraying young people full of life, excitement, and adventure. Did it feel that way?

CS: It's hard to be objective because I was so embedded in it, but the New York of 1970 was closer to 100 years ago than we are now. Before the technological revolutions with the improvements of telephones and TV, there wasn't much of a sea change as they say.

JR: Do you think that New York is completely gone, or does it still exist in its corners?

2012, Lifetime premiered a biographical film, *Liz & Dick*, directed by Lloyd Kramer and starring Lindsay Lohan in the role of Elizabeth Taylor and Grant Bowler as Richard Burton.

W. LESTER BANKS
W. Lester Banks was an American music journalist, critic, author and musician, known as one of America's most influential rock critics. Banks wrote regularly for *Creem* and *Rolling Stone* magazines, as well as the *Village Voice* and *Playboy*.

PUNK (MAGAZINE)
Punk magazine was a music magazine created by cartoonist John Holmstrom, publisher Ged Dunn and music journalist Legs McNeil in 1975. With its fifteen issues published between 1976-79, *Punk* popularized '70s New York's underground rock music scene, featuring Blondie, Sex Pistols, Lou Reed and Iggy Pop on its covers.

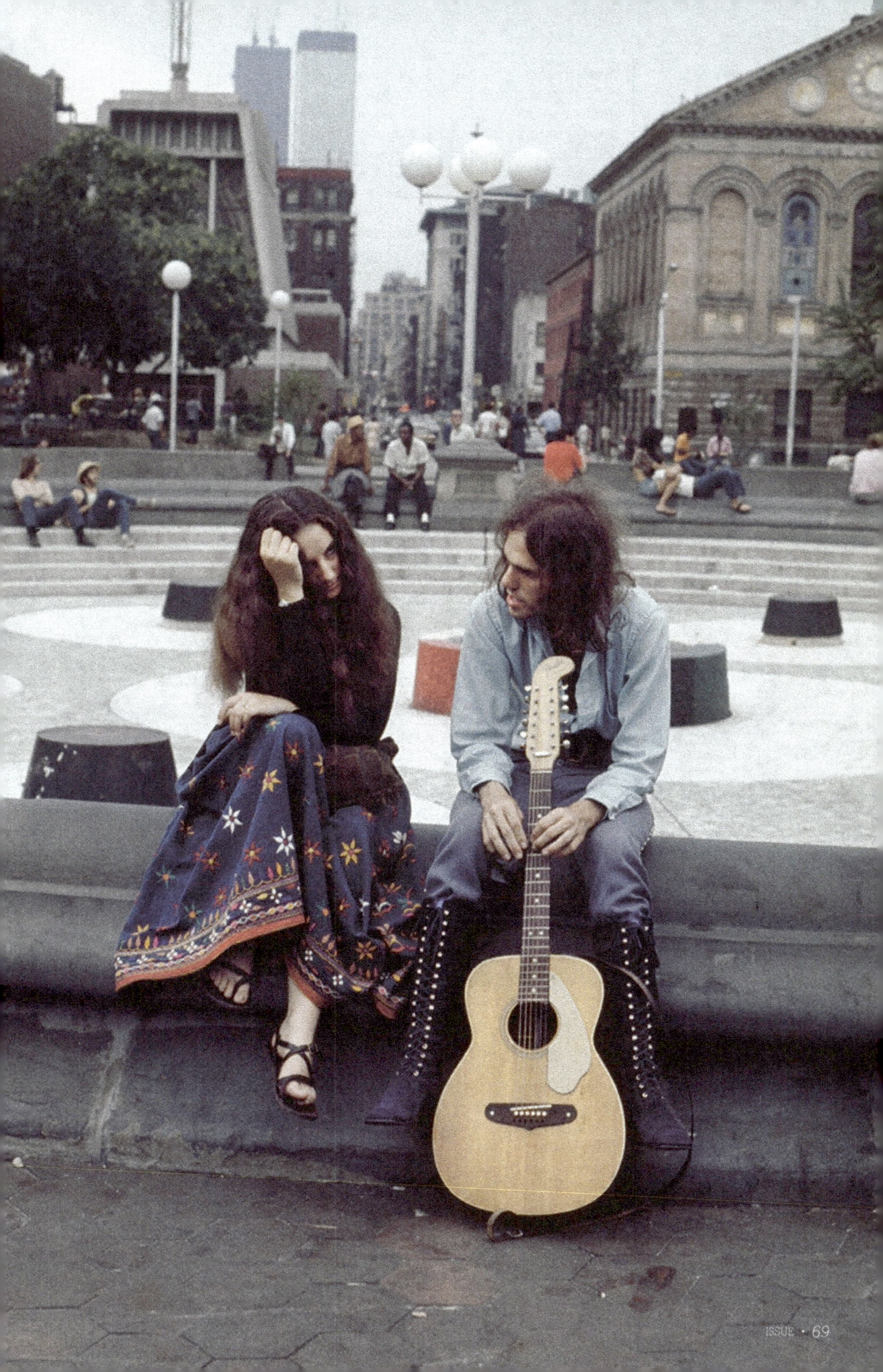

CS: I think there's plenty of it about. Physically, there's not been a huge change. We've got these glass towers, but it's not like *The Fifth Element*, yet. Maybe that's coming with the infinite things shooting up in the sky.

But, everything is getting cleaned up. Right where I live from the French Quarter, and now it looks like everything else. There's a building right around the block from Max's [Kansas City] that I used to go to that had these weird, wooden structures that looked like they were 100 years old. Then the facades got all redone, and the immune system from drugs, so I got this congenital condition. You have to be Mediterranean or Eastern European to get it, and it was time-consuming but also kind of fascinating.

JR: Did photography help?

CS: We took some

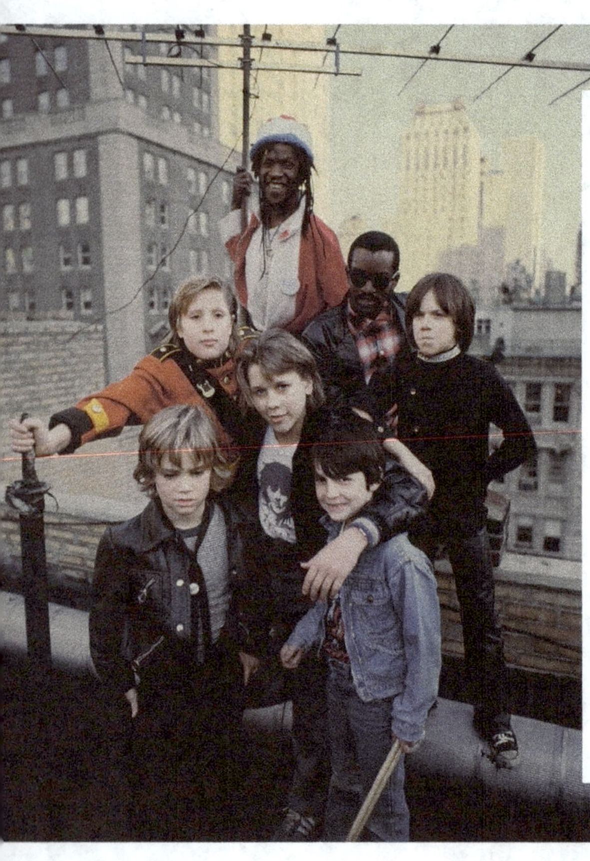

"YOU HAVE A TIME-RE-LATIONSHIP TO A SONG THAT YOU'VE LISTENED TO FOR TWEN-TY YEARS, WHEREAS PHOTOGRA-PHY PULLS YOU INTO THESE MO-MENTS THAT ARE A LONG TIME AGO."
— CHRIS STEIN

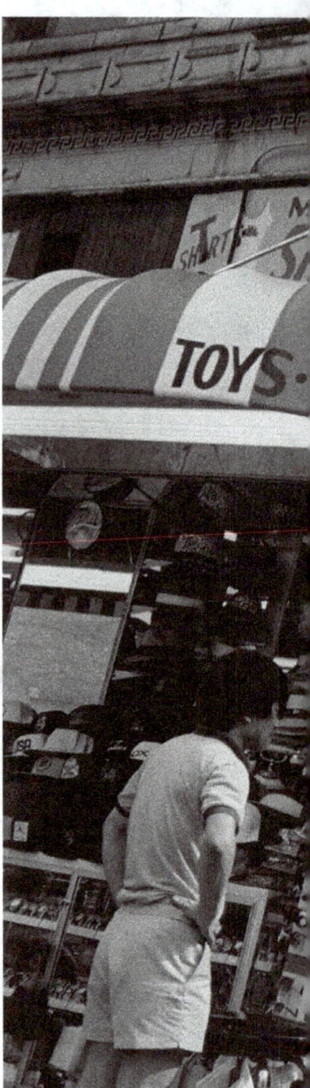

there was a really great building that was always covered with crumbling paint. They hadn't painted the damn thing for years, and then they finally fixed it up last year. And it kind of ruined it for me. It looked like something from New Orleans interiors got redone. That goes on, but overall the physicality is still there.

JR: When you mentioned your health, it reminded me that you got pretty sick in the '80s.

CS: I had wrecked my Polaroids of the hospital room I was in for three months. It was a real pain in the ass.

JR: Were you housebound for a long time?

CS: Not too long. By the time I got out,

most of it had died down. I still have scars on my back because the proteins that bind your skin together break down. It's called "Pemphigus", which is Latin for "blisters". It was

and music? Are they about the same thing, or do they come from different places?

CS: I think they're different. You get a bunch of people listening to the same

photograph, that's not as guaranteed. They may all have separate associations.

I also don't think the time travel aspects of music are as immediate as they are in photography.

long time ago.

JR: How much editorializing do you do with your photographs?

CS: They're all full-frame for the most part.

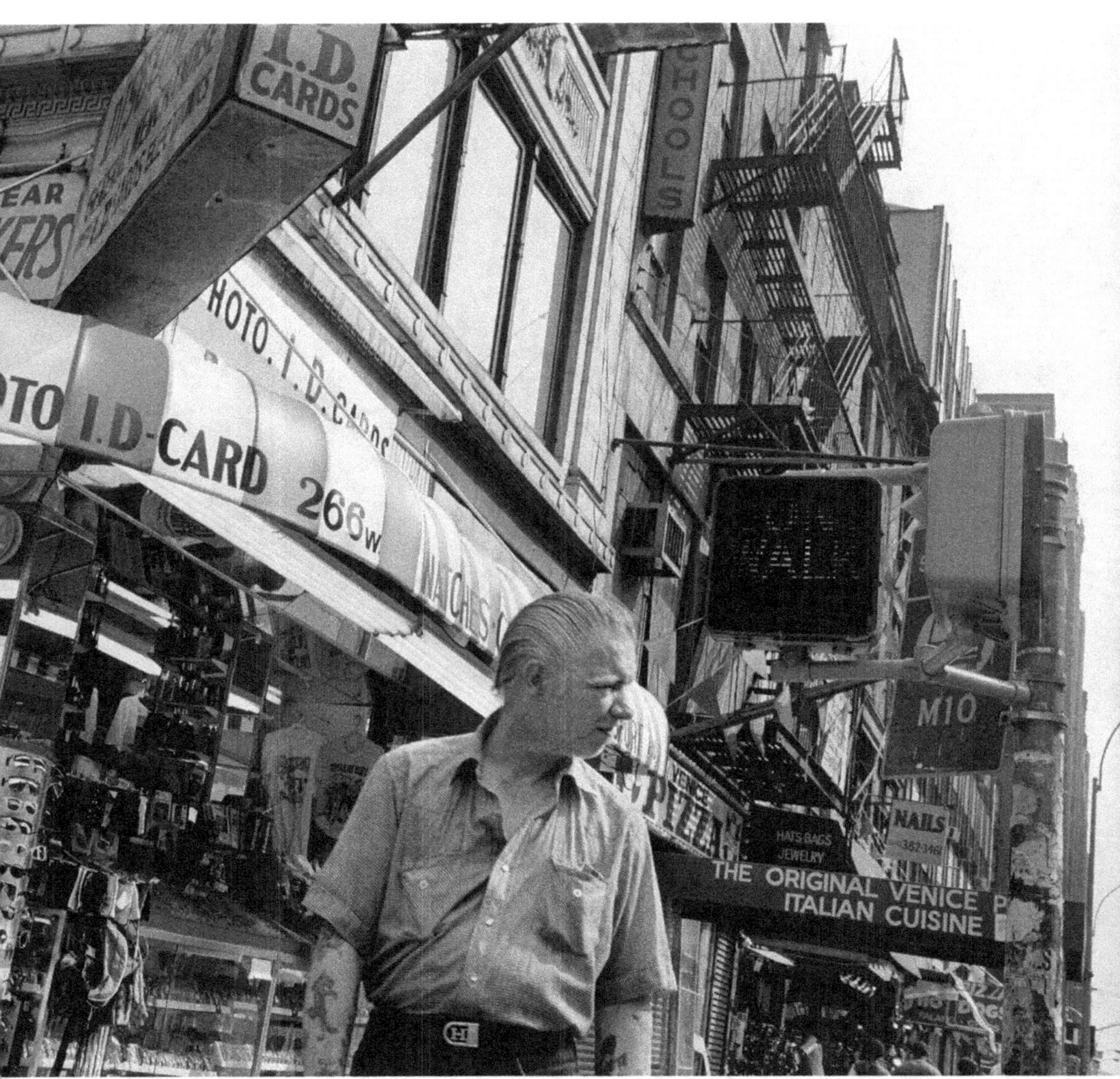

potentially fatal years ago, but now they treat it with steroids.

JR: What would you say is the difference between your photos

music, and it probably triggers the same synapses and brain locations, so there's a kind of bonding that goes on. When people look at the same

You have a time-relationship to a song that you've listened to for twenty years, whereas photography pulls you into these moments that are a

JR: That qualifies as not editorializing, right?

CS: The composition is editorializing, but that's just how you

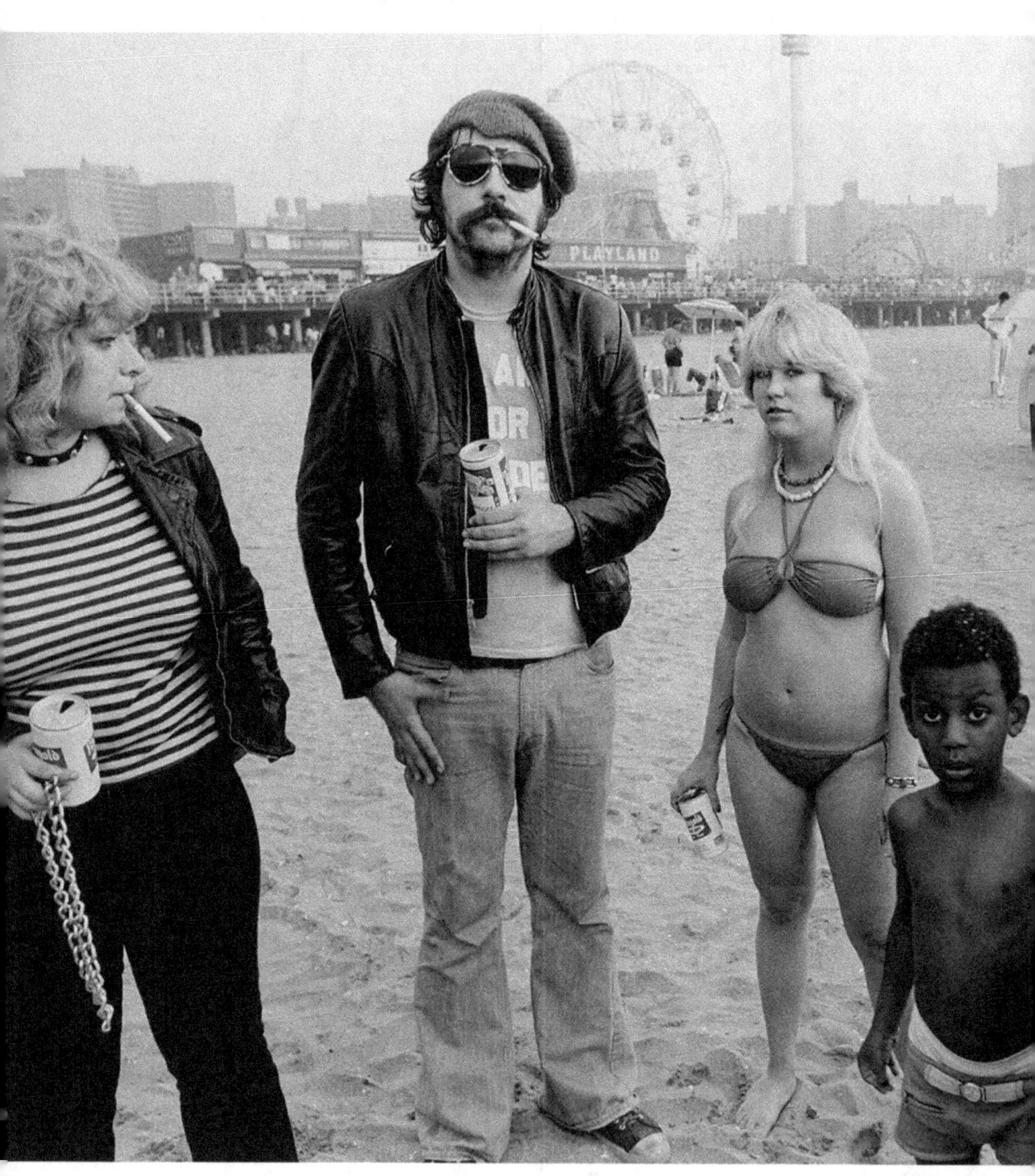

PLAYLAND

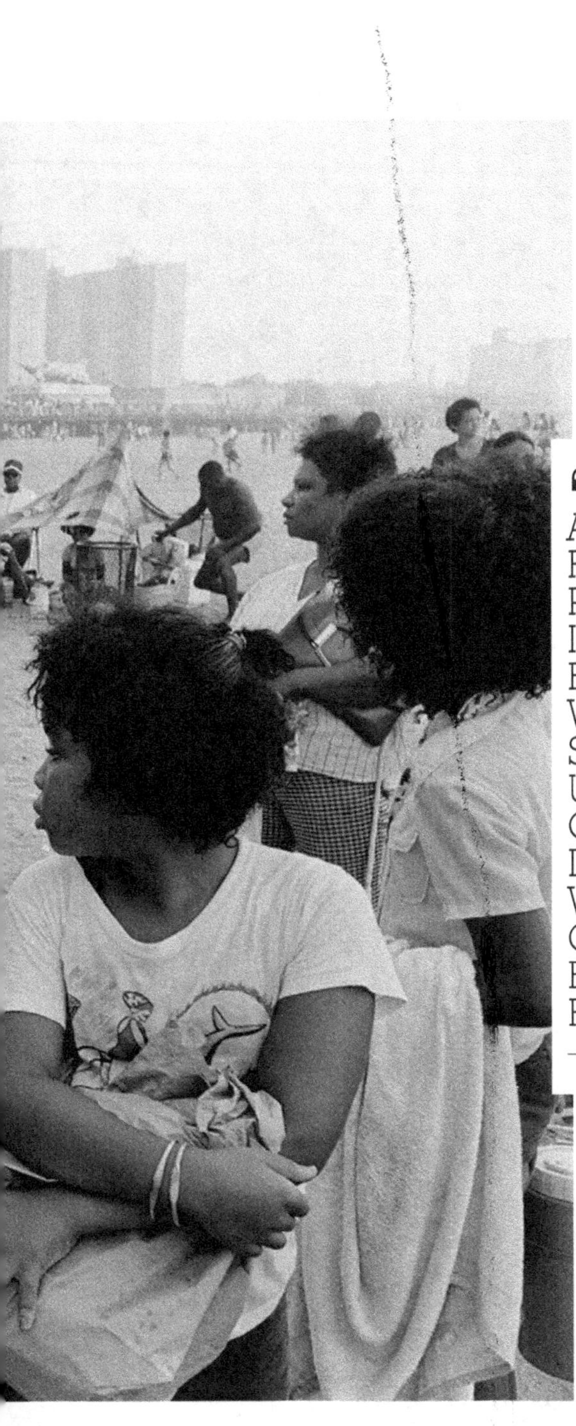

adjust the camera. I remember as a kid discovering that you could look through the lens on a camera. I didn't know you could do that because I was using a Brownie camera where you look through a second lens. The fact that you could see exactly what you were taking a picture of was something I was really happy about.

JR: Right. Because the times I've met you, you're always very happy and warm-spirited.

CS: Am I?

JR: You always seem that way. I think when you go through an extraordinary era or experience, you can be left with the joy of it, or you can let the little slights consume you so all you think of are the bad times. It seems like you just remember the good times and have a very sunny outlook on life.

CS: Life is amusing. There's a comedy routine to people saying, "Remember when we were shooting up and the guy sold us Drano and we had to go to the emergency room? Remember how great that was?" That's kind of my take on reality. I try to be optimistic about life in general.

JR: I think of your pictures as optimistic, do you see them that way?

CS: Maybe. I mean, I always found decaying stuff really attractive in a weird way and kind of fascinating. There's definitely a beauty in all that.

You go on Instagram, and there's so many photographers devoted to this dark art and gloomy stuff. I don't know if it's emo or what, but it's attractive. I don't think that genre used to be out there so much.

JR: The decay in your photographs isn't about how terrible everything was but about the possibilities to create really interesting things, which you did. You captured the milieu from which some of the greatest culture of the century came. I think that's what's so good about your photographs. They recognize that the mounds of rubble aren't bad, but are about creating a world from which amazing things can come.

CS: Yeah, I don't know. I was always drawn to it, maybe because it was familiar.

JR: My favorite photograph in your book is that one of W. Lester Banks on the beach at Coney Island.

CS: That's a classic. It's one of my favorites. I gave a very large print of that to Jon Stewart when we were on his show. He was excited because coincidently his father lived in one of the apartment buildings in the background.

JR: How did that photo come to be? He looks like somebody who'd never been on a beach before. He's enjoying it but is also incredibly uncomfortable.

CS: That's a good description. He was both uncomfortable and sort of flamboyant at the same time. It was from one of the *Punk* magazine fumetti things, the Mutant Monster Beach Party.

JR: What do you want people to take away from the book?

CS: The time travel aspect. I've seen people being fascinated

by that period, so if I can convey a little bit of that, especially to the younger people, then that's successful to me.

JR: Do you think there's a third book that you can bring out? Are you still taking pictures now?

CS: I take pictures now, and I still maintain my Instagram. I probably could put together enough stuff, but as far as the old stuff goes it's finite.

All images © Chris Stein

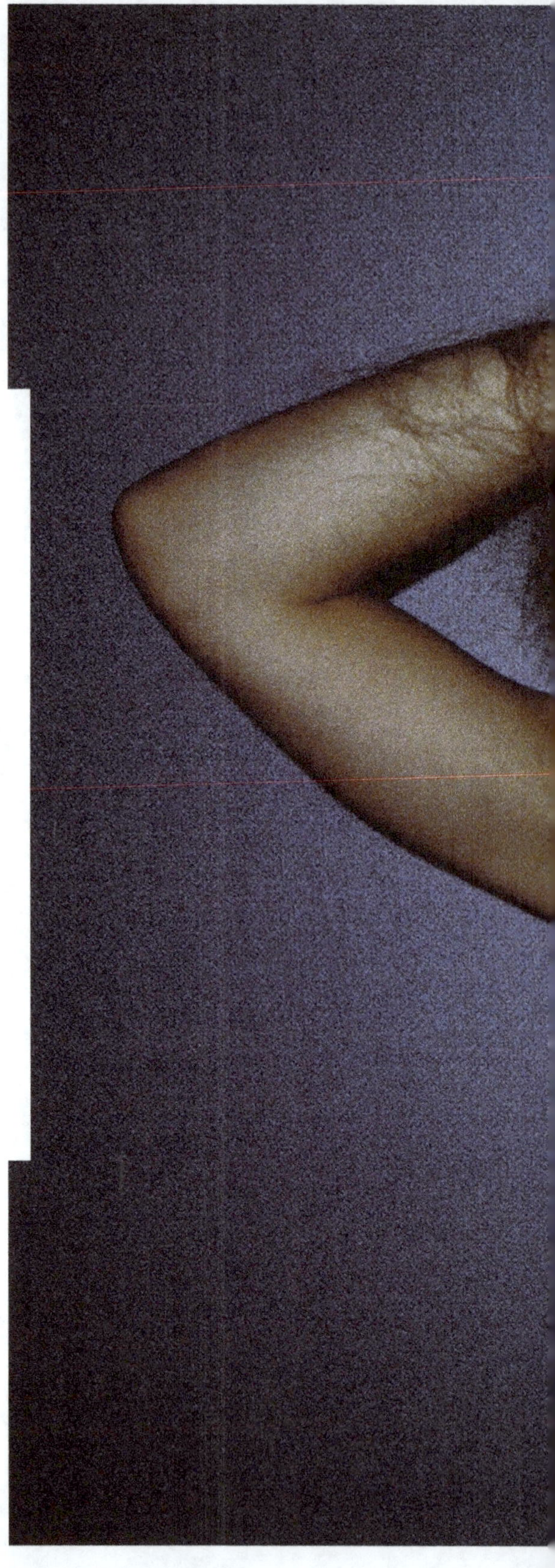

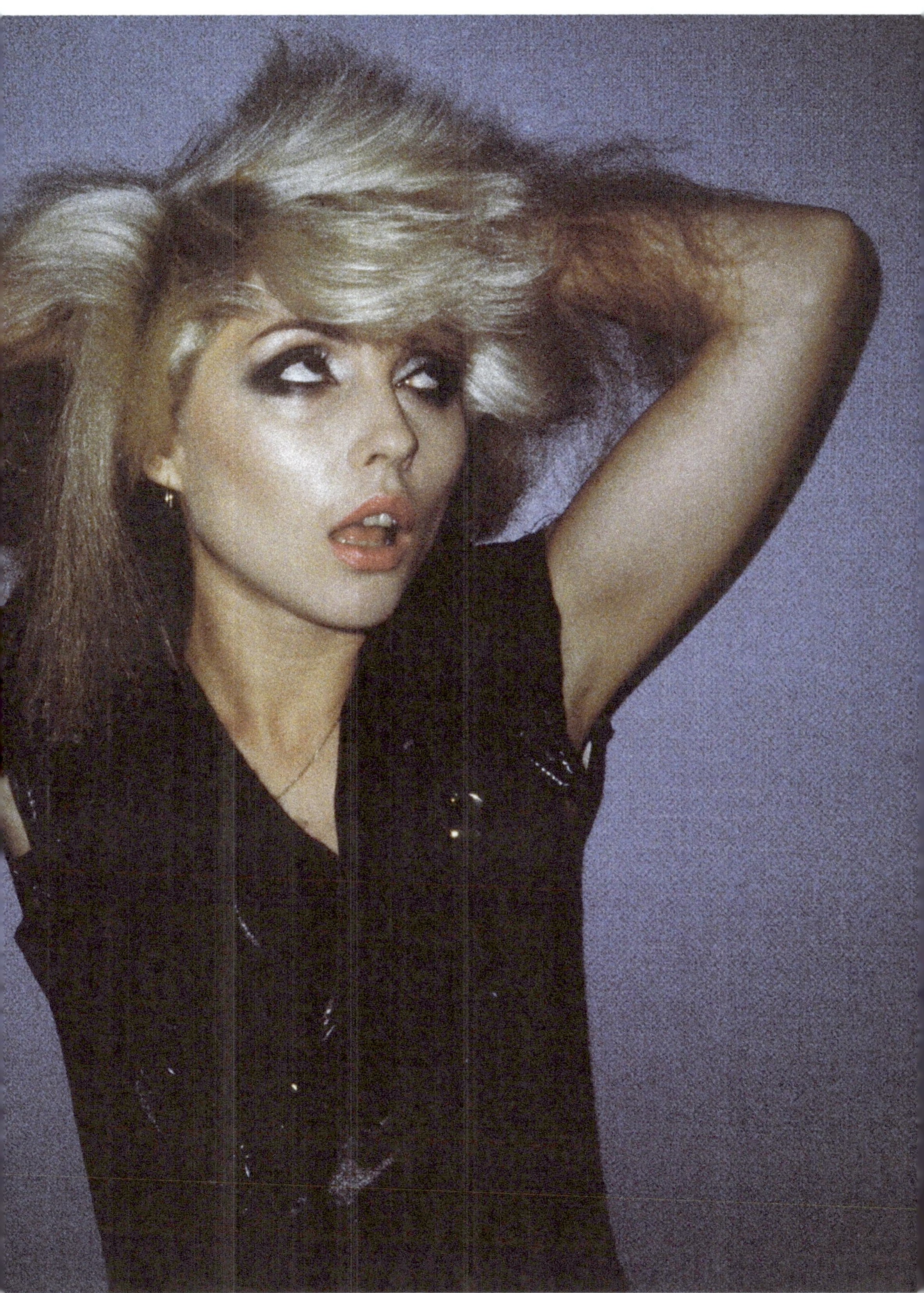

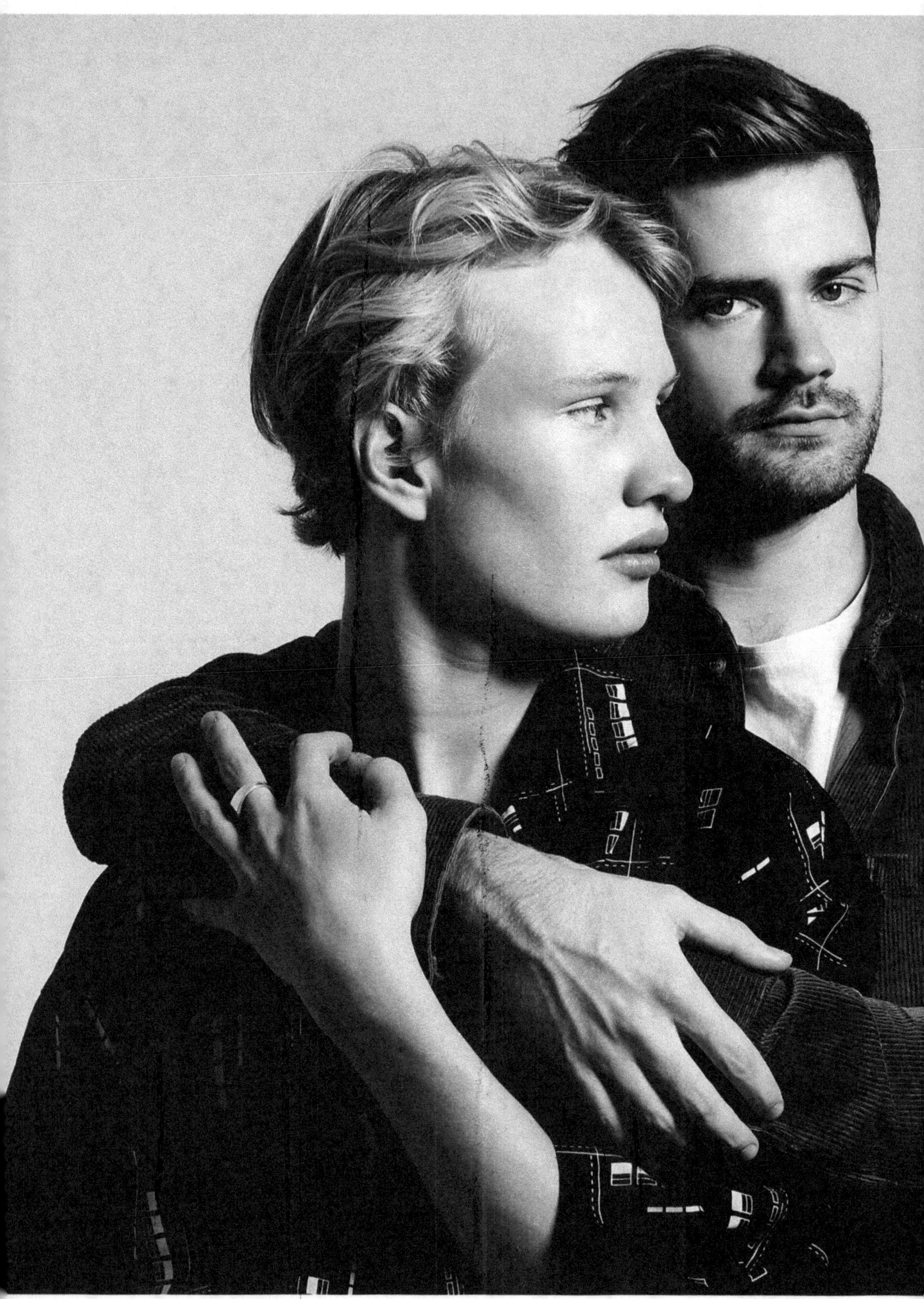

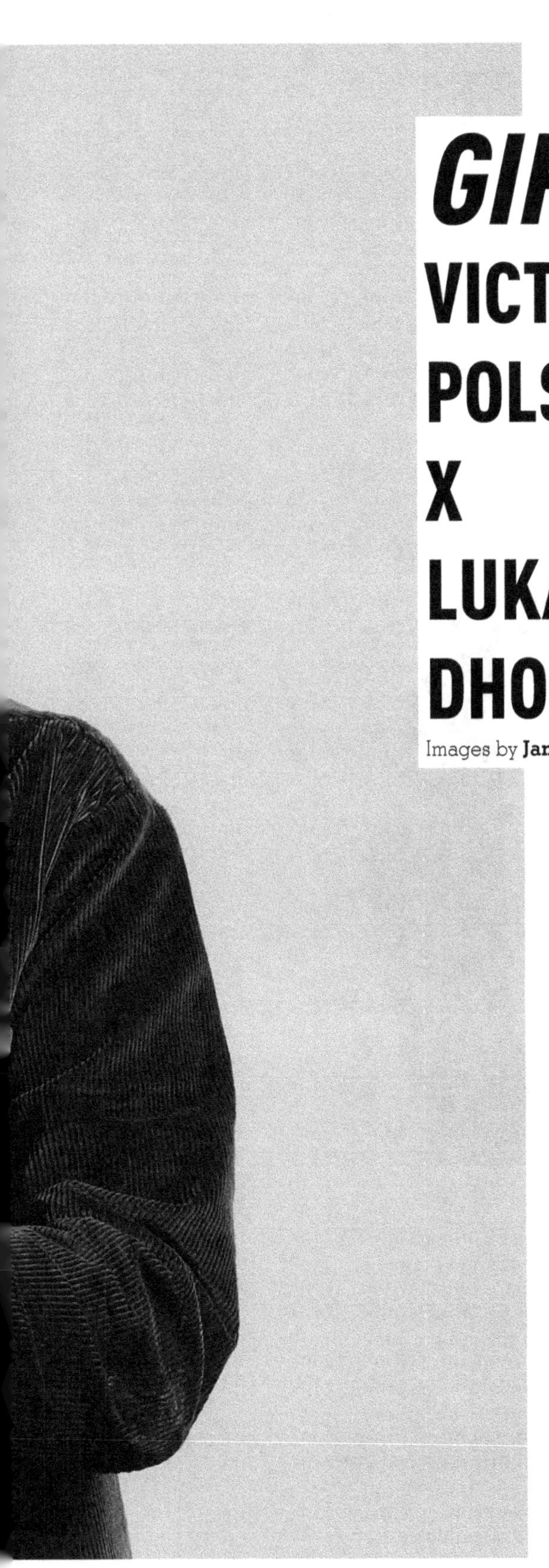

GIRL

VICTOR POLSTER
X
LUKAS DHONT

Images by **Jan-Willem Dikkers**

Director Lukas Dhont's debut feature film, Girl, *is more than just a trans story. It's a story of identity, growing up and the courageous steps required to become who you are meant to be. The Belgian film follows Lara, a fifteen-year-old girl born in a boy's body who is committed to becoming a professional ballerina. Despite being accepted into a prestigious dance academy and the support of those around her, most notably her father, Lara continues to struggle with what she sees in the mirror. Desperate to speed up the gender reassignment process while perfecting her dance technique, Lara pushes her body to its limits.*

Girl *won both the Caméra d'Or award for best first feature film and the Queer Palm at the Cannes Film Festival. It is also Belgium's official 2018 Academy Awards entry for Best Foreign Language Film. Victor Polster, the young Belgian actor who delivers a breathtaking performance as Lara, won the Un Certain Regard Jury Award for Best Performance in his first acting role.*

Polster and director Dhont discuss how they each prepared for the making of Girl *and the impact the film has had on viewers, themselves and the trans community.*

———

Victor Polster: What did you have in mind when you made the film?

Lukas Dhont: The idea for this film started in 2009 when I was eighteen years old. I had just finished at a very Catholic high school and was going to start film school. I read an article in a Flemish newspaper about a young fifteen-year-old trans girl, Nora Monsecour, who was in the ballet school in Antwerp and wanted to change classes from the boys class to the girls class but wasn't allowed. Her dream was to become a ballerina, and I immediately was very attracted to her story because for me she was an example of someone who chose the true version of herself at a very young age and was very honest with that and very ambitious at the same time.

During my Catholic high school time, I had been trying to deny a part of myself, more specifically my sexuality, to fit into the group. And so to read about the fifteen-year-old that actually did the opposite was very attractive to me. So I contacted her because I wanted to shoot a documentary about her. We met each other, but she didn't want to do the documentary because her school situation was very difficult at the time. Also, she didn't want

to be filmed because she was transitioning and didn't feel comfortable with her body being on screen. But she did agree to meet with me more.

She was a personal example of really being yourself, and at the time I wasn't "out of the closet" yet, so for me it was still very

difficult to choose myself. She helped me overcome that, and I helped her, in a way, by giving her this film. She agreed to start writing a script with me for a fiction film, which for her was a way to let go of part of her past and to deal with what was happening. From

that moment on, we started writing the script for a fiction film that eventually became Girl.

Very early on we decided to not really put the focus on the outside world or on negative reactions of the outside world. We didn't want a character that had to fight everyone. We wanted to really be

able to focus on the character and her struggles.

What was so powerful to me in the original story was the world of the ballet, symbolizing a very binary, gender-specific world in which this trans character wants to participate. I thought that made

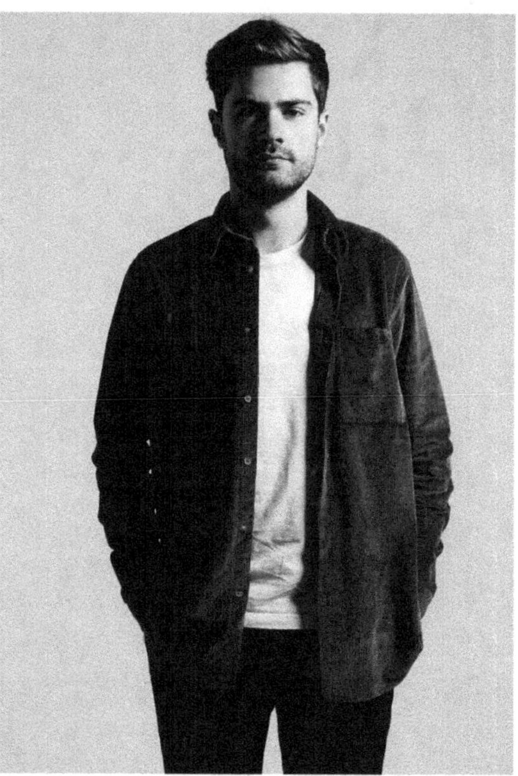

Lukas Dhont, Director of *Girl*

GIRL
Written by Lukas Dhont and Angelo Tijssens, *Girl* is a 2018 Belgian drama film directed by Dhont. It follows the teenaged Lara as she studies at a prestigious Belgian dance academy and prepares for sex reassignment surgery. The film screened in the Un Certain Regard section at the 2018 Cannes Film Festival, where it won the Caméra d'Or award for best first feature film, as well as the Queer Palm—an independently sponsored prize for selected LGBT-relevant films entered into the Cannes Film Festival.

LUKAS DHONT
Award-winning Belgian director and writer Lukas Dhont is known for his first feature, *Girl* (2018), as well as his previous short films *Headlong* (2012) and *L'Infini* (2014), all of which explore issues of gender or sexuality.

VICTOR POLSTER
A trained ballet dancer, sixteen-year-old Victor Polster won the Un Certain Regard: Best Actor award at Cannes film festival for his first acting role, portraying Lara in Lukas Dhont's *Girl* (2018).

SIDI LARBI CHERKAOUI
Sidi Larbi Cherkaoui (b. 1976) is a Belgian-Moroccan dancer and choreographer. He has made over fifty choreographic pieces and has received two Laurence Olivier Awards for Best New Dance Production, three Ballet Tanz awards for best choreographer (2008, 2011, 2017) and the KAIROS Prize (2009).

NORA MONSECOUR
The primary inspiration for the character of Lara in *Girl*, Nora Monsecour is a teenage transgender ballet dancer. She started dancing at the age of four, training professionally in ballet when she was nine. She graduated in contemporary dance at MUDA (the Institute for Dance and Drama) in Belgium, before entering the Northern School of Contemporary Dance, Leeds in 2015.

JAN MARTENS
Jan Martens (b.1984) Belgian choreographer. He studied dance at the Royal Conservatoire of Dance at Artesis Hogeschool in Antwerp and at the Fontys Dance Academy in Tilburg. Since 2009 Jan Martens has been creating his own pieces, focusing on contemporary social topics with humor and a talent for gentle controversy. In 2014, together with business leader Klaartje Oerlemans, he founded the production platform GRIP in Antwerp/Rotterdam to organise and distribute his work. From September 2014 to June 2016, Martens was artist-in-residence at tanzhaus nrw, a performing arts centre in Düsseldorf, and is creative associate at deSingel International Arts Campus in Antwerp until 2021.

BERDACHE BEGIUM
Berdache Belgium is an association formed to support parents with a transgender child. Run by parents of trans children, the association offers information and advice as well as raising awareness and working with government bodies to effect change.

for a great metaphor of the bigger picture, a society that is very binary even if it's changing a little bit.

How did I meet you?

The only information they gave was that it was the role of someone in a dance class and that we would work with the choreographer Sidi

several other people from my class, and I met you there for the first time.

After that, you contacted me and offered me an

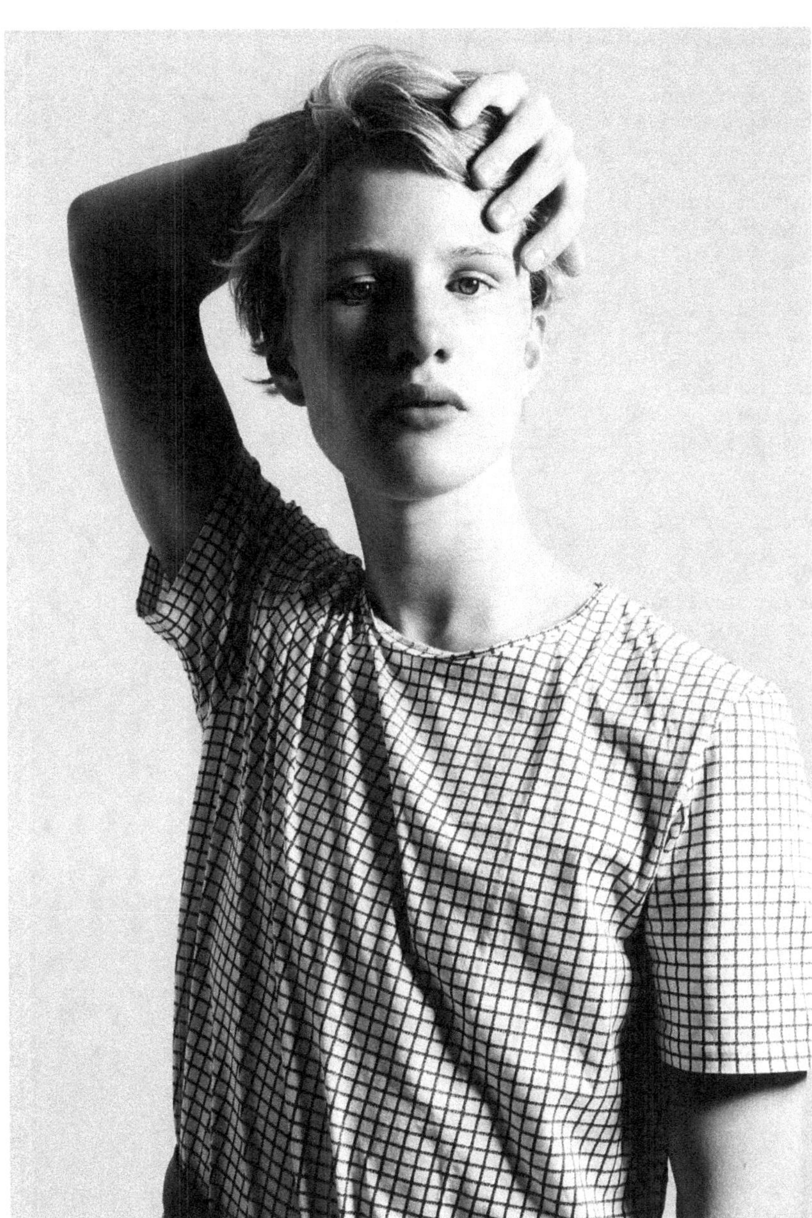

Victor Polster, stars as Lara in *Girl*

VP: I imagine you contacted the school to audition some dancers, and they got in touch with me.

Larbi Cherkaoui, which as a dancer was very interesting to me. I decided to do the audition with

audition for a more important role in the film, without telling me it was the lead. At that point I still didn't know what the film was about. You sent me certain excerpts from the script, and I decided to audition for the lead role.

The audition wasn't at all stressful. It was at your place with Arieh Worthalter, the actor who plays the father. Since I had never done a film, I was afraid it would be this thing with lots of cameras and other kids waiting their turn. But it wasn't that at all. Right away we put something together so that the relationship between Lara and her father would really be there.

LD: What attracted you most to the part?

VP: What attracted me and my parents the most when I read the script was the family, essentially the relationship between Lara and her father and her little brother, and especially the strength of her character. The strength she has already at the age of fifteen, knowing that you're in a body that does not feel like your own and that you must change it. It really fascinated me and made me want to represent this character.

What also really impressed me and my parents was that the relationship with the father was so beautiful and that the film was concentrated on this character who doesn't feel good about herself. It's concentrated on her

and not on a negative environment.

LD: Tell me about your first encounter with Nora Monsecour.

VP: My first encounter with Nora was during the dance class rehearsal. I

"SHE WAS A PERSONAL EXAMPLE OF REALLY BEING YOURSELF, AND AT THE TIME I WASN'T "OUT OF THE CLOSET" YET, SO FOR ME IT WAS STILL VERY DIFFICULT TO CHOOSE MYSELF. SHE HELPED ME OVERCOME THAT, AND I HELPED HER, IN A WAY, BY GIVING HER THIS FILM."

— LUKAS DHONT

remember she came before they started shooting, and I didn't know who she was at first. I met her, and she started coming more often, which was important for me because even though she didn't give any

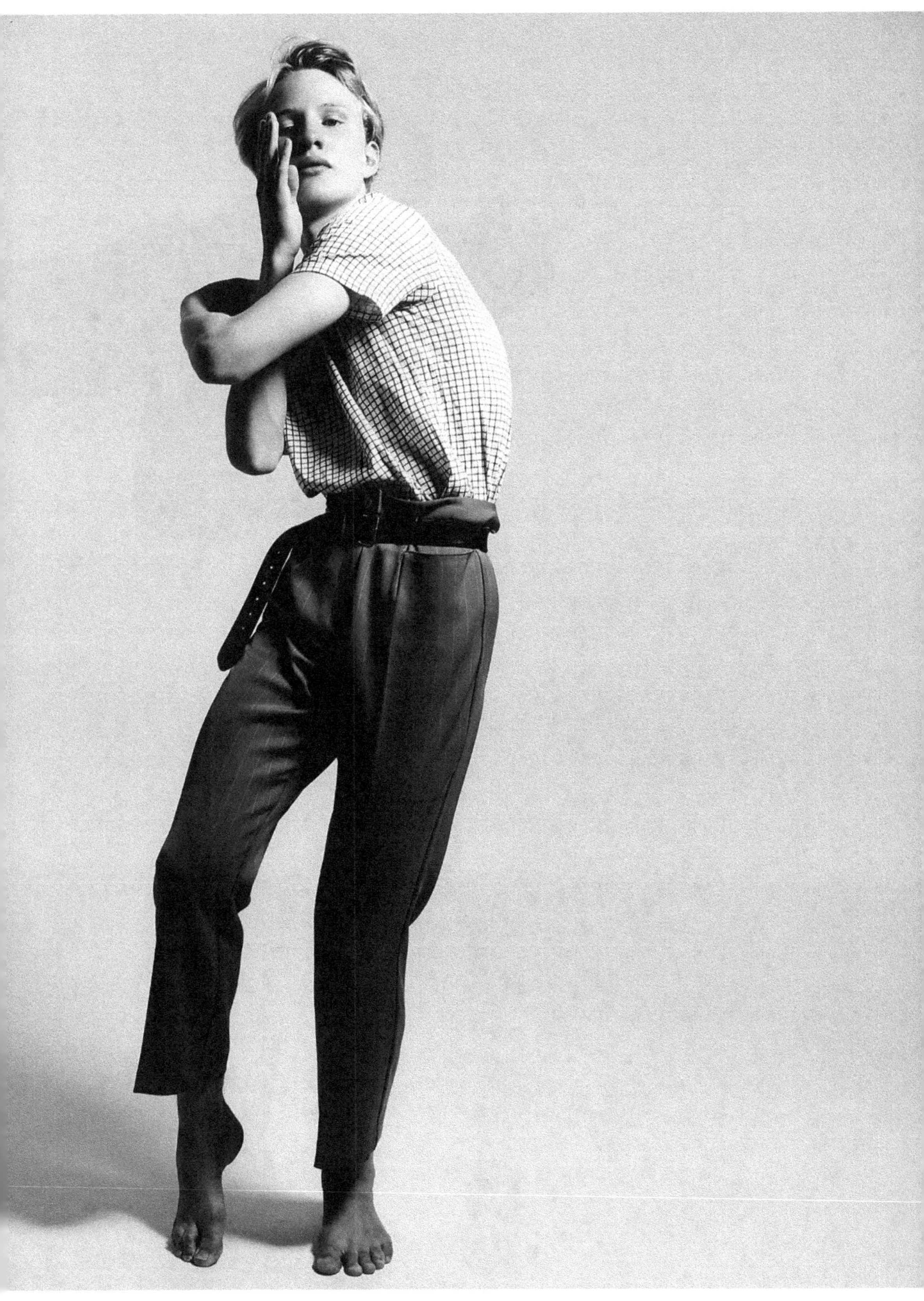

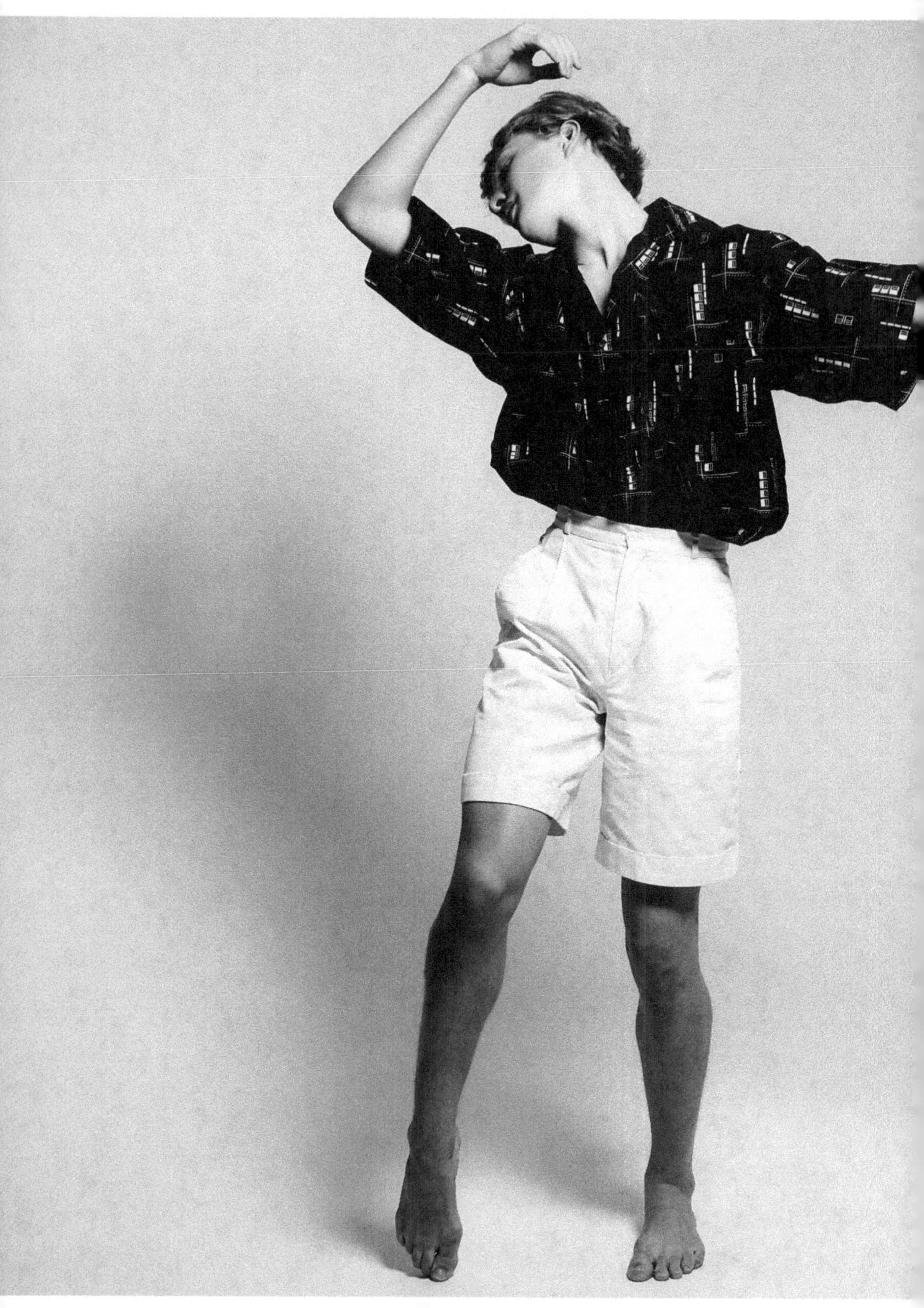

instructions, her presence was reassuring. I wanted mostly for her to believe in the film. I wanted to create a somewhat special relationship with her because she was one of the biggest inspirations I had for the film.

"THE STRENGTH SHE HAS ALREADY AT THE AGE OF FIFTEEN, KNOWING THAT YOU'RE IN A BODY THAT DOES NOT FEEL LIKE YOUR OWN AND THAT YOU MUST CHANGE IT. IT REALLY FASCINATED ME AND MADE ME WANT TO REPRESENT THIS CHARACTER."

— VICTOR POLSTER

How did you prepare yourself for the film?

LD: Because I wrote and directed this film, a big part of the preparation happened while I was writing it. I actively worked on it for four years, which is quite a long time, and in that time I did several things to really make this story as complex as it could be on every single layer.

First of all, the dance aspect because this film obviously takes place in a classical dance school. I worked closely with a modern choreographer, Jan Martens, who I followed during three years in his making process. I filmed a lot of his spectacles and rehearsals because I wanted to work out how I would film the dance scenes. Dance is not an easy thing to put on screen because it's about physicality, it's about bodies. To portray that and make it resonate with an audience in a cinema, you really have to make them feel it. For three years I really worked on that, on getting to know the dancing better and trying to put myself completely in there.

Also, when Sidi Larbi Cherkaoui came on board for this film—he's done films like Anna Karenina by Joe Wright and music videos for Beyoncé. I felt that with him I had a big inspiration I could hang on to, and that would make me dive completely into this classical area. I'm still very thankful for it because he gave me the preparation I needed to really know how I would put ballet on screen.

Next to that, I was concerned with the trans aspect, of course. Nora was the biggest inspiration, but also her parents who were very loving and accepting. They have a support group for parents of young trans people which is called Berdache Belgium, which I followed closely during the years of writing and through which I met a lot of parents and young trans kids.

Very early on I found out that every trans experience is very different. There were a lot of people like Nora, but also a lot of people that didn't have the same experience as Nora. With this film I could really only re-transmit one experience, and I wanted it to be Nora's.

We also worked very closely with the gender team of a hospital in Ghent. It is one of the two biggest centres in Europe when it comes to treatment medically and psychologically of trans people. I met with a lot of psychologists. I met with a lot of gender specialists that write about gender, transgender and the way gender is perceived in our society. All these little elements really made the script as complex as I could make it.

Then came the direction, because you had never acted before and neither had the little brother in the film. Actually,

I had only one actor that had really acted before. The difficulty was, "How do I get these young people to really stay themselves, to be very free when a camera is put on them and forty people are looking at them?"

What we did was during the three months before the shoot, you, me, Oliver Bodart (who played the younger brother Milo) and Arieh Worthalter (who played Mathias, Lara's father) did a lot of things together as a family. We went bowling, we went to restaurants, we went to movies, and it created this intimacy and confidence between us that was unbreakable once we started shooting. Even if we had twenty or twenty-five other people around us, we were like this core. I think you felt so free and had gained so much confidence that you were able to really be yourself on set and at the same time act and not feel like you would do something badly. I know believability as the character of Lara was your biggest stress.

I tried to give all the actors freedom to do what they wanted. Then I was just there to push you guys through the performances you gave. That was the biggest preparation. What was your biggest preparation?

VP: One of my big-

gest preparations was learning to dance on toe shoes. For me, being able to dance as a girl was the most important aspect. I only had three months to prepare for the film, so we did as much as possible, and at the end of my classes everyday I took extra toe classes so I wouldn't injure myself. I was afraid of injuring myself and not being able to dance afterwards.

Also, what we did with the family. Arieh and Oliver often came to my house to cook and have breakfast together. It was really important that we had that bond.

Also, my times together with Nora during rehearsals and dance scenes, which were a little less stressful because I know dancing better than acting. We filmed the dance scenes first, in six days, and Nora was there almost every day. During the breaks I spoke to her, so there was really a relationship that grew between the two of us. That gave me the confidence to act and to be less afraid of being credible as Lara. And then to be able to let myself go, like you said, because I knew there were emotions in the film that I hadn't experienced.

LD: How was your work with Arieh Worthalter?

VP: My work with

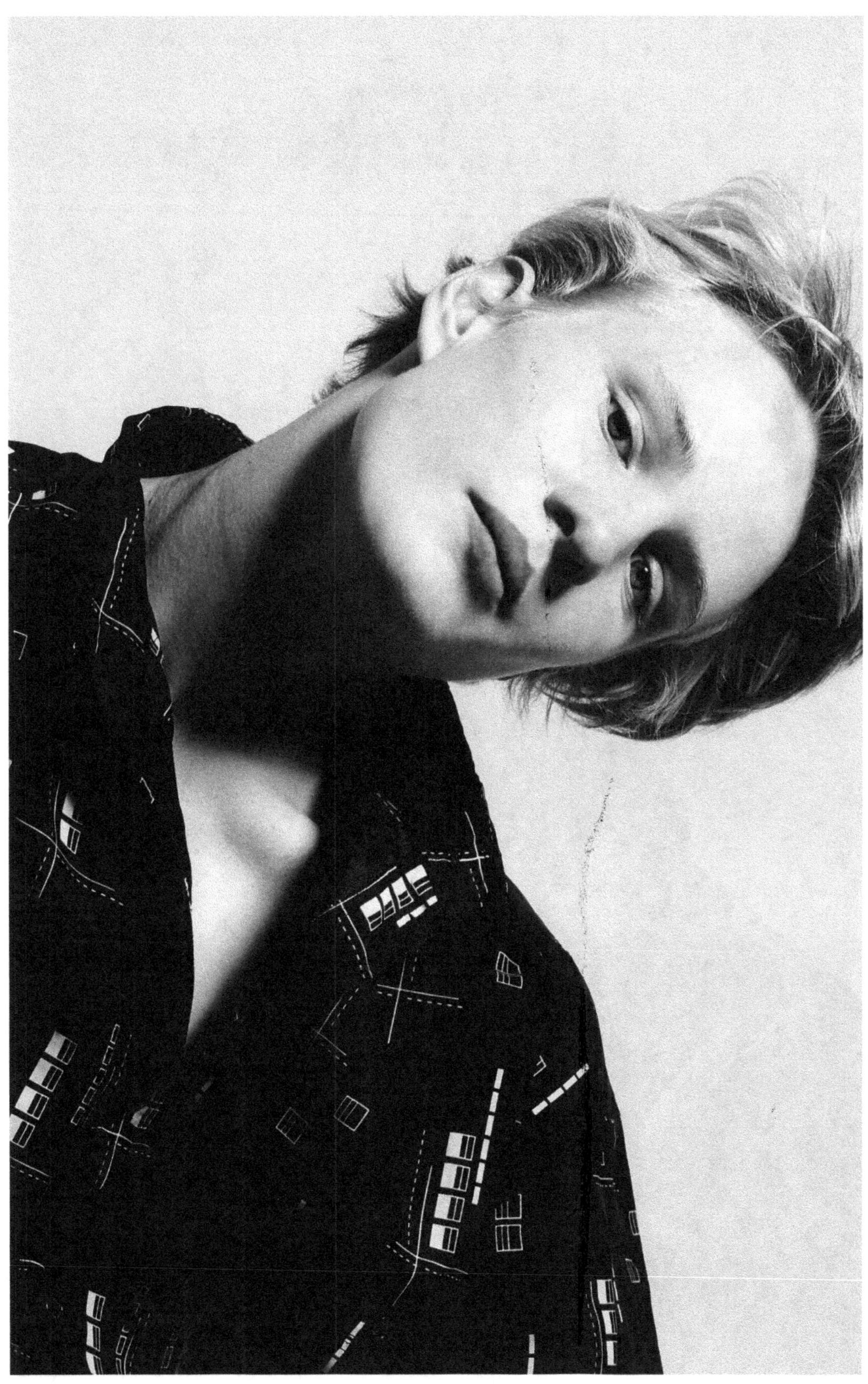

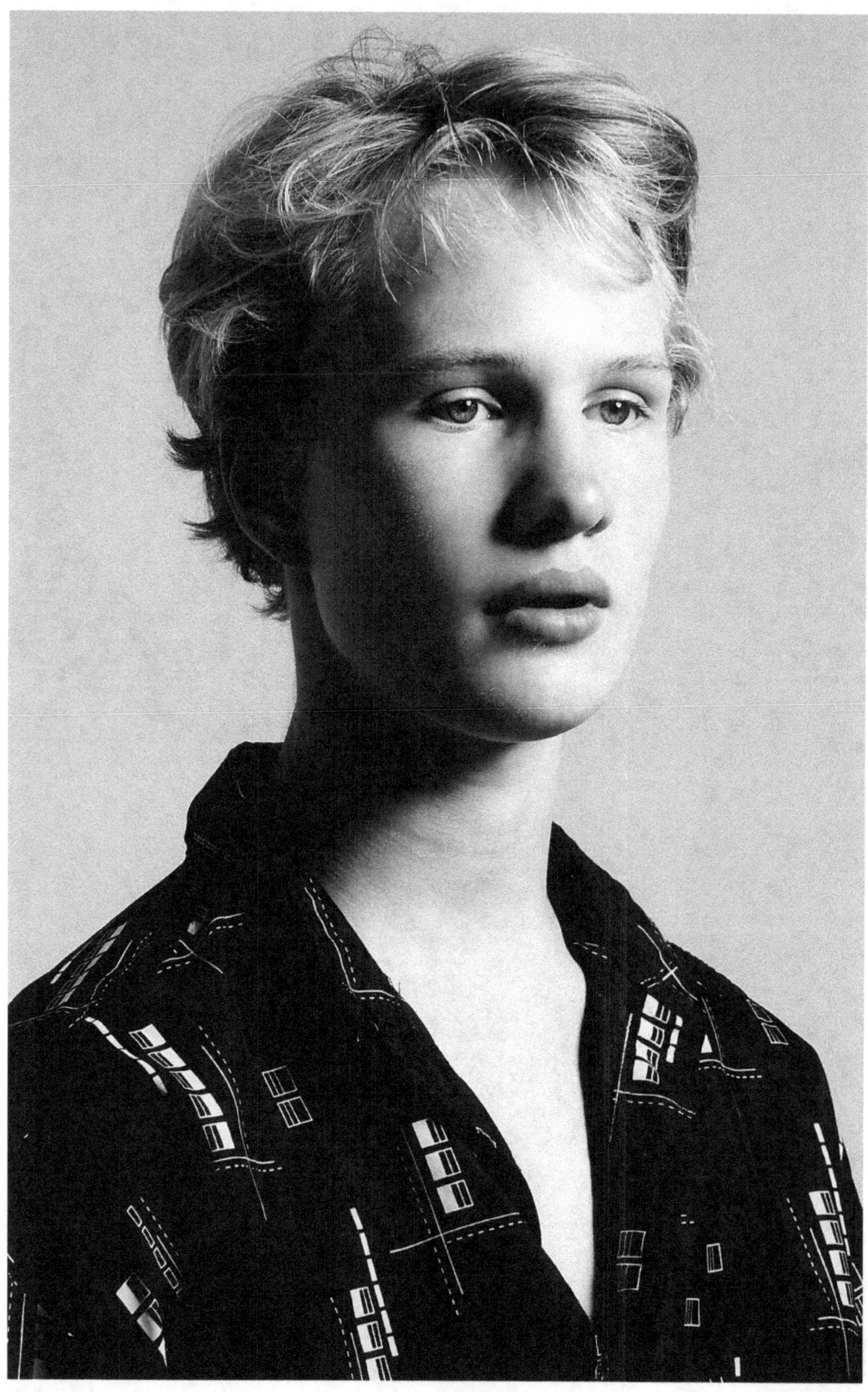

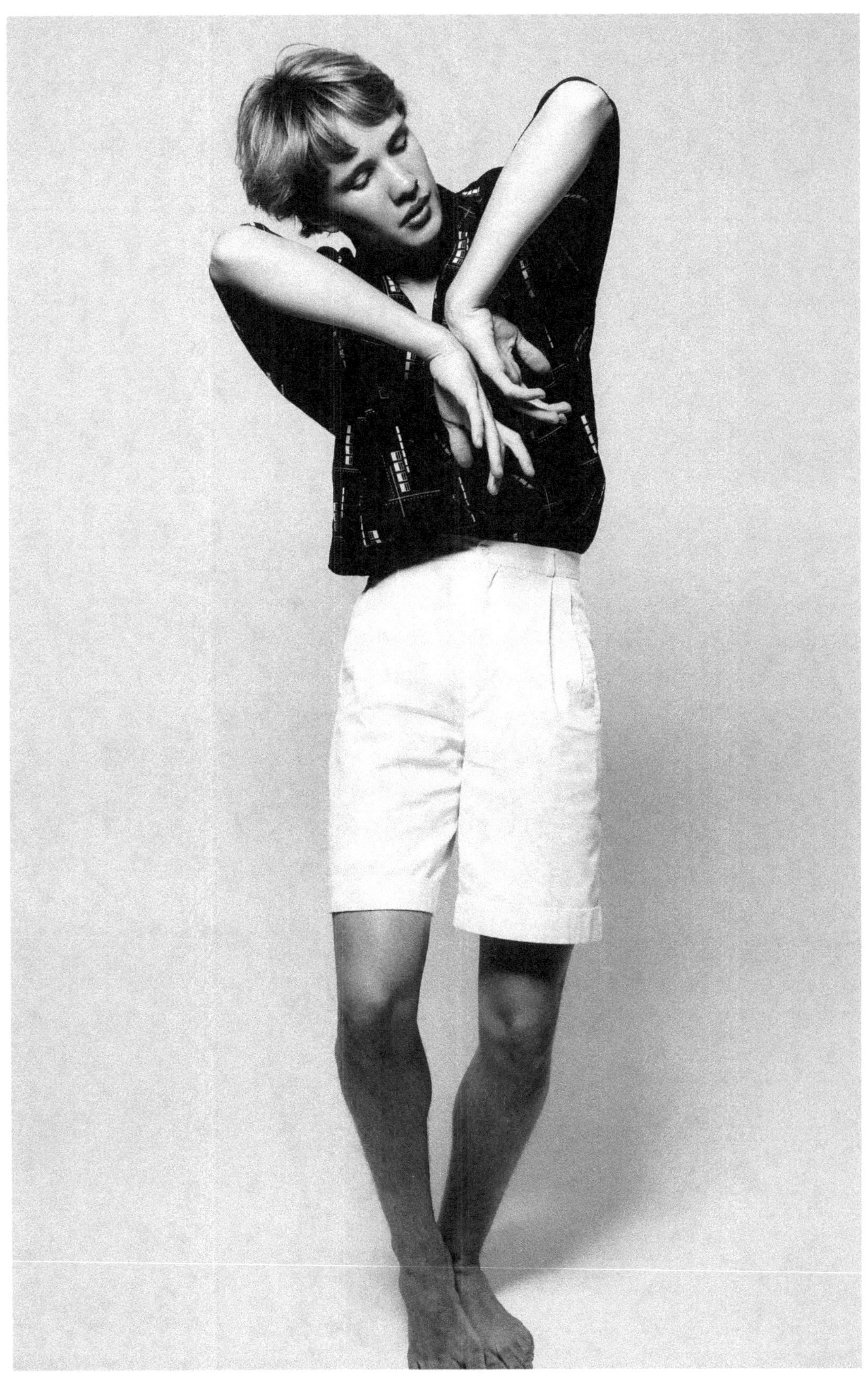

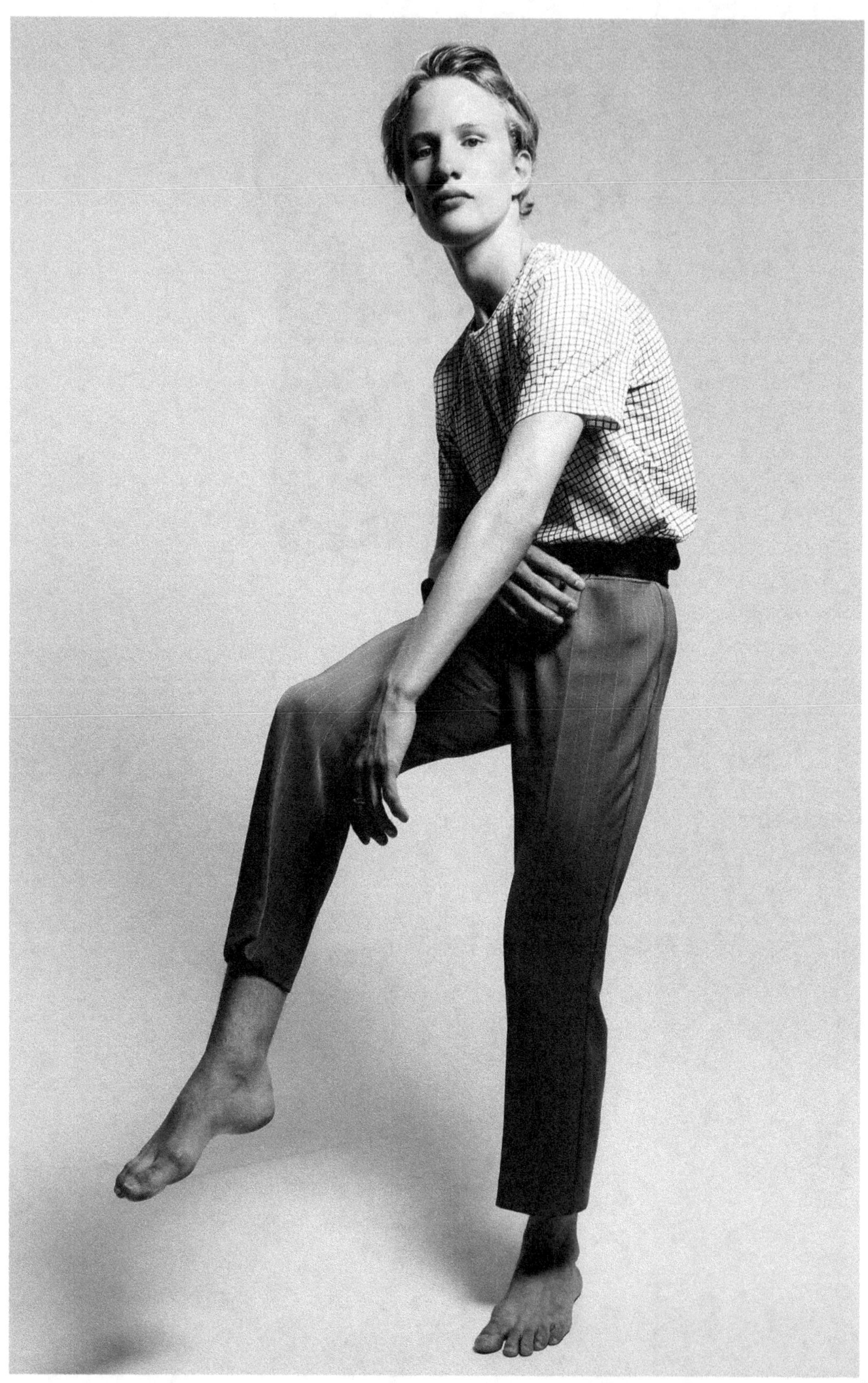

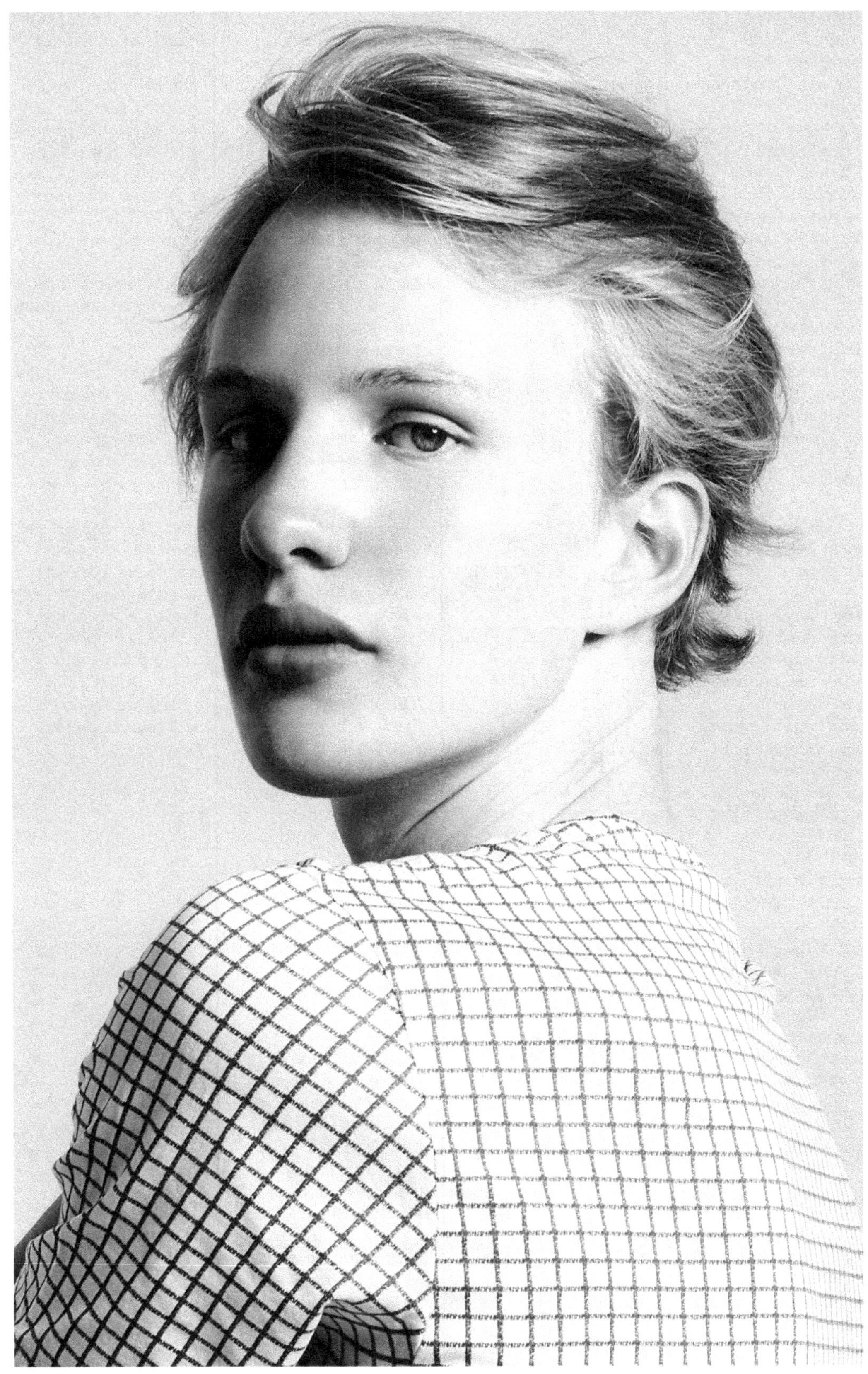

Arieh went very naturally, right from the very first day when I did the audition. We cooked, and we tried to see if there was already a father-daughter relationship. Each time we took it further, so that at the end he was really like my own father because I saw him every day, which was necessary for the film. It was something real because the relationship I had with him during filming is still there.

LD: Did you get a lot of reactions through Instagram and Facebook from young trans people?

VP: There were a few when the film came out from people who were transgender, and they were all positive. I was super happy because it was, of course, an audience I wanted to reach, and I was afraid I wouldn't be credible. I was so happy and proud that these people had been touched. I also had messages and reactions from young people who are sixteen years old like me, and so I was super proud that they were touched. You?

LD: We did a big tour of film premieres in France, Belgium and the Netherlands. We also were here in Telluride, Colorado, which is when I met a young person like you, fifteen years old, who came to watch the film. She was

shaking after she saw it because it really touched her core and struck a chord. I'm still in touch with her. I think the film awoke something in her that she had tried to hide for a long time.

We've had young people come to watch it who are really emotional, who feel like there is someone put on screen that they really had to see. Lara is a tough character. She's not the easiest character, but they really are moved by seeing this character on screen.

Can you tell me about May 12, our premiere, and the reaction after that? Not only from the audience but also between us, with Nora and you there

VP: In Cannes? It was the world premiere of the film, and I think everyone was a little stressed to see what people would think. I know I was. And then everything went really well—even better than well—because at the end the whole audience was on their feet. It was a relief to see that people were touched by the film. Almost the whole team was there, so it was really a magic moment because we could see what we had done over several months finally on the screen in front of a real audience.

I was super happy that Nora was also at Cannes because I think she was touched too. At the end of the film when

I went to see her, she simply said, "Thank you." That was all she said, but it was a magical moment and one of the most beautiful compliments I received because for me it was important that she be touched by the film.

LD: What was your favorite moment since Cannes?

VP: A moment I really loved was when the other dancers saw the film because there were many people from my class, and I was stressed about that. That was a very beautiful moment, and there were lots of others. Each time there's a screening, I'm still nervous to see if people will like it, and it's still unbelievable how it touches people.

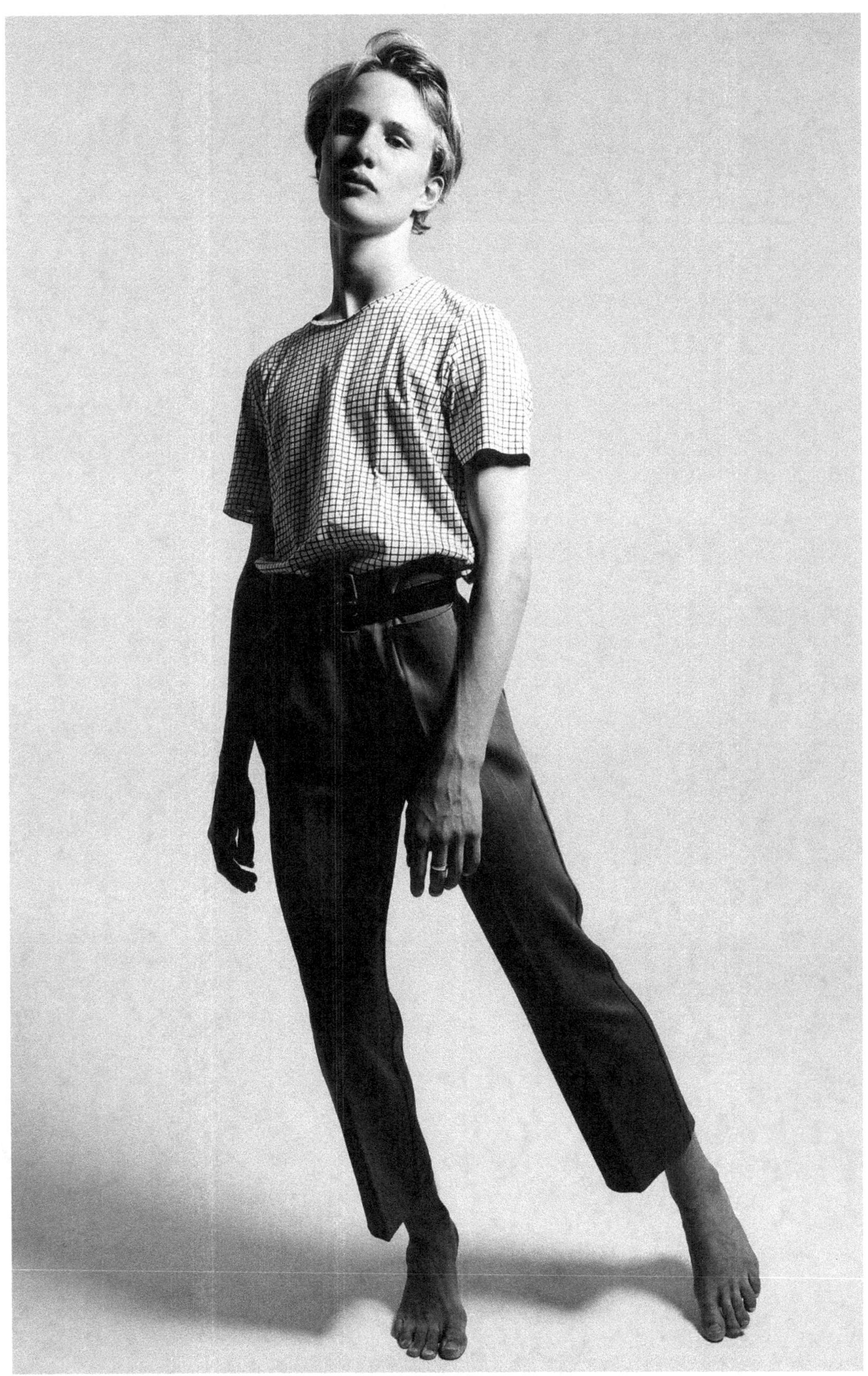

KILO KISH

Interview by **Aly Wicker**

Images by **Jan-Willem Dikkers**

An architecture dropout turned fashion major, Kilo Kish picked up music as yet another creative outlet on top of design and visual art. She has since released a full-length debut album Reflections in Real Time *(2016) and collaborated with musicians such as Childish Gambino, Vince Staples, The Internet and Gorillaz. Her newest EP,* Mothe, *is not-so-subtly interested in metamorphosis—a subject that Kish has always riffed on with her swelling list of talents. While her 2016 debut showcased the rapper's conversational flow,* Mothe *sees Kish in a period of transition with her newfound singing voice taking center stage over hazy synths.*

Between directing music videos and the launch of her new clothing label AGGY!, Kish took a break to discuss her intentions for Mothe, *creative capacity and the role of spirituality in keeping her grounded.*

———

AW: Now that *Mothe* is out, what have you been up to?

KK: I just finished the music video for "Void." I'm debuting my new brand, AGGY!, at Complex-Con. I'm also working with Yasmina Kahn on figuring out the production side of performing *Mothe* live. Yesterday, I directed a video for my friend Sosupersam.

AW: Do you also direct your own music videos?

KK: I at least co-direct all of them, and I come up with the concept for most of them. Elliot Sellers and I worked on the "Void" concept together last year but didn't have time to do it. We ended up putting it to "Void," which is actually perfect for it.

I'm usually involved from top to bottom, in terms of color and the way I want my videos to look. I always do wardrobe, and I sit in on all the edits.

AW: You've spoken a lot about metamorphosis and how *Mothe* was a change in perspective from your last album. As an artist, your approach is very much about limitless evolution. Do you feel your personality morphes as well, or do you regard it as a constant?

KK: My perspective changed a lot.

> **"I WANTED TO OVERALL FEEL FREER, LIKE I WAS COMING THROUGH THE OTHER SIDE OF SOMETHING."**
> — KILO KISH

Reflections in Real Time had a lot of questions and internal dialogue. With *Mothe*, I wanted to overall feel freer, like I was coming through the other side of something. I tried to change the way that I saw and created things. I wanted it to be more organic and not overthink it, so I purposely set parameters within my own personality so I could stay open enough to create and perform it well.

My personality changed a bit, but there's the constant wanting to top myself and being analytical about what could have been better or more interesting. My manager Justin says, "You're one of those people that are never satisfied." I can be satisfied with the fact that I achieved what I wanted, but there's always another level.

AW: Was there a shift in your process?

KK: The process is pretty much the same. I wait until the title comes to me, and then I start working on it from there. I wait around and work on other stuff, and once I have a title, I go in and try to think of visual identity and do research. Then I do music after that.

I think I give all my projects an equal amount of energy and focus, but I don't judge this as harshly as I would judge a record. With an album, I would focus

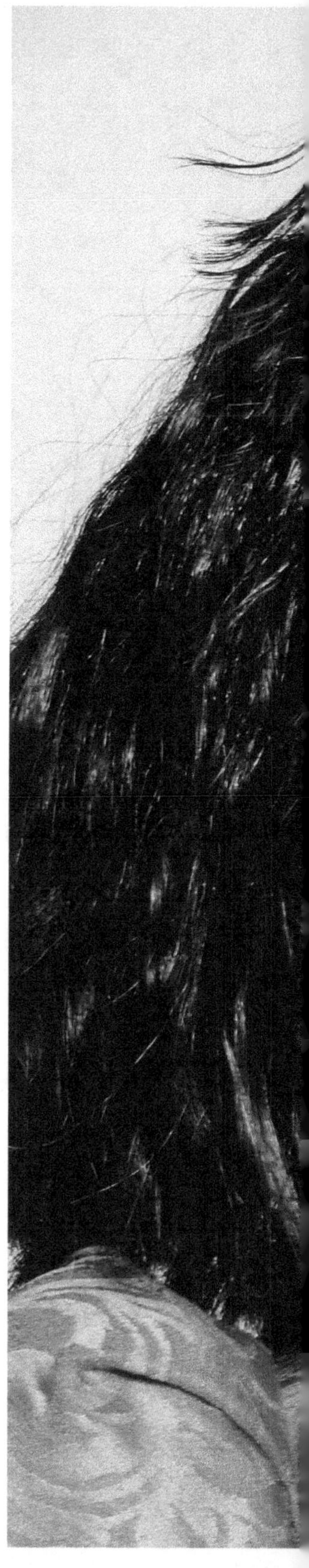

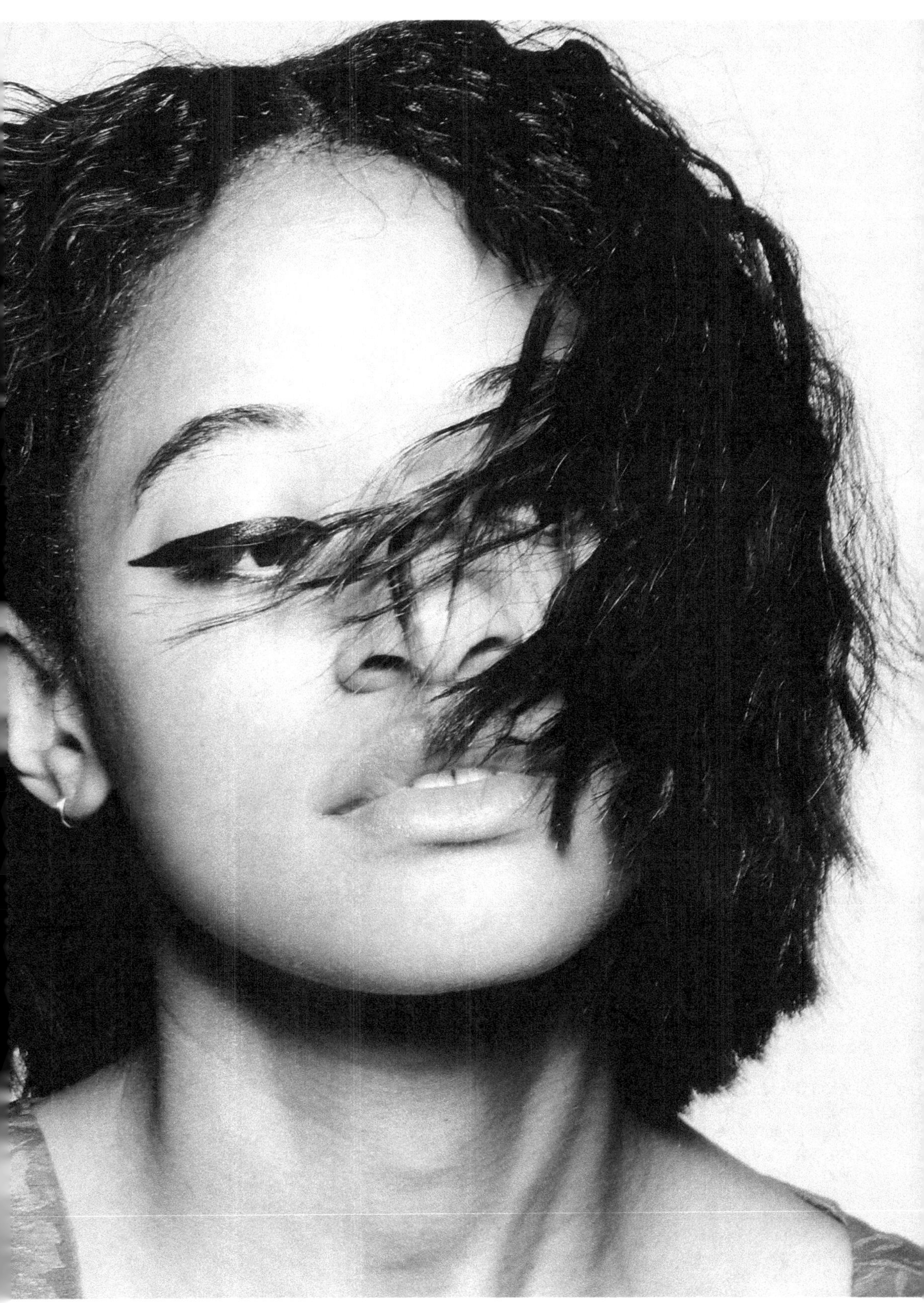

a lot more on making sure the whole pallet is within the same vein. With an EP, it's more about trying out ideas versus making something super solid.

EPs are also good bridges between two albums that are super different. They baby-step your listeners into another chapter. That's what I choose to use my EPs to do.

AW: You mentioned how you always start

> **"I CAN BE SATISFIED WITH THE FACT THAT I ACHIEVED WHAT I WANTED, BUT THERE'S ALWAYS ANOTHER LEVEL."**
> — KILO KISH

with the title. It's genius because then you don't get bogged down by the minutiae of what the lyrics are going to be. You start at the top and work down.

KK: I like doing that personally, but I know so many people do it the opposite way. Then there are people who write and write endlessly, and when they find a vibe they curate a collection of music.

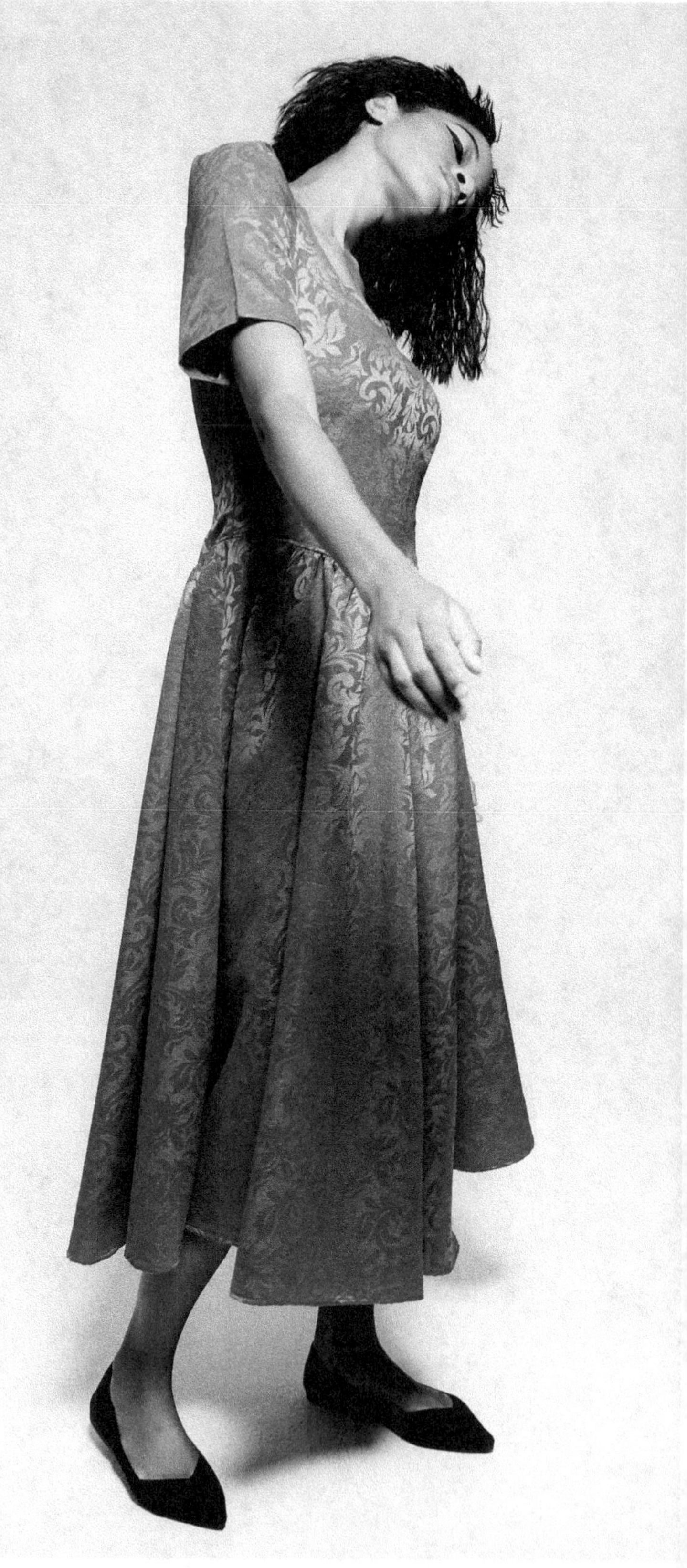

KILO KISH
Kilo Kish, the artistic moniker of Lakisha Robinson, is an American singer, rapper, visual artist, and fashion designer based in Los Angeles. She released her debut album, *Reflections in Real Time*, in 2016 and has just released her newest EP, *Mothe* (2018). Kish has collaborated with likes of Vince Staples, Gorillaz, A$AP Rocky, The Internet and Childish Gambino. Her new fashion brand, AGGY!, premiered at the 2018 ComplexCon.

YASMINA KAHN
Yasmina Kahn is an American architect based in Los Angeles. She has collaborated with brands such as Stüssy and artists like Kilo Kish.

SOSUPERSAM
SOSUPERSAM is the moniker of professional DJ, danger, and businesswoman Samantha Duenas. She has released 2 EPs: *Gardens* (2016) and *Priority* (2018).

ELLIOT SELLERS
Elliot Sellers is a director who has created music videos for the likes of Kilo Kish, Ty Dolla $ign, Cults and Lil Jon.

COMPLEXCON
Held in Long Beach, California, ComplexCon is a curated convention and music festival led by board members such as Pharrell Williams and Takashi Murakami. The convention showcases a curated variety of pop culture, art, food, style, sports, activism, innovation and education.

But I don't have a collection of music that hasn't been put out. I don't have 200 songs just chilling somewhere.

AW: You seem hyper-aware of your creative process and of not being intimidated by how hard that process can be. Is there any aspect of your art that seems to come especially easy?

KK: If something is not straight or a color is slightly off, it's easy for me to notice. This actually causes me more problems than good because it becomes something I need to make sure gets fixed.

It's also easy to create references because of the way I catalog information. I can be inspired by something I saw when I was fourteen and recall the details quickly. I'll search it and show people like, "This is what I mean."

Also just coming up with creative ideas is really easy, as well as making last minute adjustments. I've been DIY for so long that I pretty much learned how most industries work in the sense that I can draw from what I know to make quick changes and come up with creative solutions. If I need to make t-shirts or get a dress made, I can figure it out. The hard part can be bringing those ideas to other people, and depending on whether or not they

> **"IF YOU'RE TOO HUMBLE ABOUT YOUR WORK THEN YOU WON'T EVEN PUT IT OUT OR BELIEVE IT MATTERS. YOU HAVE TO BE THE ONE WHO GIVES IT VALUE FIRST."**
> — KILO KISH

agree it can become a problem in itself.

AW: Speaking of, do you look for specific qualities in the people you collaborate with?

KK: For me, it's openness to do the unexpected or atypical. Also thoroughness. I'm super thorough in my research and detail-oriented, and I prefer to work with people who are extremely diligent in that as well because it makes everything easier. I know they're taking as much care in the project as I am and have similar values in terms of wanting to push the boundaries.

With a lot of things there's the possibility that "people will like it more if I do it this way" or "it'll get more traction if I do it that way." Also I could make more money if I were cutting corners in production. It really comes down to being on the same page and putting creativity before other interests.

AW: Do you feel it's more beneficial as an artist to be humble or to be proud of your work?

KK: I think within our industry it may be better to be proud because if you're too humble about your work then you won't even put it out or believe it matters. You have to be the one who gives it value first, and then other

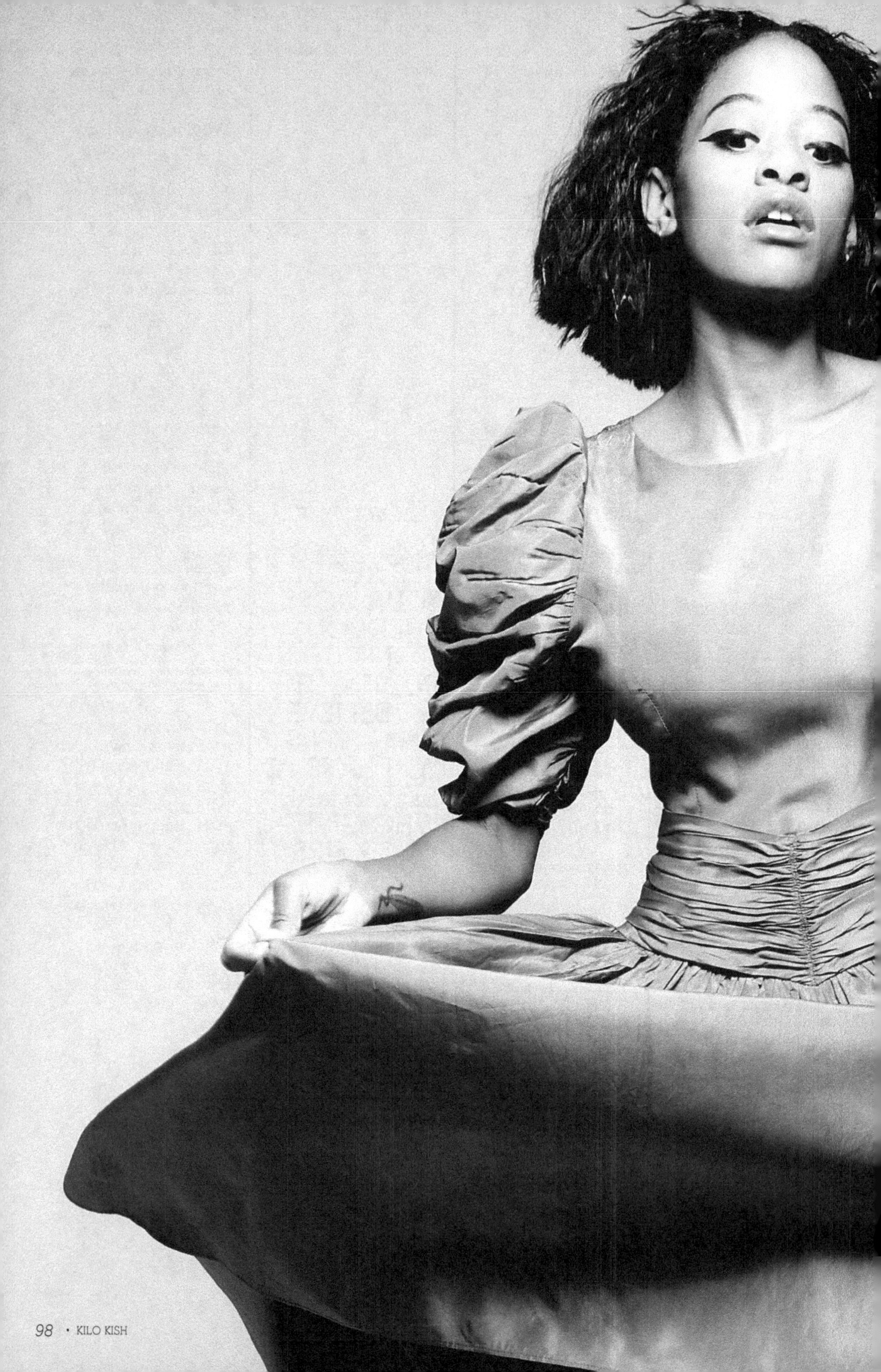

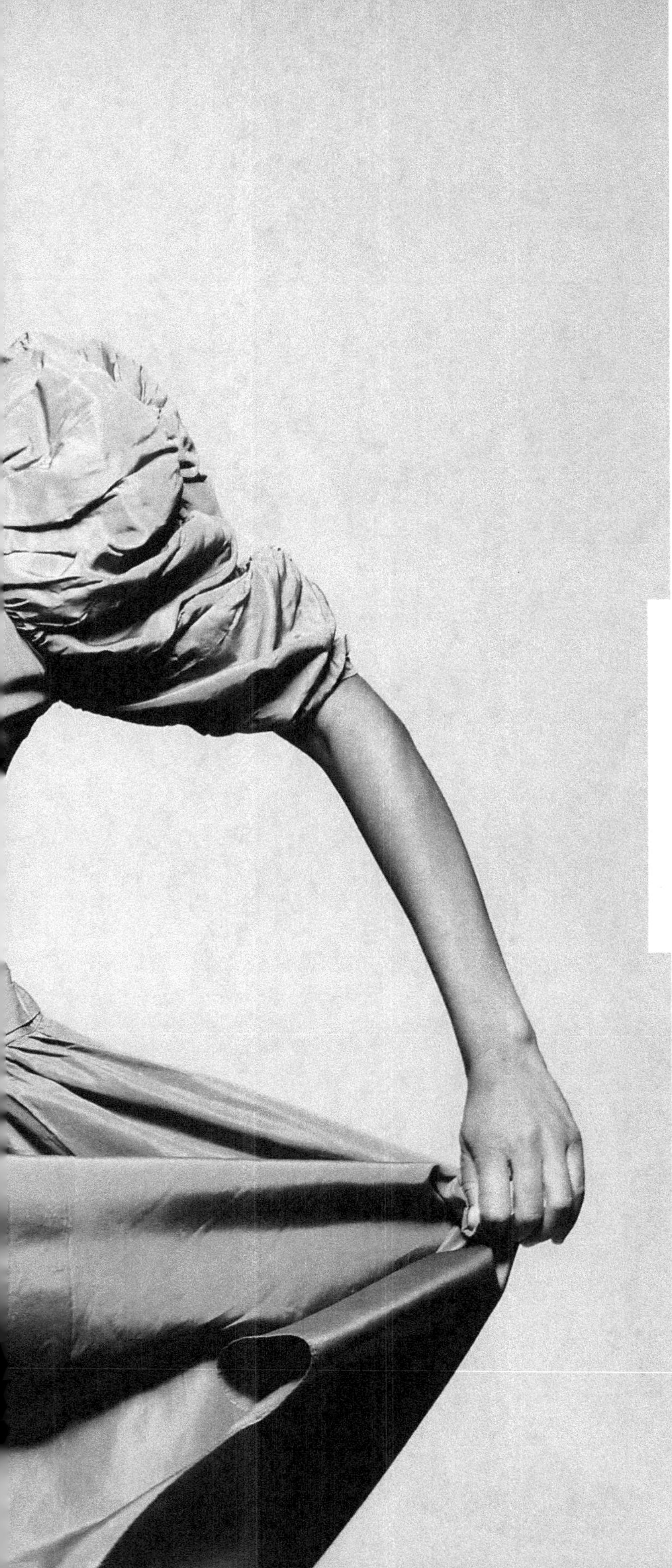

people will then sub-
sequently see it and
give it value.

Philosophi-
cally speaking, it's
probably better to
be humble because
we're in 2018. There
is so much reference
at this point that it's
really hard to make
anything extremely
unique. I can name
so many references
for everything I've
done, and it's not all
musical. We can't say
that we don't have
banks and banks of
reference when we
have the internet. I

**"IT'S VERY
HARD NOT
TO HAVE ANY
PARAME-
TERS AND TO
JUST HAVE A
BLANK PIECE
OF PAPER."**
— KILO KISH

think it's better to be
realistic about how
much we're actually
adding.

AW: That's interest-
ing because I know
you really try to shut
off too many outside
influences when you
make an album.

KK: Yes, but that's just
me. I'm very sensitive
with what comes
into my body. I can
feel the difference
between when my
mind is overloaded
versus not.

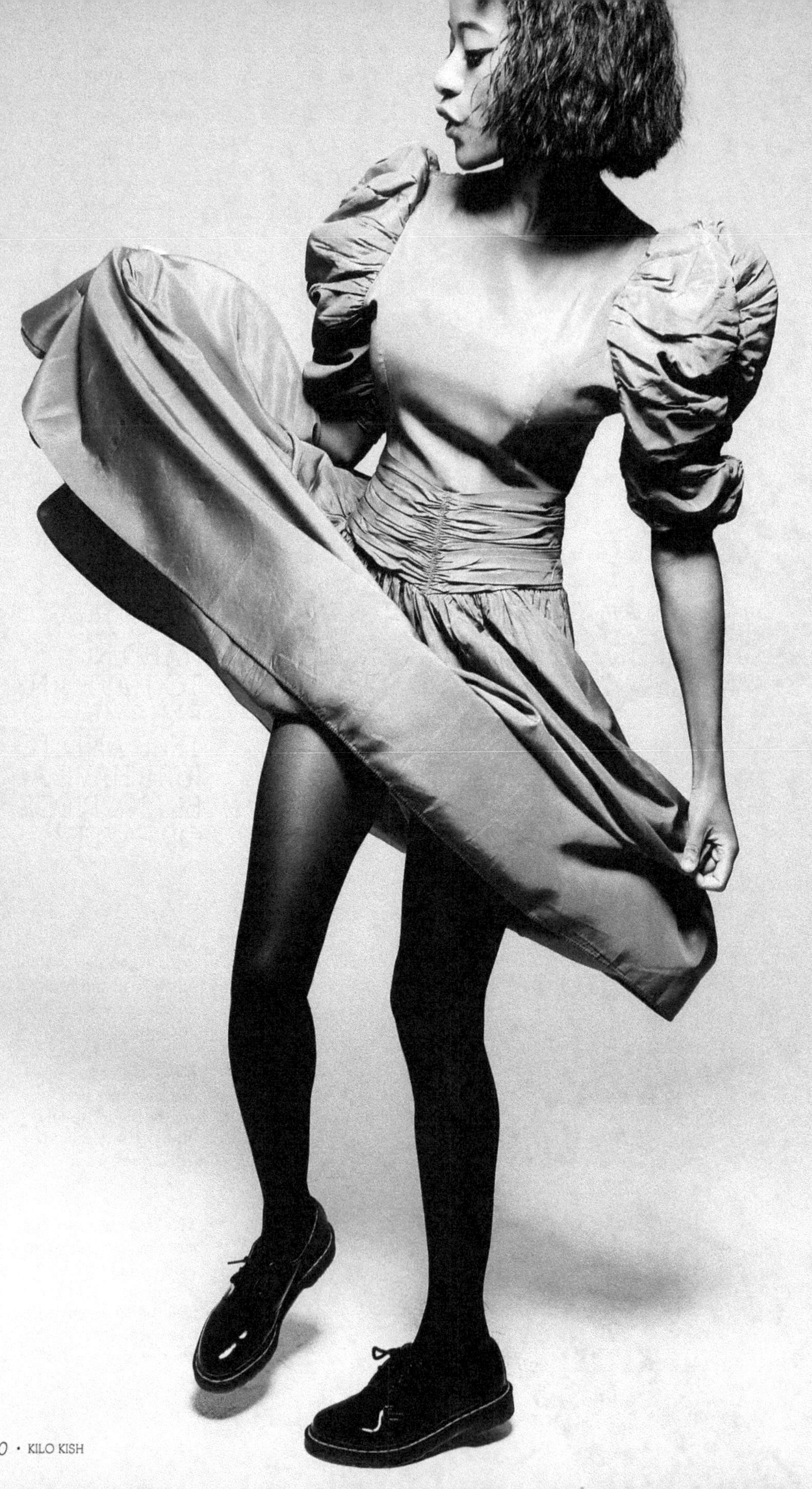

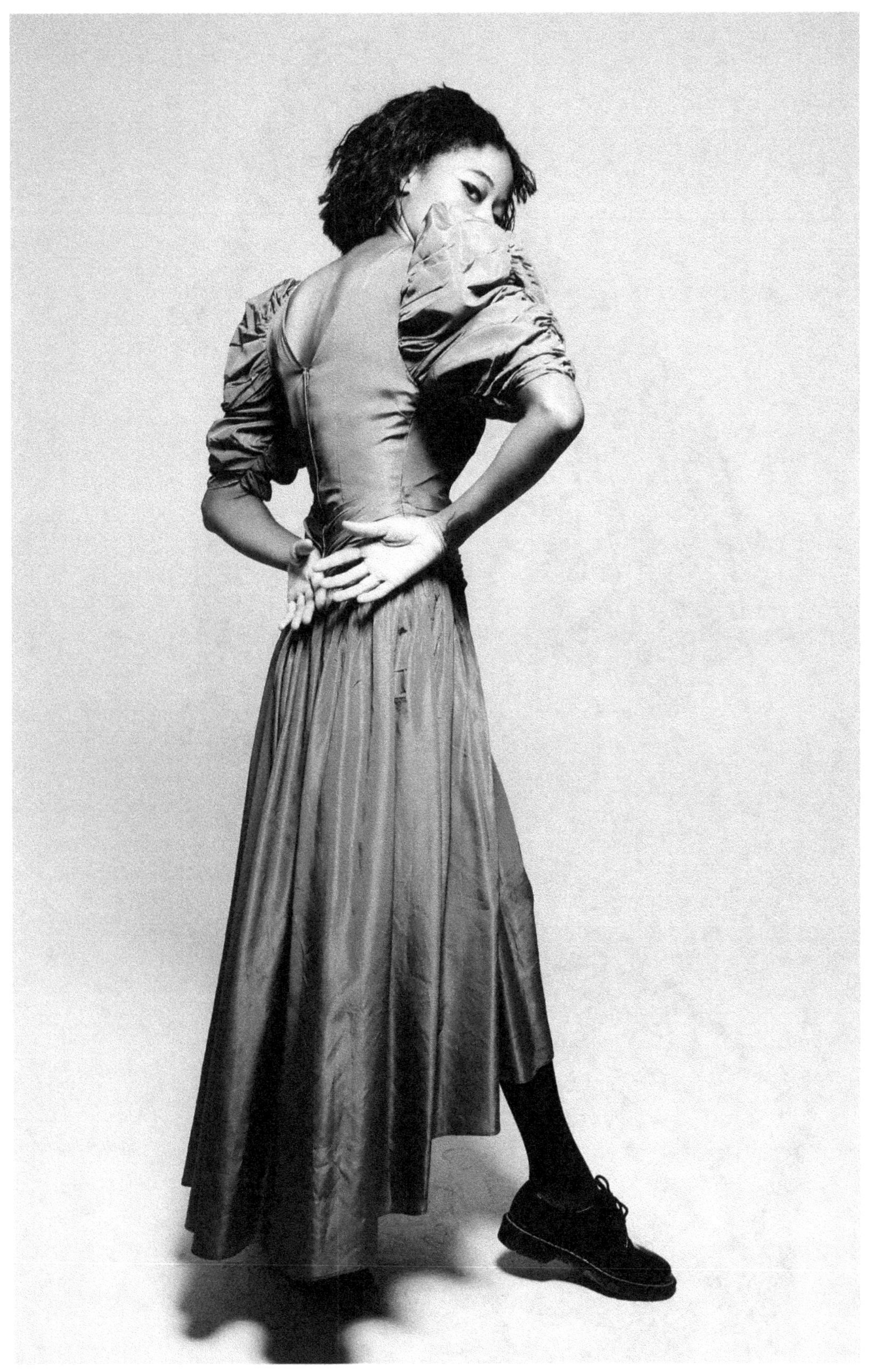

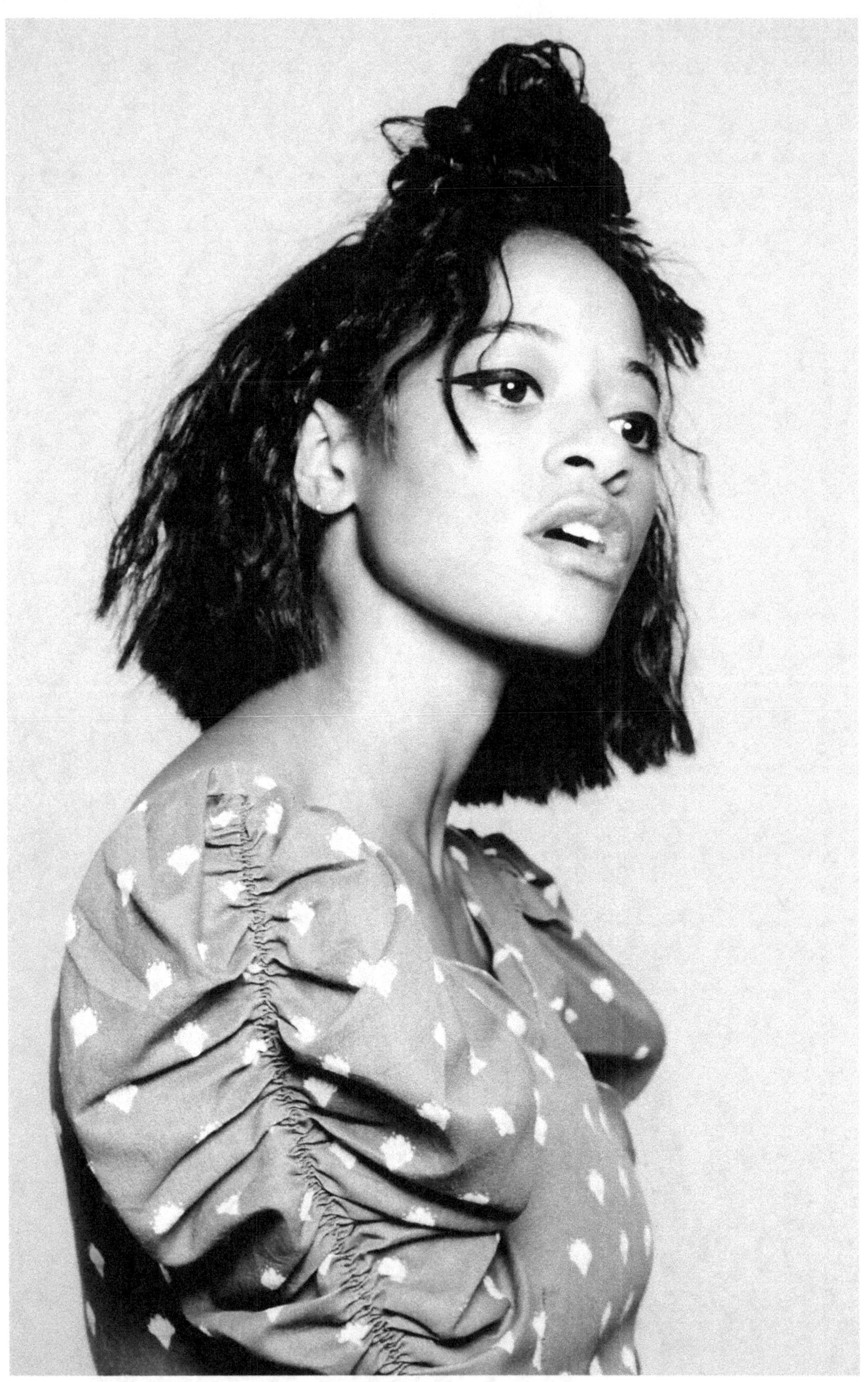

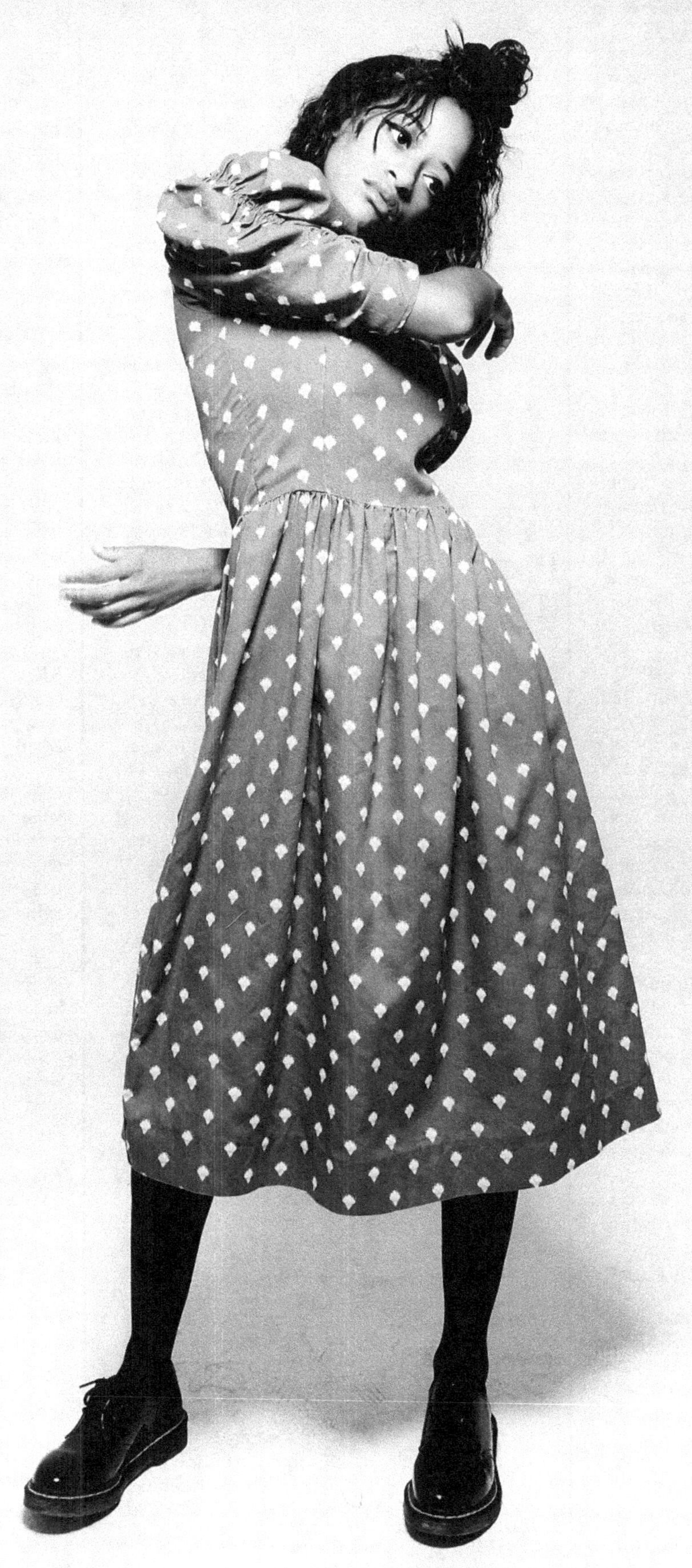

I have so many safeguards in the way that I work. I'll plan a project two months before I work on it, and it probably won't come out for another six months after that. I want to make sure everything actually happens and that I'll have enough stamina since I do so much of it on my own.

AW: You do so many different kinds of art. When you have simultaneous projects, do you find yourself talking about the same themes? Or do you try to take a break in topics from one genre to the next?

KK: It carries through sometimes. For example, when I was doing *Reflections in Real Time* I also did a gallery show. The projects were unrelated, but the themes about social media and its implications carried through to the show.

When I do things close in succession, it can carry through. Which is why I won't work on music right now while we're working on stuff for *Mothe*. I don't write or listen to that much music until I know I'm ready to start another album.

There are varying levels of total creativity amongst musicians. Some love to sit down every day and make a piece of music. Then they have other people collaborate with them on album artwork

> **"I THINK IT COMES DOWN TO NOT LETTING YOUR EVER-CHANGING EMOTIONAL STATE REGARDING YOUR WORK GET IN THE WAY OF CONTINUING TO DO IT."**
> — KILO KISH

and videos, and they have a creative director to design their show space. But for me, I have to be all of those things, and I think a lot of indie artists are that way as well. It can be draining to do that while making a fashion brand at the same time. I try not to hold too much information at the same time.

I really believe that within your brain you have 100%. It's not 100% to this and another 100% to that. You have 100% total. If you want to devote 50% to music and 50% to fashion—or 50% to music and 25% to your toxic relationship and 25% to whatever else—those are all depleting your total amount of energy. I try to conserve as much as I can.

AW: Would you ever produce music for other artists?

KK: I'd be quicker to work on videos or visual identities because I have no producing expertise besides what I've learned from working with my own producers. I sit in on sessions, and I give input when the beats are being made for my record, but being the producer is too many options for me. It's soundbank after soundbank. Even when I make music, I get bored super easily. I can't sit there for hours and hours listening to the same thing over and over.

I see myself more

as a visual artist or a designer than a musician in the way I approach my music. I just happen to use the things I know from other things, and I'm able to make good music. But I think that the world of being a musician is super hard, and I don't think I would ever be that great at making beats. I've tried, and I just don't have the patience for it.

AW: It goes back to what you were saying earlier about how you like setting attainable parameters for yourself.

KK: It's very hard not to have any parameters and to just have a blank piece of paper. People and brands are always like, "Do whatever you want!"

I'm like, "No, what are the actual parameters? What is the budget? How much space is there?"

These are important things to know so that I can even get started because "whatever you want" could mean anything in the entire universe.

AW: Do you have a favorite song on *Mothe*?

KK: I like "Like Honey" the most because I like the mix the most. It's the closest to what I thought the project would sound like, but you never know until it's done.

With *Reflections*,

I tried super hard to achieve a specific idea, and then it was kind of achieved but also kind of not. With *Mothe* I learned to accept that the fun part of making music is not knowing what you are going to get.

AW: Anyone who's been at something tenaciously for a while, such as yourself, must confront necessities like trial and error. How do you navigate discouragement or uncertainty?

KK: I can be very moody and artsy. I can be a martyr to my art. I can be obsessive. I can be very creative and purposeful. I think it comes down to not letting your ever-changing emotional state regarding your work get in the way of continuing to do it. One day you might have the best day of your life, and the next day you might be like, "I suck at everything". I think that's just being a creative.

At least I'm aware that it's a tumultuous process. With the back-and-forth of emotional states and status—people either paying attention or not paying attention—there's no way to do it and not have varying emotions. When you have the feeling of "I don't know if I'm going to keep doing this," the answer is always "yes."

I'm probably going to be an artist forever. Even if I don't always make music, I'll find some other creative outlet, whether that be through brands or creative direction. I don't necessarily have these goals of being an international pop star. I want all of my work to be good and to be impactful, and it's a lifelong quest and project.

There will be things that are the highlights in your life story, and other things will be a paragraph. No particular project is going to be the one. It's the body of work that's important.

AW: That philosophy shows in how many different things you do.

You've collaborated with Childish Gambino, and he's known to bury himself in his work and emerge with a finished project that makes people wonder how he finished it so quickly. Has that been your approach too?

KK: Donald and I are quite similar in that way. I used to be a lot more social when I lived in New York, but LA has a different way about it where you see people less than normal. I got used to not having my core group of friends out here and got super into my work.

It gives me a lot of purpose to wake up early. I'll wake up, go for a walk, and get

started immediately. I don't stop until it's at least dinner time.

AW: You've mentioned a little bit in other interviews your spiritual background, which is interesting because in this industry not many people believe in or acknowledge spirituality as a facet of life, much less their personhood. Do you have a current practice or belief system that informs your art?

KK: Growing up in the South, I went to church every Sunday and was super Christian. Then I kind of didn't do any of it when I moved to New York. I didn't acknowledge that whole part of myself, or I guess I was just busy.

Then midway through making *Reflections*, I got really depressed. I think also just being twenty five, I had so many questions. It was bogging me down. I can go into bouts of existential depression just because I have thoughts that other people don't necessarily talk about. At that point, I hadn't expressed my questions through the album yet—I was in the process of doing that. I also was reading tons of weird philosophy books which can be quite dark. Life can be depressing if you are looking at from such a harsh perspective.

I think I needed something outside of

what I was working on, outside of people. I needed something outside of our planet to latch back onto and to ground myself with again. I began going back to church a bit. It helped me to reground myself in a time that I felt really wiry and loose. I was doing fine from a career standpoint, but mentally I was spinning out a little bit.

Because it was so helpful, I've just continued. I continue to pray now and watch church stuff online and listen to music. I've gone to therapy before, and I've done so many different things for my own anxieties. But I feel that, at least for me, it aids in keeping me very balanced and grounded.

AW: Your stage presence is very expressive and reminded me of someone having a conversation with themself in the mirror. But how do you experience it?

KK: It's fun to perform now. I didn't used to like it that much because I wasn't sure what vibe to put forth, and I wasn't comfortable being myself. I was more so trying to make sure people thought I was nice or good. I also thought I had to be engaging in cliché ways. You go on stage and say, "How's everybody doing tonight?" and "I hope everybody's feeling alright!" It felt really uncomfortable

because I don't like small talk.

It's also fairly recent that I sing. Being a perfectionist, I was worried about, "What if the notes aren't exactly right?" I had to look at it from the basis of conceptual art, and once I applied what I knew about art to the musical performance space, it got a lot easier.

Now I don't judge each performance on whether it's the best representation of who I am—it is always the best representation of who I am because I'm doing it. It's easier now that I've changed my perspective. I'm able to be that angsty teenage part of myself on stage all of the time, which is fun.

AW: What did your younger self want to be?

KK: I wanted to be a chef when I was a kid. Then I wanted to be an architect, which is what I thought I was going to go to college for. I did a pre-college program at Pratt and realized that I'm the worst at ruler-based things. Then I went to college to be a fashion designer.

When I was a teenager, I had a jewelry company and would screenprint shirts with stencils to sell to my friends. I had a fictitious name I filed when I was fifteen or sixteen.

AW: So entrepreneurial so young.

KK: There was that company where kids created cookies that were sold in the mall. Do you remember that?

AW: I forgot about that! They were so cool.

KK: To me that was being entrepreneurial. I was like, "He's sixteen, and he has a company already!" I was already being judgy to myself very young.

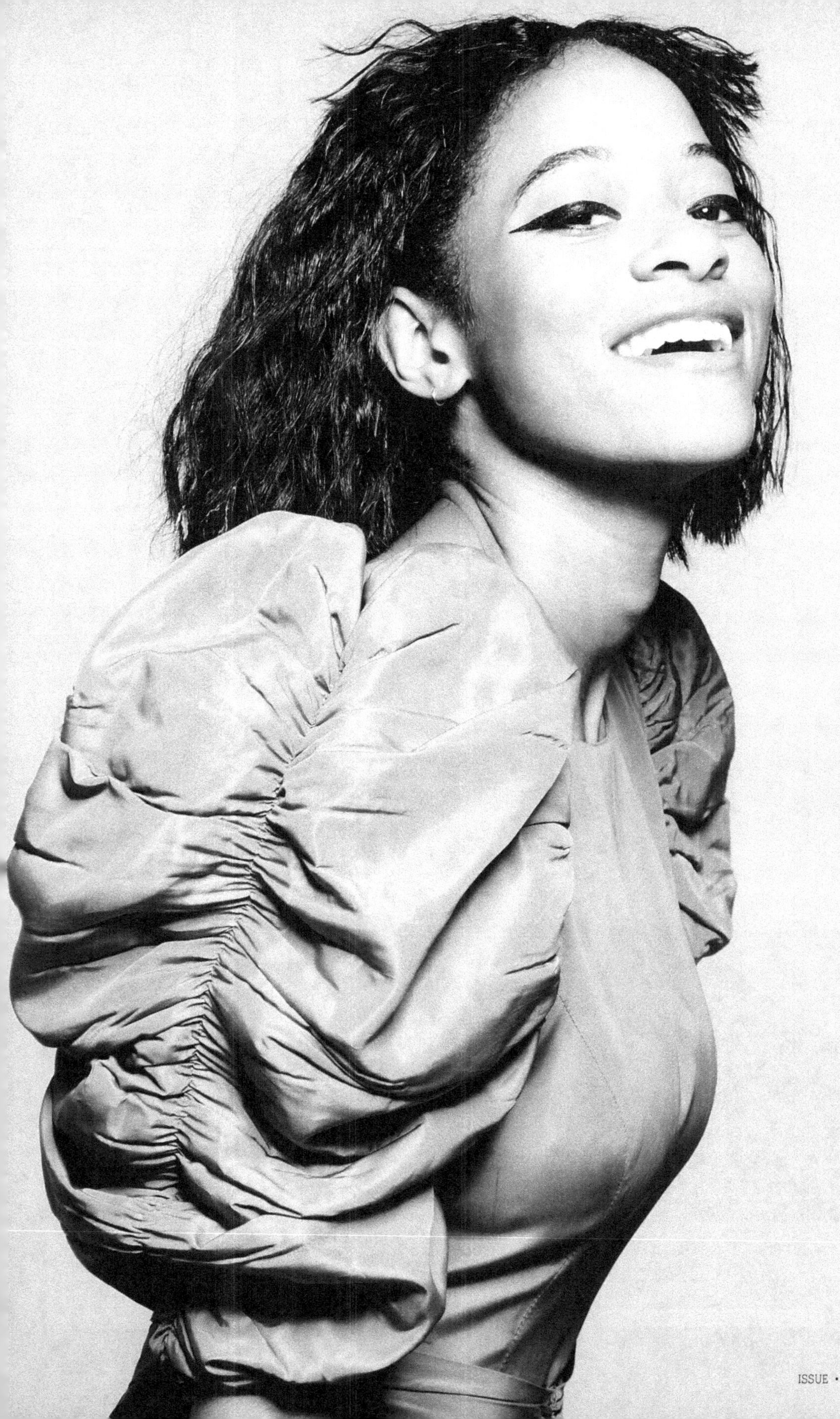

YOUR PASSION: My passion is to uplift the stories of the most vulnerable through storytelling in activism and art. Spread peace, love, light and revolutionary goodness.

KENDRICK SAMPSON

Currently making waves as 'Nathan' on the popular HBO comedy Insecure *(fans on Twitter call him 'Lyft Bae'), Kendrick Sampson is no stranger to playing* mous (2017–) *and award-winning action series* The Flash. *Outside of acting, he's not afraid to use* *justice reform and uniting oppressed communities. He speaks about his love of storytelling, maintaining*

> ## "MY CAREER IS JUST A PIECE OF MY PURPOSE. IT DOESN'T DEFINE ME, AND I KNOW I'M HERE TO UPLIFT THE VOICES OF THE MOST VULNERABLE COMMUNITIES AND PEOPLE OF COLOR. THIS IS MY PURPOSE IN LIFE AND MY CAREER SERVICES THAT."
>
> **— KENDRICK SAMPSON**

diverse characters from comedic to thrilling. His work includes the Golden Globe-nominated crime drama How to Get Away with Murder *(2014–), popular comedy series* White Fa *his voice and is heavily involved in the Standing Rock movement and Black Lives Matter, as well as advocating for criminal* *perspective and why we need to celebrate—rather than overlook—our differences.*

——————

Where are you from?
Houston, Texas.

Education: I read 'n' stuff.

Ambitions: Storytelling, ending white supremacy, spreading love and light and peace, producing good art.

Favorite food: Creole.

Favorite band: Rubber.

Favorite movie: Changes all the time! *Pan's Labyrinth, Zootopia, Coco.*

How did you get involved in this line of work? Through a lot of hard work and support from my mom. She made me find my own agent at age eleven when I said I want to act.

Artist you would most like to work with: Steven McQueen (Director).

Turn-ons: Beauty, purpose, confidence, melanin, curves, love, imperfections, revolution, diversity, adventure, challenge, hygiene,

Turn-offs: Hate, desperation, gossip, abuse, bigotry, misogyny, transphobia, xenophobia.

What was your first break? I'm still waiting on it. I don't know it depends. I think it's gone on several phases, *Vampire Diaries* and *How to Get Away with Murder, Insecure, Ball Pen*. Different stages of breaks. Breaking through.

What have you been in? Those! And *White Famous*. I played a British dude named Robbie. In *Vampire Diaries* I played Jesse. In *The Flash* I played Brainstorm, and in *How to Get Away with Murder* I got to play Caleb. And now in *Insecure* I'm playing Nathan.

How do you feel about this career? I was like, which one do I want to do?

I decided that storytelling was my strength, and that's what I loved. And I loved all of it. Even the annoying aspects of it, just because I knew the end result was storytelling with creating. That's my passion, and that's the best way I can serve the world.

How would you describe your specialty or type? I want to be more of a character actor, that's what's exciting—playing a bunch of different characters. But I also love playing things that

What would your ideal job be? My ideal job would be a project that I create and am producing, and then I can act in that. That would be a dream and a goal come true, one that I'm working really hard on, and I can't wait until that happens.

Do you consider yourself to be lucky? To be honest, I don't believe in luck. I believe I'm blessed, I believe I'm purposed, and I'm walking in that, and whatever happens with that happens. Even in hard times, that is still a blessing. I'm doing my best to be inten-

> ## "I GET TO PLAY A BUNCH OF VERY DIFFERENT CHARACTERS WITH DIFFERENT ACCENTS FROM DIFFERENT BACKGROUNDS, AND PEOPLE OF COLOR DON'T GET TO DO THAT VERY OFTEN."
>
> **— KENDRICK SAMPSON**

feel like it's good. I get to play a bunch of very different characters with different accents from different backgrounds, and people of color don't get to do that very often. I've been super, super grateful, and I hope it continues.

How did you decide to become an actor? I did a T-chart in ninth grade. I'm not going to say I always wanted to be an actor, but since maybe sixth grade. When I got to ninth grade I was deciding between that and law, so I did a T-chart. I did the pros and cons and I are really close to me, where I have to play with my vulnerability and be portrayed in that light. I don't know. There are many diverse different characters that I can play.

Who is your favorite actor you look up to? So many. I have a lot of buddies that I love: Rosario Dawson, Matt McGorry, Mark Ruffalo, Shailene Woodley. I don't know Will Smith but I look up to him. I look up to a lot of my buddies just because of how they use their platform and their artivism, and they are also great talented actors.

tional and purposed in that, whatever that is and whatever comes my way. I'm very grateful for everything.

What advantages do you have? Perspective, I think. I know that my career is just a piece of my purpose—it doesn't define me—and I know that I'm here to uplift the voices of the most vulnerable communities and people of color. That is my purpose in life, and my career services that. So it doesn't depend on it. My whole life isn't my career, so my perspective is probably my biggest advantage.

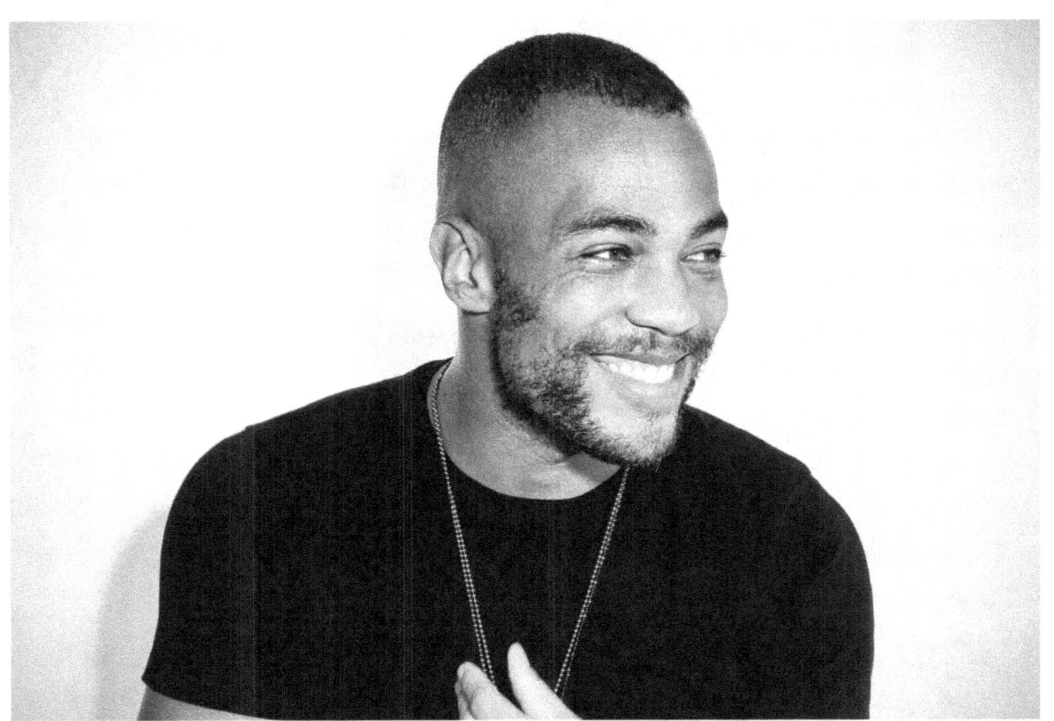

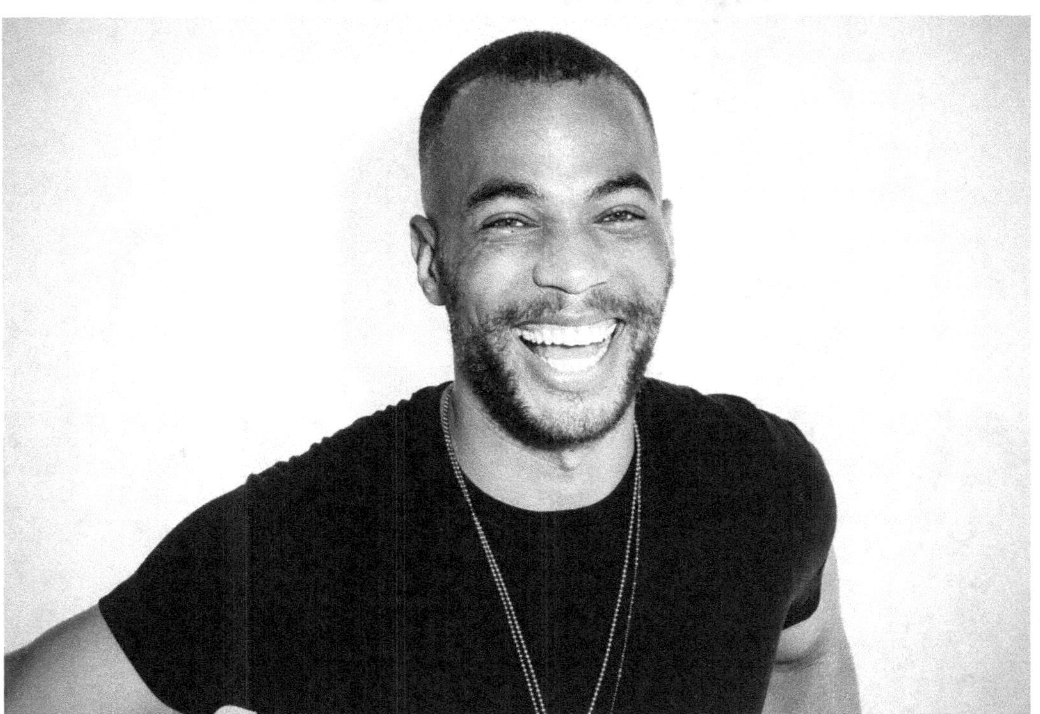

Too many to name:
YOUR INFLUENCES: James Baldwin, Fred Hampton, Fannie Lou Hamer, Delores ~~Herta~~ Huerta, Bamby Salcedo, Will Smith, Viola Davis, Susan Sarandon, Jane Fonda, Denzel Washington, Assata Shakur, Cesar Chavez, Fredrick Douglas, Zapatistas, Sitting Bull, Patrisse Cullors, Melina Abdullah, Linda Sarsour, Carmen Perez, Bernie Sanders, Steven McQueen, Guillermo Del Toro, Jesus Christ.

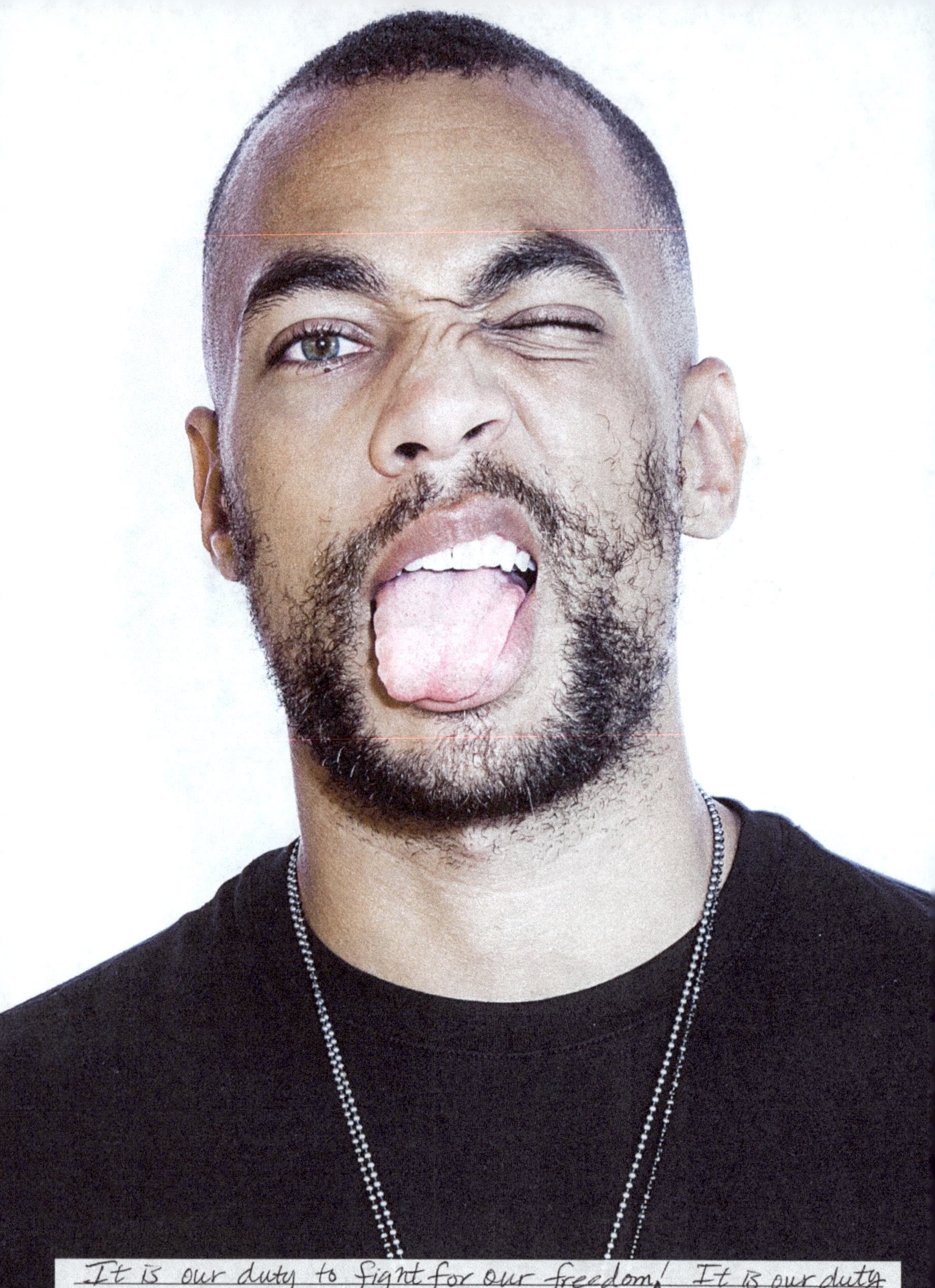
It is our duty to fight for our freedom! It is our duty to win! We must love and support each other. We have nothing to lose but our chains. Ase.
— Assata Shakur

a Primetime Emmy Award nomination for Outstanding Lead Actress in a Comedy Series.

HOW TO GET AWAY WITH MURDER
How to Get Away with Murder (2014–) is an American drama television series created by Peter Nowal and produced by Shonda Rhimes and ABC Studios. Viola Davis stars as Annalise Keating, a law professor at a prestigious Philadelphia University who becomes entwined in a murder plot. Davis has received critical acclaim for her portrayal. She became the first black woman to win an Emmy Award for Outstanding Lead Actress in a Drama Series and also won two SAG Awards for Outstanding Performance by a Female Actor in a Drama Series, as well as two Golden Globe nominations.

Would you rather have a car or diploma? I don't have a car, and I don't have a diploma. I don't know. Maybe a diploma. Maybe.

How do you feel about how interconnected the world is becoming? I think there are pros and cons to it. I think the pro is that we see things happening all over the world, and we can be inspired by somebody all the way across the world, but

How do you feel about having children? I think I want them, and I think it's a huge responsibility and test of character.

What challenges do you feel the world is facing today? Jesus Christ. Well … that lack of Jesus Christ. Lack of love and respect, too much fear, too much hate in this country, too much white supremacy—and in many

es enough, and that leaves us to hate each other and think that because somebody's different they might be coming in to take what I've got because they have an advantage or something like that. And then I have to find a way to hate them, and there's not enough celebrating each other and coalition-building and love.

What are you most grateful for? I am most grateful for Jesus. And my mama. I love my mama.

> # "WE'RE NOT CELEBRATING EACH OTHER'S DIFFERENCES ENOUGH, AND THAT LEAVES US TO HATE EACH OTHER AND THINK THAT BECAUSE SOMEBODY'S DIFFERENT THEY MIGHT BE COMING IN TO TAKE WHAT I'VE GOT."
>
> — KENDRICK SAMPSON

also—especially with the news and stuff like that—it's overwhelming. It gives us less of an excuse not to communicate and then puts more pressure on communicating, and it's stressful, but at the same time it's beautiful and advantageous in a lot of ways.

What does the future look like to you? The future looks beautiful and diverse. My goal is that the future will look like one where the most

oppressed voices are the most important.

countries I guess. Too much socio-economic disparity and not enough celebrating of differences. I hear too many people say, "I'm color-blind, and I don't see gender, and I don't see color" and all that kind of stuff.

That's a problem because if you don't see gender, and you don't see color, then you don't see the beauty and the diversity in the world. We're not celebrating each other's differenc-

What is your favorite way to communicate? My favorite way to communicate is through storytelling in every aspect—in my activism, in life and in my career. And I'm super long-winded with it because I love every detail, so people are like, "All right get to the point." And I'm like, "Look, what you've got to know is what kind of red it was!"

What is your favorite book, film, and music right now? I loved *The Shape of Water* last year. I don't know, there's so many. I guess that's really hard. I just read *My Love, My Love* by Rosa Guy. That was really good. *The Alchemist* [by Paulo Coelho] is still one of my favorite books of all time. Right now I'm listening to Ozuna and his new album *Aura* and Beyoncé and Jay-Z because I just went to their concert. And Kendrick Lamar. Mine changes every day.

BREEDA WOOL

Breeda Wool is gathering plenty of attention for her current on-screen role—that of Lou Linklatter in Stephen King and David E. Kelley's acclaimed TV series Mr. Mercedes. *Before portraying the tattooed, motorcycle-riding Lou,*

> ## "I HAVE MOMENTS OF INTENSE AND DEEP GRATITUDE THAT I GET TO PLAY MAKE-BELIEVE AS A GROWN UP AND PEOPLE GIVE ME MONEY TO DO IT."
>
> **— BREEDA WOOL**

Wool cut her teeth as a dancer and street performer, and later became a fan favorite for her role as Faith Duluth on the hit series UnReal. *She chats about watching her own sex scenes with her dad, working as a therapist and playing gender-fluid characters on screen.*

Where are you from? Champaign-Urbana, Illinois. Or Shampoo-Banana, Illinois.

Education: BA, psychology, theater.

Favorite food: Spaghetti.

Favorite movie: *Mulholland Drive.*

Favorite band: The Kinks.

Your idea of heaven: Dancing with my family and singing Irish music.

Turn ons: Committed hand gestures and sustained eye contact. Being good at art, loving your vocation.

Turn offs: Lashing out at others when you're insecure.

What was your first break? I'm still waiting for it. No, just kidding. I did my first film because I was dating an Irishman. My friend from college, a guy from Belfast, got me the film, which was with

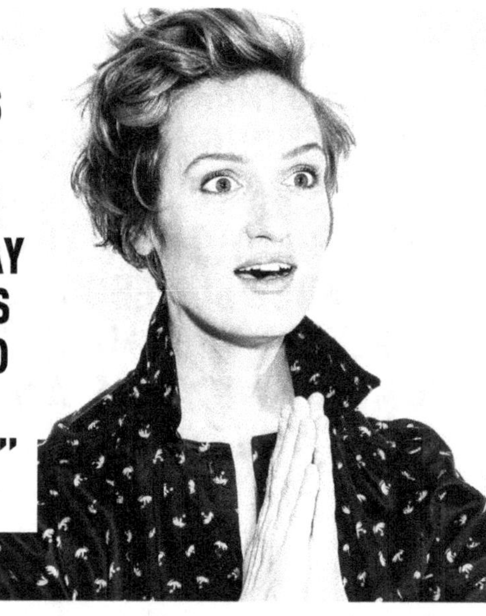

Lauren Wolkstein who has gone on to make extraordinary films. We made a movie where I was a guitar-playing homeless cowboy. I remember I got my boobs out and I had an orgasm on screen, and the first time I watched the film was with my dad. I thought it was going to be really cool like, "Mom, Dad, I've made it. I've done

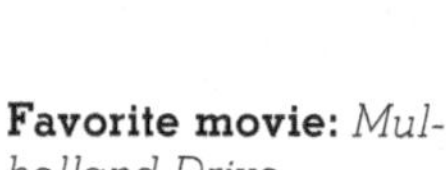

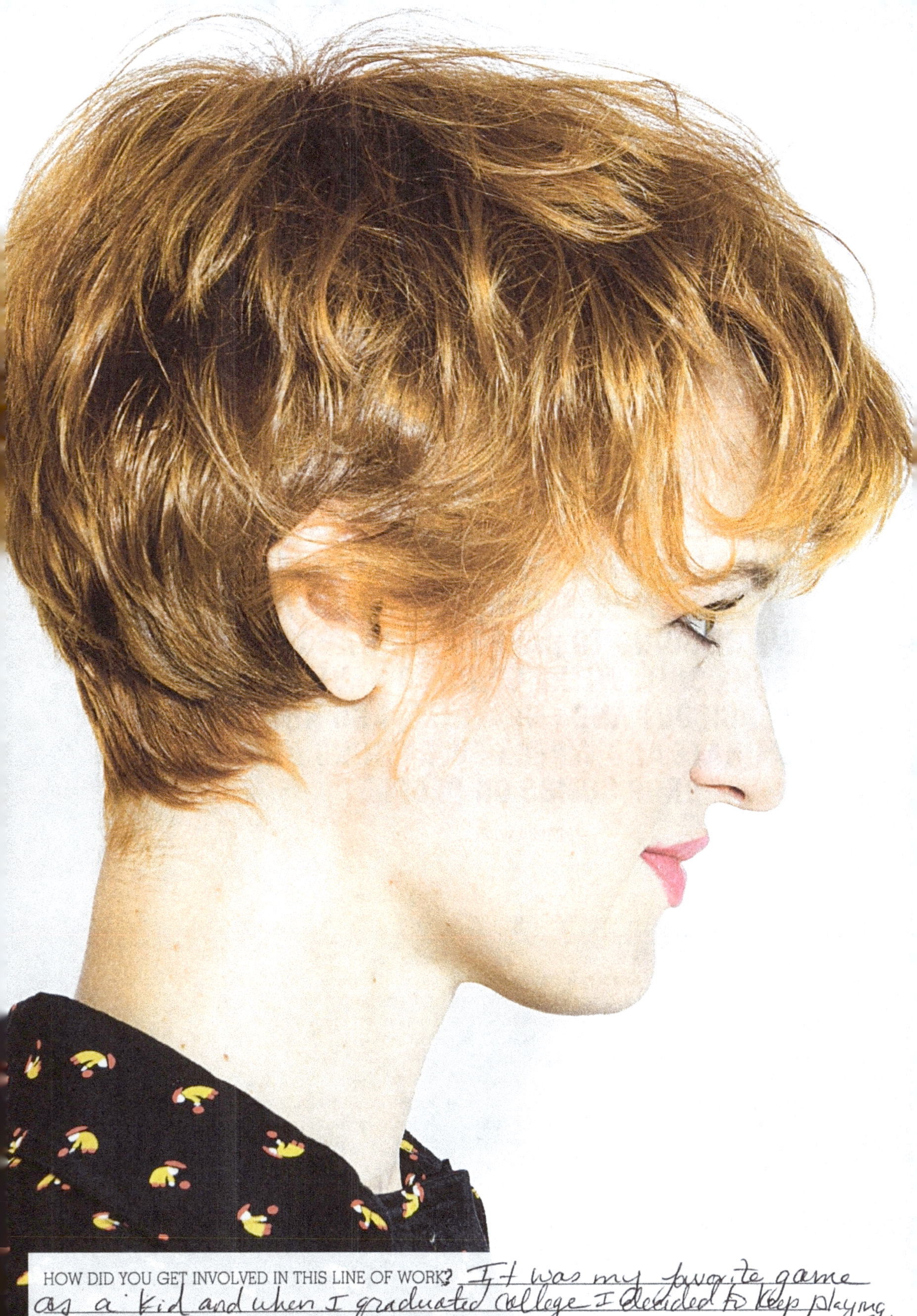

HOW DID YOU GET INVOLVED IN THIS LINE OF WORK? *It was my favorite game as a kid and when I graduated college I decided to keep playing.*

something," and then I'm watching this intimate moment with me and this other woman, sitting next to my dad. We didn't look at each other at all during the film, and then at the end of it my father, who is also an Irishman, was like, "It's amazing."

So that was the first thing I did, and it started the path of my parents encouraging me for years and years to come.

What have you been in? I was a street performer. I did

and my name's Lou Linklatter.

How do you feel about this career? It's simultaneously horrifying and stable and maddening. And then I have moments of intense and deep gratitude and awe that I get to play make-believe as a grown-up and people give me money to do it, and I get to go onto sets with groups of people and all they want to do is play make-believe, and we make up stories and tell them to people

ing it or directing it, which is something I'd like to do someday, and I've done some of that already—that it was some sort of service job. And I guess I've learned that that's not true, or that it's kind of cool to do something for something else. A little maturity in my life.

How would you describe your specialty or type? I don't think I have a type. I think I can empathize with a lot of different people. I definitely play a lot of gender-queer people,

up salacious show content. The show was created by Marti Noxon and Sarah Gertrude Shapiro and was inspired by Shapiro's award-winning independent short film *Sequin Raze*. The show's fourth and final season was released on Hulu in July 2018.

PENNY MARSHALL Carole Penny Marshall is an American actress, director and producer. She rose to fame in the 1970s for her role as Laverne DeFazio on the television sitcom *Laverne & Shirley* (1976–83), receiving three Golden Globe nominations for her portrayal. Marshall progressed to directing films in the 1980s, making her directorial debut with *Jumpin' Jack Flash* (1986) before directing *Big* (1988), which became the first film directed by a woman to gross more than $100 million at the US box office.

> # "THE AGE OF THE FEMININE IS COMING THROUGH, WHERE IN ORDER TO SURVIVE WE'RE GOING TO HAVE TO CARE ABOUT SOME SHIT. WE'RE GOING TO HAVE TO REACH OUT AND EMPATHIZE, AND NOT DOMINATE AND WRECK EVERYTHING AND DROP BOMBS ON PEOPLE."
>
> — BREEDA WOOL

movement and dance things for years. I did Shakespeare in New York, and then I did a TV show called *Un-Real* where I played a wonderful lady named Faith. I was on a show called *Betas*, and now I'm on *Mr. Mercedes* on the Audience Network, and it feels like a masterpiece. It's Stephen King and David Kelley, and it's this beautiful portrait of a serial killer and a detective. In the story I'm the serial killer's only friend and I ride a motorcycle and have neck tattoos,

and then wherever you are out there, you experience something and maybe we can experience something together and I don't feel so alone in the world and we are all in it together. So yes, I like it.

How did you decide to become an actor? It was my childhood game. I always thought that being an actor was like a service job and that unless I had autonomy over my own art—from either writing it, creating it, produc-

and I have done that since I was a kid. I played Bottom in *A Midsummer Night's Dream*. I was Mercutio in *Romeo and Juliet*. I was often placed in sort of gender-fluid situations.

Whether that says something about me or reflects something back to me personally, sure, why not. I'll take it. I'll take those reflections. But I also think it's fun and exciting to extend myself into states of mind that I'm not familiar with at all. I actually love that even more.

Who is your favorite actor, one that you look up to? Phillip Seymour Hoffman is somebody I really love. Penny Marshall—I wouldn't mind walking that path at all. She ended up directing *Big* and *A League of Their Own*. I like Meryl Streep. Doesn't everybody? Because she always makes

be employed one year and be unemployed the other, which makes it super hard to plan ahead. But I also have a degree in psychology, and I worked in a psychiatric center in Staten Island for a while. I don't know if you've ever been to a therapist but that job is…whoa! I don't think I'd want to do that. Just

yourself to be lucky? Shockingly so.

What advantages do you have? I'm born of two loving parents in a country not at war and in an upper middle class, educated family. I have so many advantages, and I have so many entitlements that I try to become clear and aware of. I know not everyone starts with the same starting point, and I think as a citizen it's important to know how you have a leg up. What you should do is think, "If I'm ahead in

go back to school for physics or electrical engineering or something? Maybe, I don't know. If you are hiring an electrical engineer intern I'm available.

How do you feel how interconnected the world is becoming? I think it is the antidote to a dying age of fossil fuels. That sharing and reaching out. Every great leap forward in technology comes with a great leap forward in human consciousness, and I'm very excited about this particular

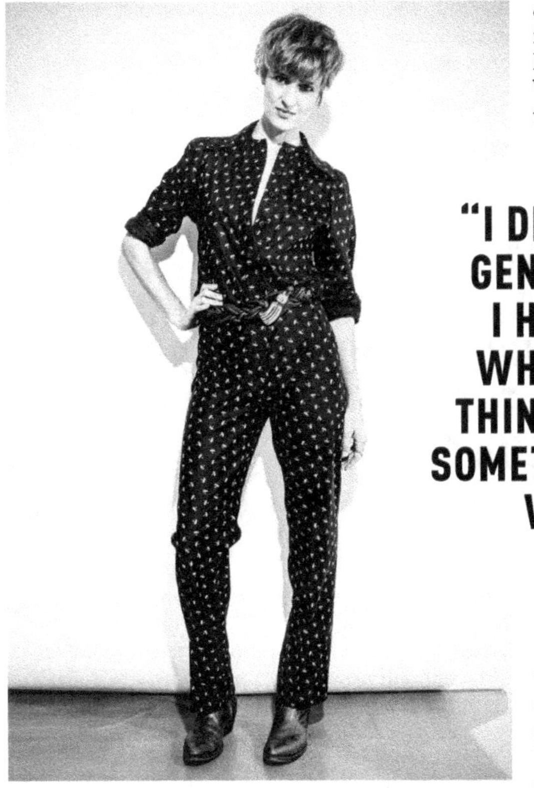

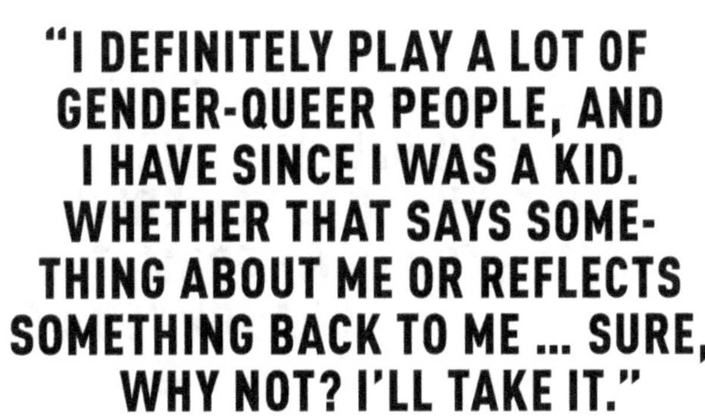

it not about her, it's always about the story. Brendon Gleeson, who I work with on *Mr. Mercedes*. That man makes me feel good about my career choice.

What would your ideal job be? My ideal job is this one, it's this acting job. It's insane, and I could

sit around being like, "Hmm, how can I love and care and help you from a professional point of view?" It seems really intense, and you'd have to have really good clear boundaries, which is not something that I'm well-practiced at.

Do you consider

this way, I need to turn around and look at my surroundings" and go, "let's go team, everyone lets go" and help and provide for that. I do not think that any of my born advantages are of my own making.

Would you rather have a car or diploma? A diploma. My father was a scientist. I went in to college as a physics major. I always have this weird thought in my brain, like I never had a "plan B" for this acting thing. Would I

technology that has come around in the last fifteen years and what that will mean for human consciousness.

It seems scary and seems like it is going to be awful and destructive, but I actually think that it is the antidote to our own destruction. The age of the feminine is coming through where in order to survive we're actually going to have to care about some shit. That is one thing that is inherently human is surviving and adapting. In order to do that we're going to have to reach out and empathize and not dominate and wreck everything and drop bombs on people.

What does the future look like to you? I am intensely hopeful and optimistic. I am in my most intense depressive state of existence. But at my core I feel it's going to be okay, which is a weird thing to feel in the wake of intense sadness, but I feel like we're built for togetherness. I personally have had a lot of crazy shit happen in my life, lots

that's your future. That's my future.

How do you feel about having children? I like the idea of adopting a baby, a lot, so I've looked in to that. I think it's magical to squish your DNA with someone you love and then make a thing that is a reflection of you and your soul and all your ancestors and all that shit, but it's also super magical to find somebody who already exists, who needs the epigenetic factor of influencing someone's life and then having that change who they

you feel the world is facing today? We have more atomic weapons. Since World War II many countries have developed enough weapons to kill everybody on earth. Right now we're in this place of the great peace, and part of the great peace came about because of the deep understanding of the ability that we now have to destroy ourselves. It's like if you have a gun in the house—human beings have a gun in the house.

But I think that what is happening is we've had enough gen-

What is your favorite book, film and music right now? I'm reading James Baldwin's collection of work in the compilation *The Cross of Redemption*. I highly recommend that to anybody.

I'm making music right now with my partner. He is part of a band called The Brinks so we made our first song. I feel very shy about. It's fun when you do something artistically different or new because it feels like you're in middle school, and you have a crush on somebody and you have just

of death, people taking their own lives, people dying suddenly.

The future is still amazing, it's still a party, and it's incredible. The most incredible thing is that the more you educate yourself about where you came from, the more that you can change your future. I'm just in the process now of really trying to educate myself on how I got here and then figure out how I can change it because I do not think of myself as a powerless person. So if you figure out how to change something,

are…that's also amazing and magical.

But I like breastfeeding. It's really cool. Like spraying breast milk out of your breasts. Who wouldn't want to do that? I don't know. I'm an actor so I do have some narcissistic tendencies. So having something come out of my vagina, looking at it, it looking like me, it looking back at me and me being like, "Oh everything's right with the world." I guess that is kind of cool too. I don't know.

What challenges do

erations go by since World War II that we no longer understand that guns can kill people. I feel like we're a generation that isn't aware and understanding of the power that we've accomplished and possess. I do think we have the tools to become hyper-aware and hyper-knowledgeable about ourselves and our potential and possibilities.

What are you most grateful for? My mom.

What is your favorite way to communicate? Physically.

kissed them for the first time. That is how I feel about making music right now. I've also been listening to Patti Smith and Morrissey.

Can I extend the film question to TV? I just watched Sandra Oh's *Killing Eve*. I'm obsessed with the actress who plays the killer. I recommend watching that show, and *Mr. Mercedes*, obviously. Self-promotion.

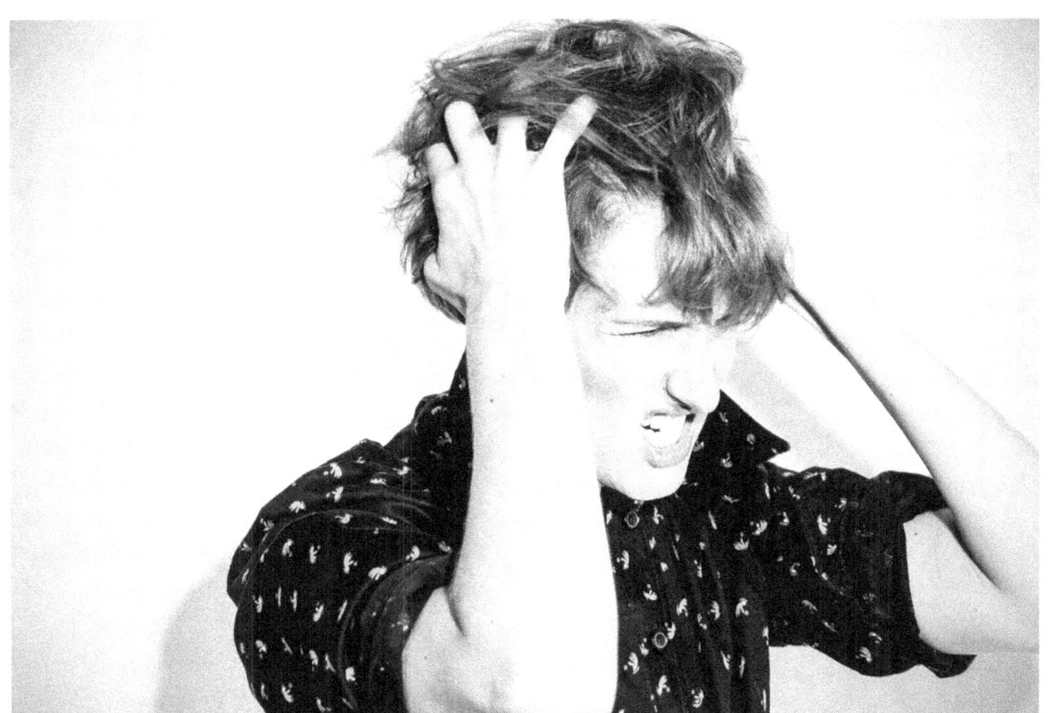

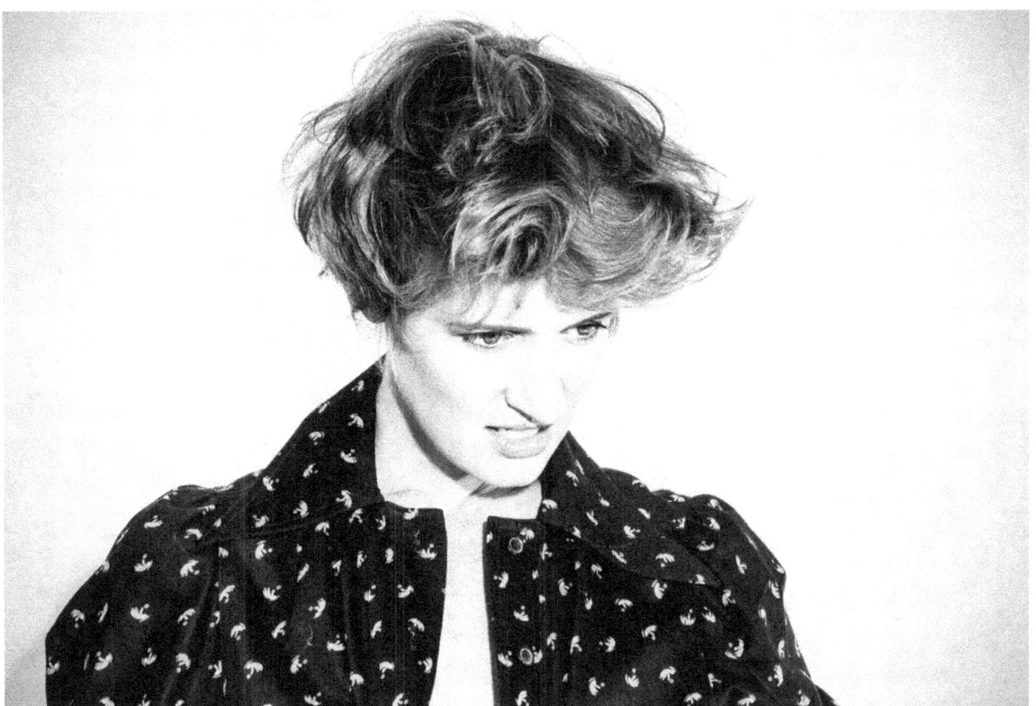

YOUR PASSION:

The most expressive thing you can ever do is commit. To commit to something is the most dificult and rewarding thing I have ever done. I've commited to being an artist and for me that means telling the truth to the best of my ability.

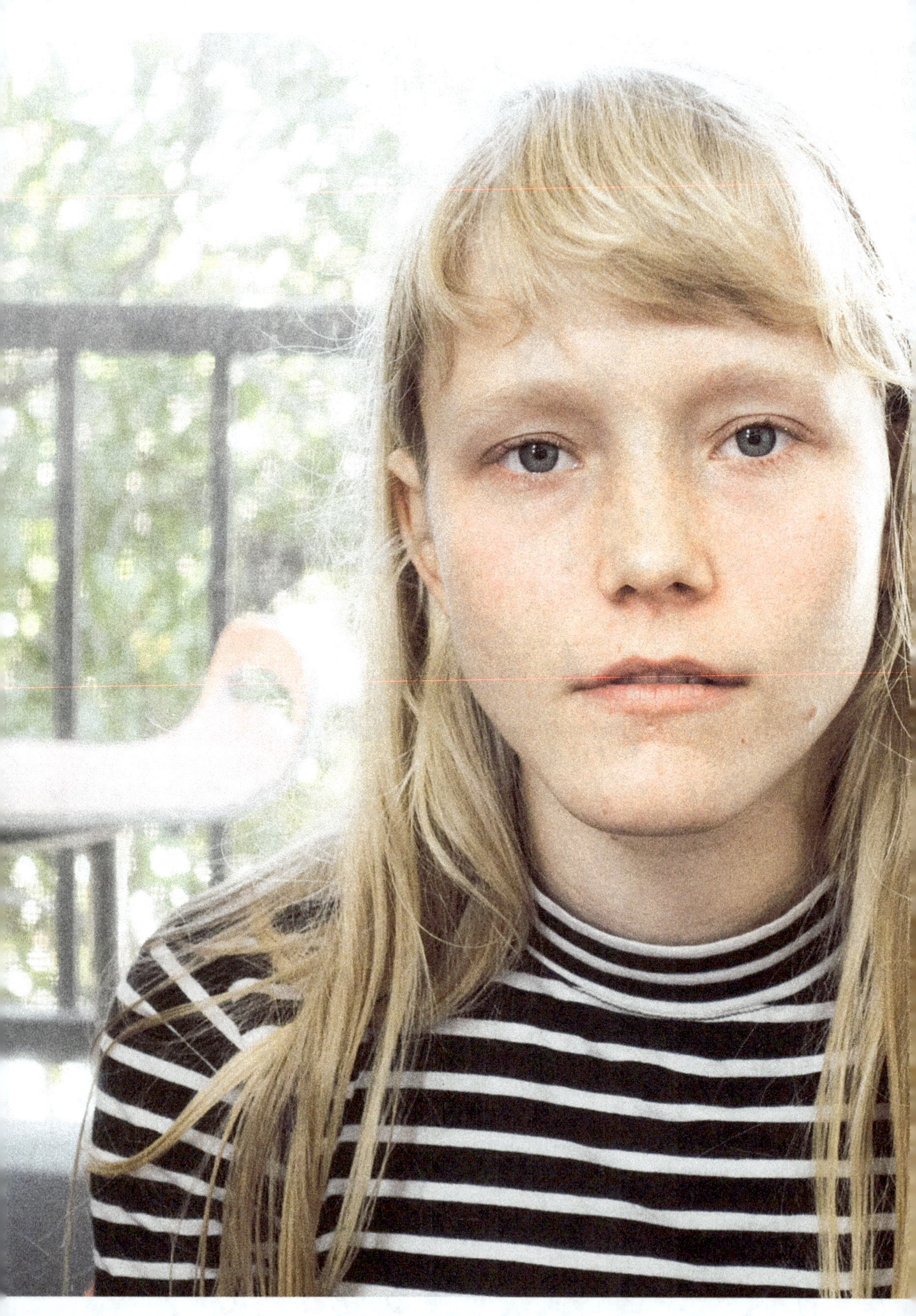

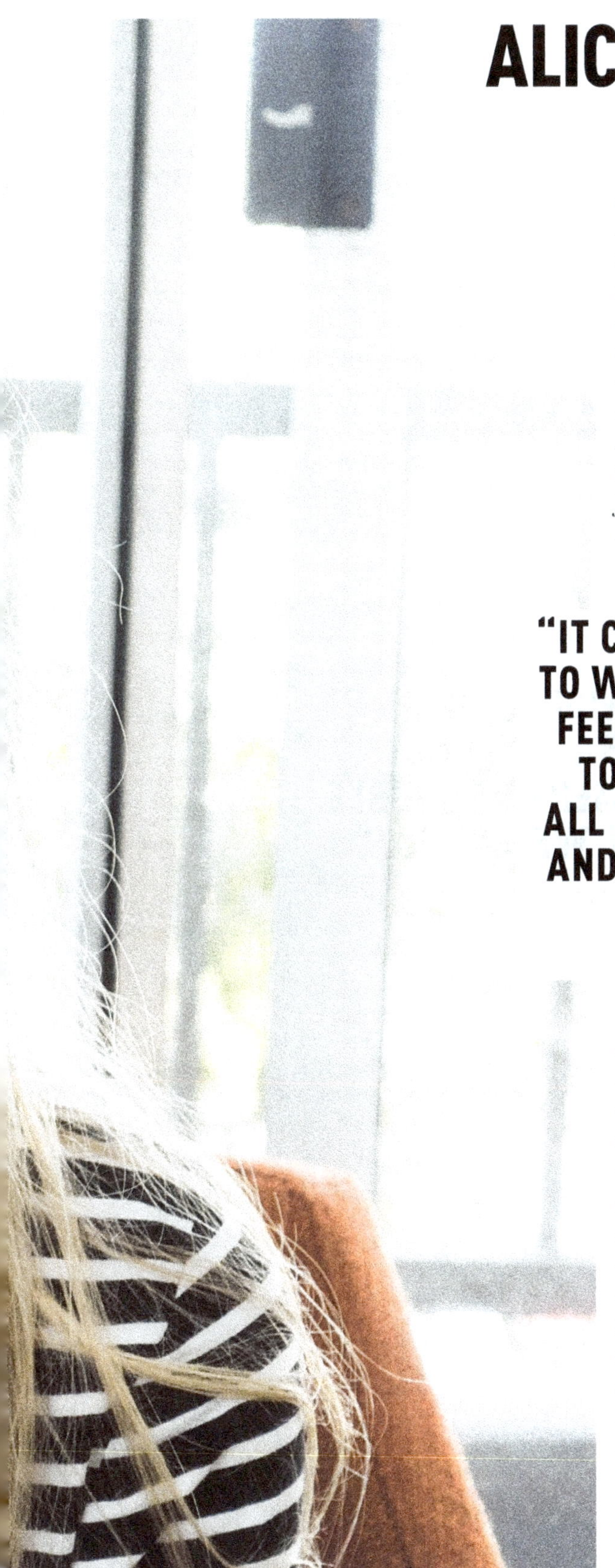

ALICE PHOEBE LOU

Berlin-based artist Alice Phoebe Lou cares deeply about how her music connects with others. Beginning as a fire dancer turned street musician, Lou still enjoys taking her music outdoors, where resonating with a random stranger is more meaningful than a paying audience. Recently, she's been making music that reaches audiences through film. Lou wrote and recorded the title track for Alexandra Dean's

"IT CAN BE OVERWHELMING TO WRITE A SONG WHEN YOU FEEL AS THOUGH YOU NEED TO HOLD THE WEIGHT OF ALL THE SOCIAL, POLITICAL, AND INEQUALITY PROBLEMS IN THE WORLD."

— ALICE PHOEBE LOU

critically-praised Bombshell: The Hedy Lamarr Story *(2017), executive produced by Susan Sarandon and winner of the New York Film Critics Online award for Best Documentary. Lou's song "She" received its own recognition on the Oscars shortlist for Best Original Song, and she released a mesmerizing music video for it which premiered on NPR's* All Songs Considered. *Lou discusses how her track for* Bombshell *came about and why she encourages other musicians to try busking.*

———————

Where are you from? I'm from Cape Town, South Africa.

When did you start making music? I played piano as a kid, but I was more into dancing. I was a performing arts kid, always putting on plays. I started writing songs as an angsty teenager and eventually was writing proper songs when I moved to Berlin.

Who did you listen to growing up? My parents always had something on the record player—PJ Harvey, Cat Power, Morcheeba, Portishead, Patti Smith.

songs on the street, and people reacted really well. It seemed like a fun thing to try so I gave up my ideas of going to university in Cape Town and carried on playing on the streets. That's when I realized this music brings me immense joy. So I figured I'd carry on and see where it led.

What role would you say busking played in your development? Everything. Busking teaches you so much about crowd dynamics and how to create an immersive bubble where people feel welcomed. It's about creat-

How would you say your relationship with the busking community has changed as your career evolves? A lot of buskers who come through Berlin know my music, because Berlin's the kind of place people pass through during the summer. I'm a little bit infamous now which is frustrating because I just want to be a nameless, faceless person sometimes. The appeal of playing to strangers is that when they care, it actually means something.

I try my best to play on the street as much as possible even

> ## "BUSKING TEACHES YOU SO MUCH ABOUT CROWD DYNAMICS AND HOW TO CREATE AN IMMERSIVE BUBBLE WHERE PEOPLE FEEL WELCOMED."
>
> **— ALICE PHOEBE LOU**

I was influenced a lot by my parents' record collection.

When did you decide this is what you were going to do? It wasn't something natural to me, like "I'm going to be a musician!" I traveled around Europe as an eighteen-year-old, and I was actually performing on the streets as a fire dancer. I found that you can travel Europe with very little money and live this bohemian, nomadic lifestyle, which was amazing for me.

In Berlin, I tried doing a couple of cover

ing an environment that moves people and finding direct channels to people's emotions.

I always recommend people busk, even if they have been performing for decades. I've convinced people to busk, and it's always a hard experience even for really seasoned musicians because it's humbling in a very scary way. But it teaches you so much about yourself and people in general, and definitely about the effect of music on people's emotions especially when you're surprising them with street music.

while touring, and life has been getting busier. Unfortunately, I've had quite a bad problem with a stalker. I couldn't play much on the street last year because every time I showed up he would be there. Hopefully we'll be having help from the German government, and people can get him to leave me alone so I can do what I enjoy doing and not be perturbed.

You opened for the legendary Rodriguez on his South African tour. Had you known his music growing up?

Sixto Rodriguez, known simply as "Rodriguez," is an American singer-songwriter from Detroit who wrote and recorded music in the early '70s. In spite of weak reception in the US, and unbeknownst to Rodriguez, his music gained popularity in South Africa, Australia, Botswana, New Zealand and Zimbabwe from the mid-'70s onward. His story is the basis for the Academy Award-winning film *Searching for Sugar Man* (2012). Rodriguez has since gone on to tour extensively and release new live recordings.

I definitely had. He was someone whose record was in every slightly lefty household. The documentary paints him as our biggest star, and I think that's a little sensational. But he definitely influenced a lot of South African people's lives, and it was amazing to go on tour with him.

It was strange as well because he's got such an anti-establishment rhetoric, and that's kind of why people were into his music at such a difficult time in South Africa's history. But when you go to the concerts it's 99% white people, a lot of whom aren't really doing anything to change the social circumstances that still exist in South Africa.

But it gave me a lot of perspective playing to thousands of South African people when most of my shows have been overseas. It was like a weird homecoming.

You've received a lot of recognition for your song "She," which is featured in the fascinating documentary *Bombshell: The Hedy Lamarr Story*. How did that come about? Alex and Adam, the director and producer, reached out to me. Most of the film's music is older, and I think they wanted to end the film on a more uplifting song sung by a current female artist.

I suggested a few things and ultimately wrote a song that seemed to fit them best.

It's not like my other songs. It's got a different energy to it. The first time I saw it at the Tribeca premiere was crazy because I was so into the documentary because it's about a fascinating, inspiring person. By the end of it I had totally forgotten my song was in it, so when I started hearing my song it was like, "What's going on?"

What are some things that you like to address through your music? In my late teens, I was disillusioned that my songs needed to have so much gravity and weight. It can be overwhelming to write a song when you feel as though you need to hold the weight of all the social, political,

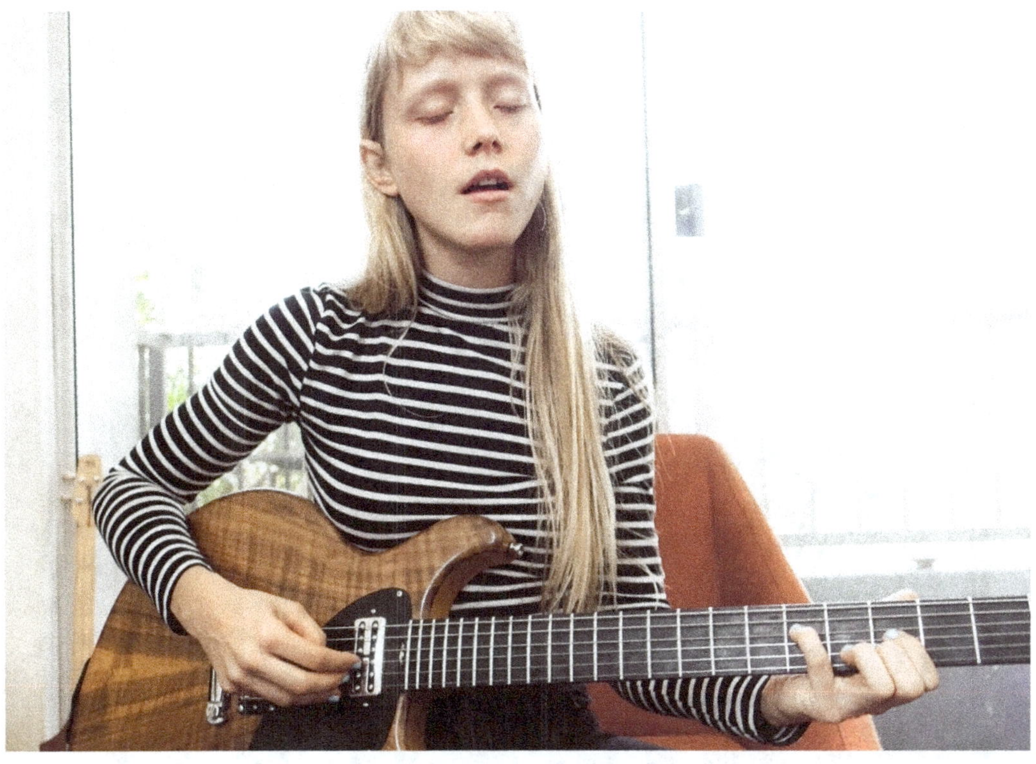

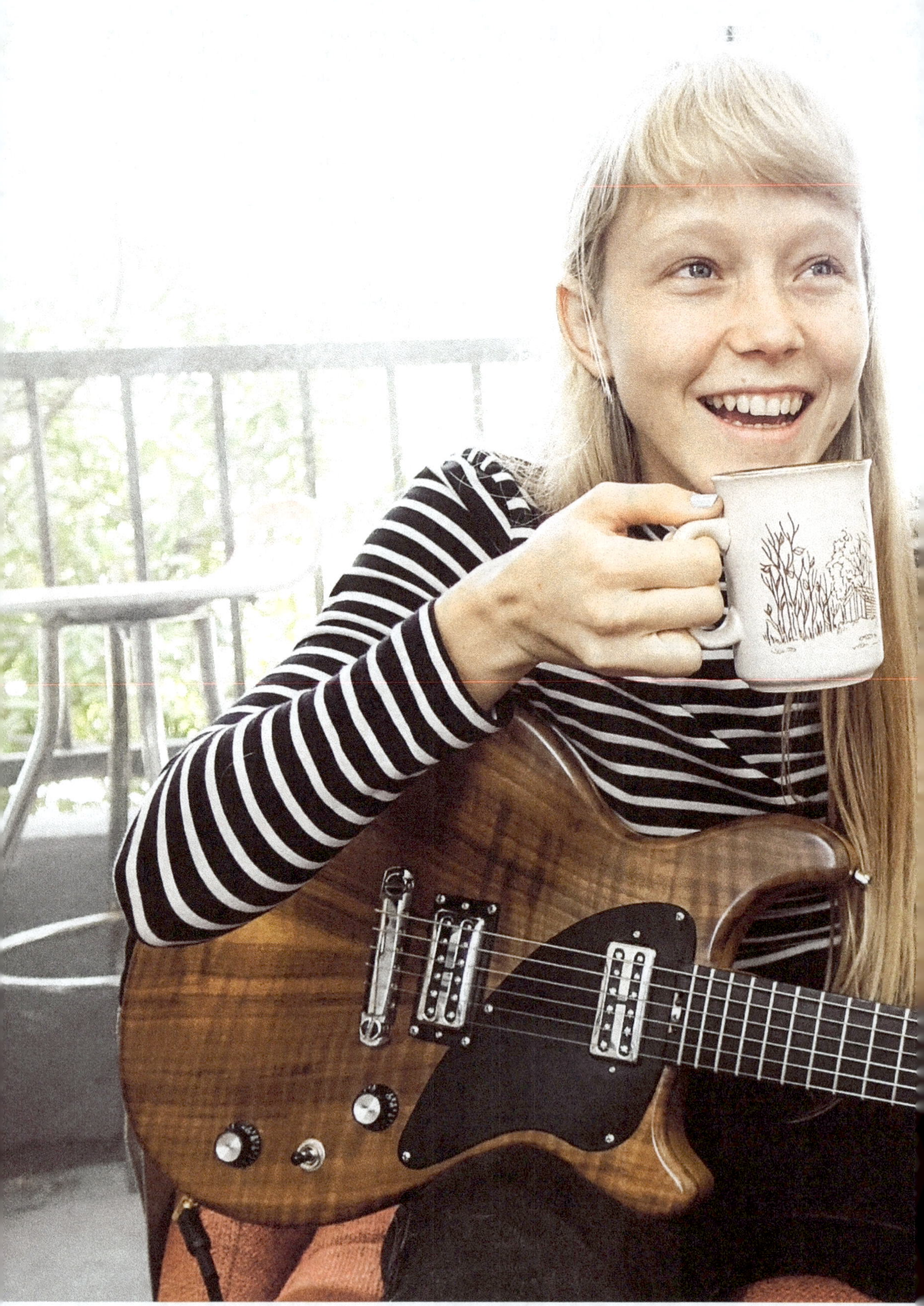

and inequality problems in the world.

It's less important to me now to didactically say things or comment on problems in society, as opposed to making music that moves people. My songs are very personal, but at the same time they could be personal to anyone. Writing songs anyone can relate to and feel something—that's all that really matters to me.

You're working on recording a new album. What can you tell me about it? It's exciting

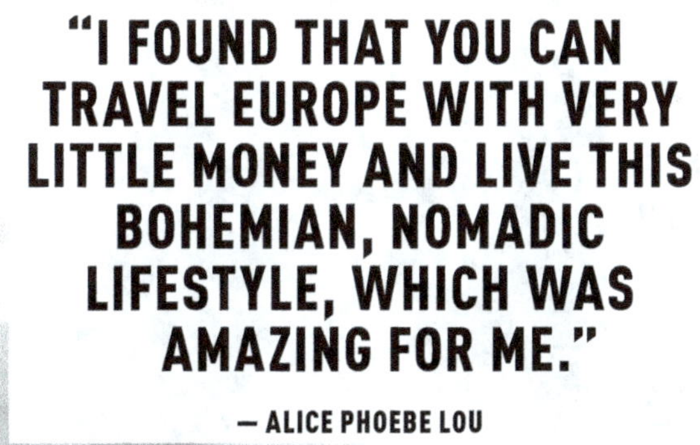

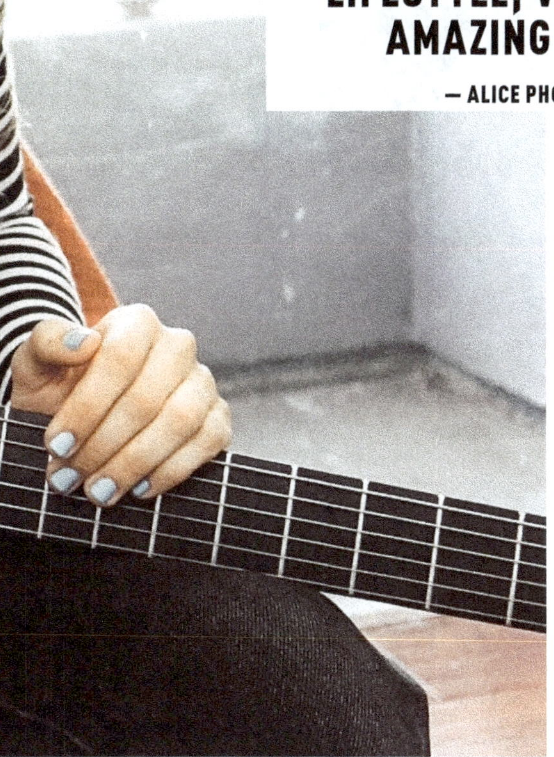

because for the first time in a long time I'm working on something with no stress, just good things. We spent two weeks in an incredible studio in Northern California close to Stinson Beach. It was like living in a castle with all the gear in the world that you could ever want, plus an incredible producer and musicians working so hard with me to finish the album. I have only good feelings about it.

Who would you most like to collaborate with and why? I like to throw parties in Berlin, and the point is to create an evening where my friends traveling through Berlin, who would otherwise play in a tiny little bar, can be more appreciated than that. For me, that's the most inspiring way of collaborating—not just aspiring to collaborate with established people, but to create things in your own community.

What are your interests and passions outside music? I love organizing events. I'm also booking a stage at a festival this year and branching out into those kinds of things. My emphasis is on community and bringing out the best in the people around me, as they seem to do to me.

I love cooking. I love discovering new places. I love playing places that are totally outside of my comfort zone. The weirder and more random the show, the more interested I am.

What's your favorite book film and music right now? I'm very inspired by Haruki Murakami books generally, but right now I'm reading a book by Anaïs Nin. She's an incredibly inspiring writer from the '30s and '40s, before feminism was even called feminism. Jodorowsky's *Dune* is a favorite film. I'm inspired by my friends' music at the moment. There's a lot of South African musicians doing amazing things.

JESS GABOR

Los Angeles-born and bred actor Jess Gabor is set to hit TV screens as the newest cast member on Showtime's long-running and extremely popular series Shameless (2011–). She plays

her dream acting role, her ambitions as a photographer and why she's too optimistic for her own good.

"BECAUSE OF SOCIAL MEDIA, THERE'S A LOT OF NARCISSISM AND A LOT OF PEOPLE ARE VERY SELF-INVOLVED— IT'S ALL ABOUT YOUR IMAGE AND NOT ABOUT WHAT YOU'RE SAYING TO THE WORLD."

— JESS GABOR

the character of "Kelly Keefe," a tough as nails military brat who becomes involved with eldest brother Carl Gallagher (played by Ethan Cutkosky) and takes over his life. She chats with us about

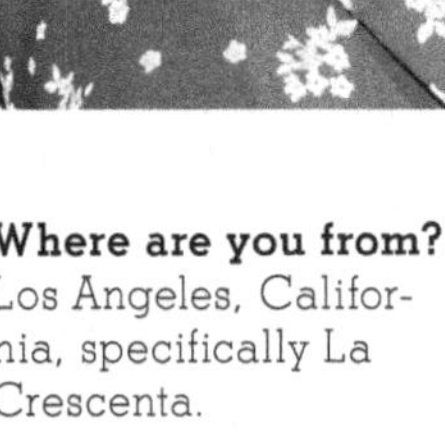

Favorite food: Cheese.

Last book read: A Life in Parts by Brian Cranston.

Turn ons: Considerate, reliable, a sense of humor.

Where are you from? Los Angeles, California, specifically La Crescenta.

Education: BA at Loyola Marymount University and Moscow Art Theatre.

Ambitions: Photography (35mm film).

Turn offs: Caring about weight and calories, being closed-minded, unkind.

Your idea of heaven: A nice, sexy man feeding me chocolate.

What have you been in? Oh God! Probably

JESS GABOR
American actor Jess Gabor began her career with roles in student films and independent projects before landing the reoccurring role of Kelly Keefe in Showtime's Shameless in 2018. This is her first major acting role.

SHAMELESS
An American comedy-drama television series developed by John Wells, Shameless debuted on TV network Showtime on January 9, 2011. It is an adaptation of the British series of the same name and features an ensemble cast led by William H. Macy and Emmy Rossum. The series depicts the dysfunctional family of Frank Gallagher, a single father raising six children. The series' ninth season premiered on September 9, 2018, making Shameless the longest-running original scripted series in Showtime's history.

TATIANA MASLANY
Tatiana Maslany (b. 1985) is a Canadian actor known for portraying multiple characters in the science fiction television series Orphan Black (2013–2017). In 2016 she won a Primetime Emmy Award for her work on the show, becoming the first Canadian actor from a Canadian series to win an Emmy in a key dramatic category. Maslany has also appeared in the television series Heartland (2008–2010), The Nativity (2010) and Being Erica

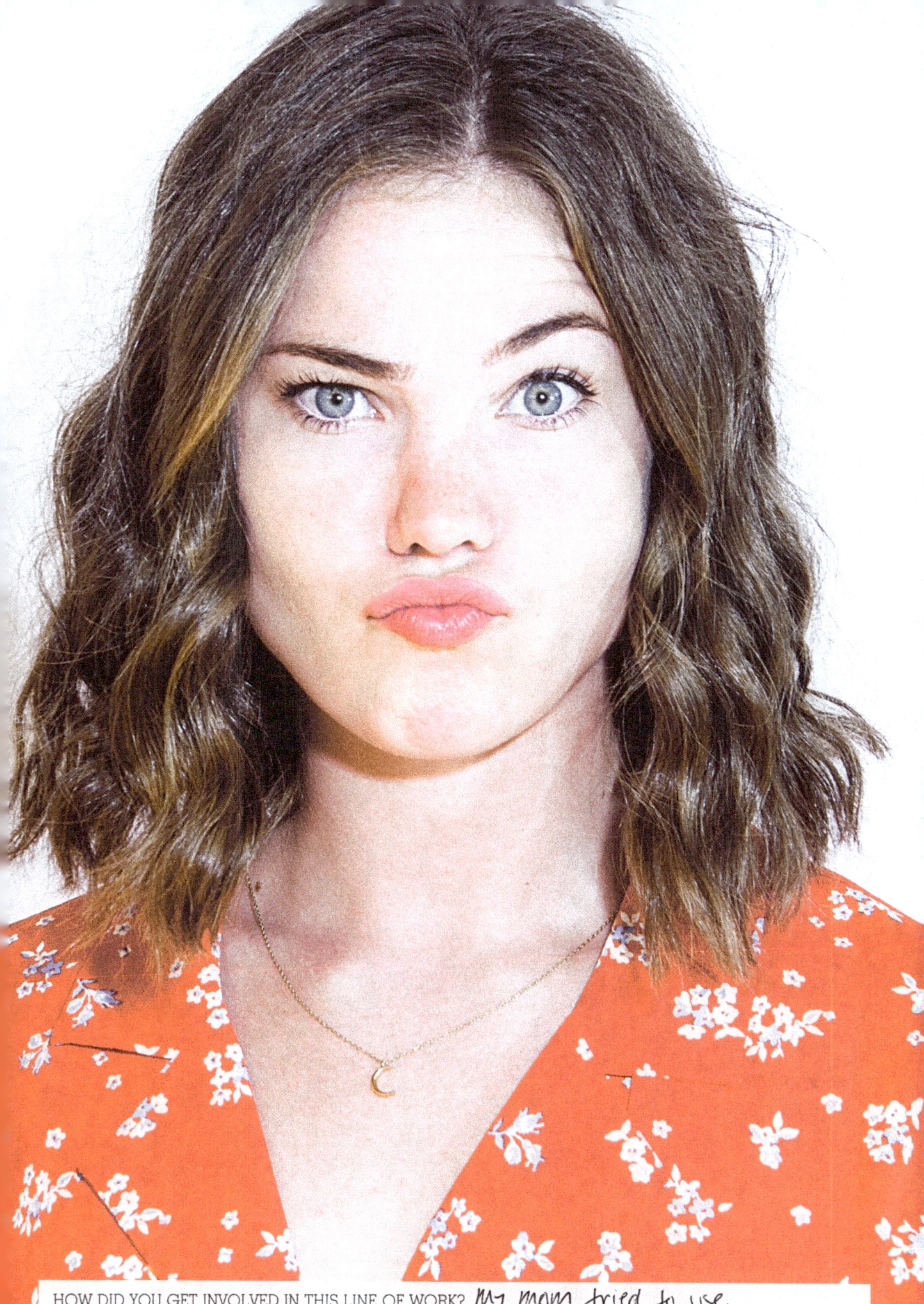

HOW DID YOU GET INVOLVED IN THIS LINE OF WORK? My mom tried to use reverse psychology to make me not want to act... didn't work☺

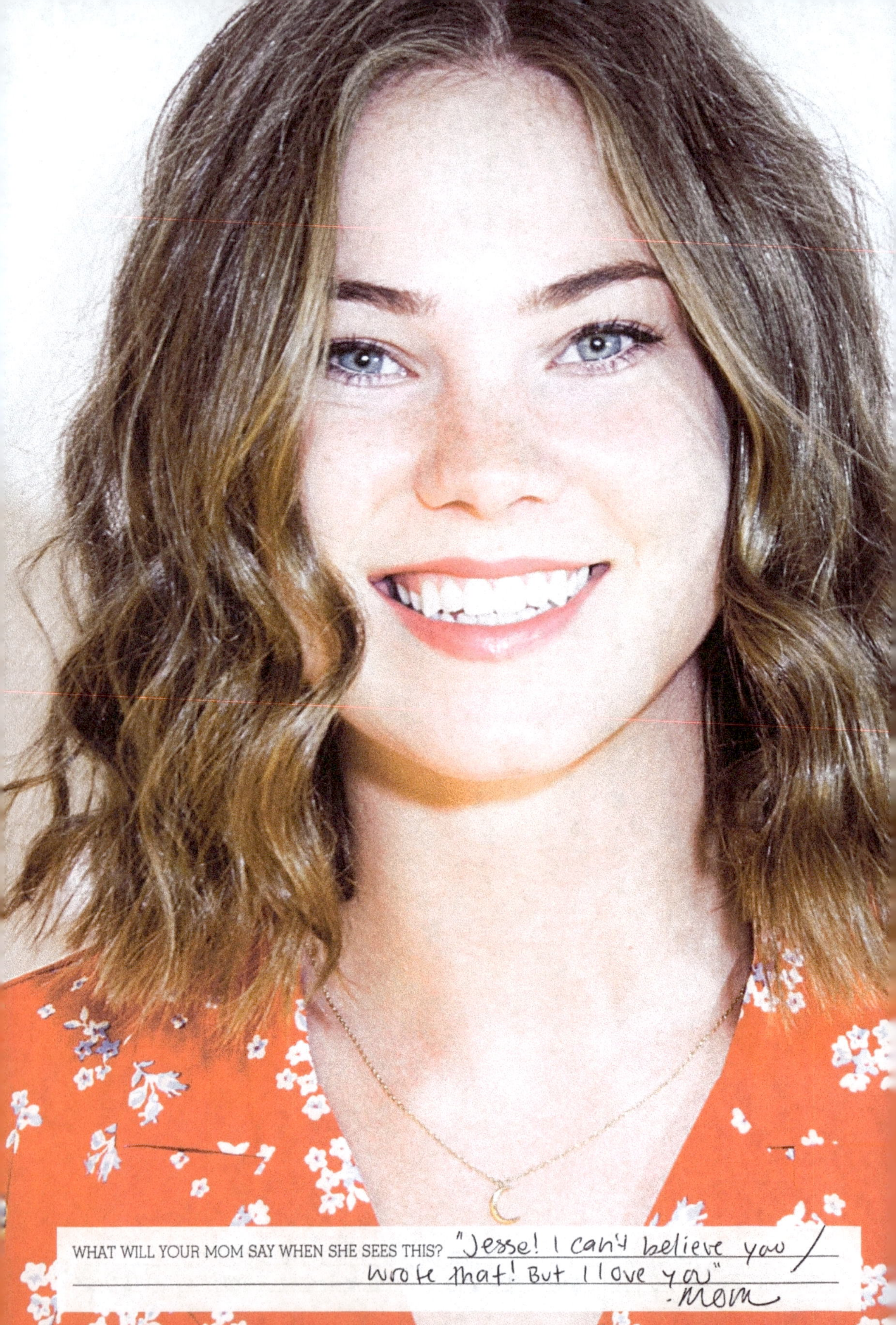

WHAT WILL YOUR MOM SAY WHEN SHE SEES THIS? "Jesse! I can't believe you
wrote that! But I love you"
-mom

(2009–11) and starred in the films *Picture Day* (2013), *Cas and Dylan* (2013), *Woman in Gold* (2015) and *Stronger* (2017).

STARTERS
Starters (2012) is a novel by Lissa Price. The book takes place in a futuristic Los Angeles, where wars are waged with biological weapons that have killed anyone not vaccinated against them. The only ones that survive the attack are either under twenty or over sixty years of age. Starters has been published in German, Greek, Dutch, Italian, French, Portuguese, Turkish and Spanish.

more than seventy student films, then a couple of TV shows, a couple of movies here and there, and right now I'm on *Shameless*.

How do you feel about this career? It's challenging, man. It's really challenging, but it's the most creative and amazing field that I could possibly be in.

How did you decide to become an actor? My mom works for Disney, and she put me and my sisters in all of her movies as extras, as reverse psychology to try to make us not want to be actors. It didn't work

right now. I'm also a really big fan of Tatiana Maslany. I'm following her career a lot.

Do you consider yourself to be lucky? Hell, yeah. I think luck is a combination of hard work in each opportunity. I've been blessed with a lot of amazing opportunities, and I've put in a lot of hard work.

What advantages do you have? I'm probably too optimistic for my own good. I'm really positive. I have a really great family and friends that are very supportive.

Hopefully happy, healthy and working.

How do you feel about having children? I'm down. Not now. I'm twenty-one.

What challenges do you feel the world is facing today? Because of social media, there's a lot of narcissism, and a lot of people are very self-involved because it's all about your image and not about what you're saying to the world. I think there's a lack of education that we need to really look into.

**What are you most

> ## "YOU CAN LEARN ABOUT THINGS TODAY THAT YOU'D NEVER BE ABLE TO LEARN ABOUT YEARS AGO, AND YOU CAN BE VERY IN TUNE WITH WHAT'S HAPPENING IN THE WORLD, WHICH IS WHAT WE NEED RIGHT NOW."
>
> — JESS GABOR

because I was like, "This is what to do."

How would you describe your specialty or type? In any makeup, in any wardrobe, you could be anything.

What would your ideal job be? There's this book called *Starters*—it's a young adult science fiction novel. It's incredible, and there is this main character called Callie. My dream is to play Callie.

Who is your favorite actor you look up to? Definitely Meryl Streep,

Would you rather have a car or a diploma? A diploma.

How do you feel about how interconnected the world is becoming? There's so much information at all times that it's hard to manage it all, but I think it's incredible. You can learn about things that you'd never be able to learn about years ago and be very in tune with what's happening in the world, which is what we need.

What does the future look like to you?

grateful for? My family. I love my family.

What is your favorite way to communicate? Face-to-face, or I'll call somebody. I'm really bad at texting.

What is your favorite book, film, and music right now? My favorite book is *Brave New World* by Aldous Huxley. Favorite music: I'm a DJ gal, I'm a raver, so I like Porter Robinson and Kaskade. Movie: *Life is Beautiful* by Roberto Benigni.

RECENT ISSUES

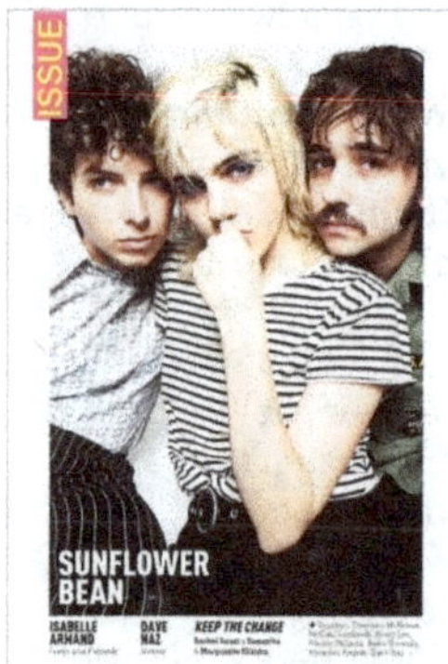

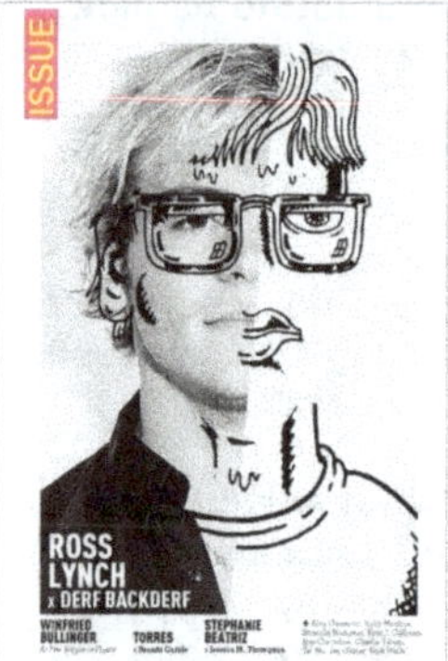

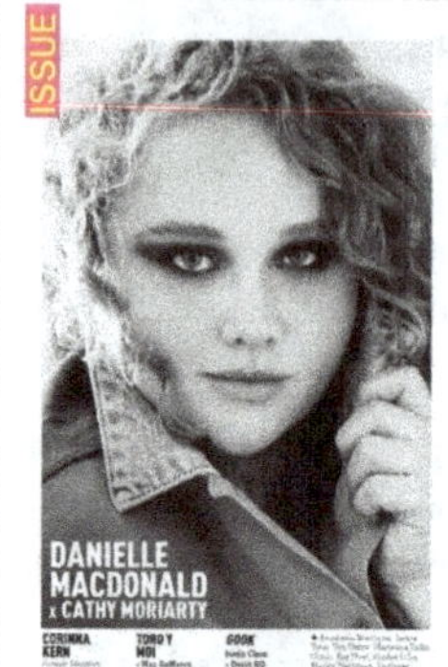

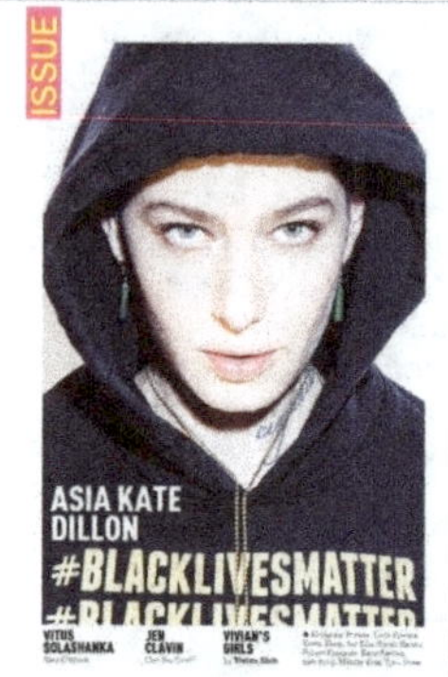

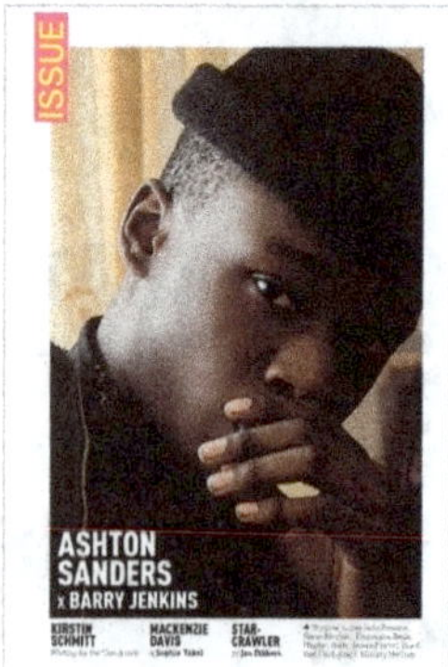

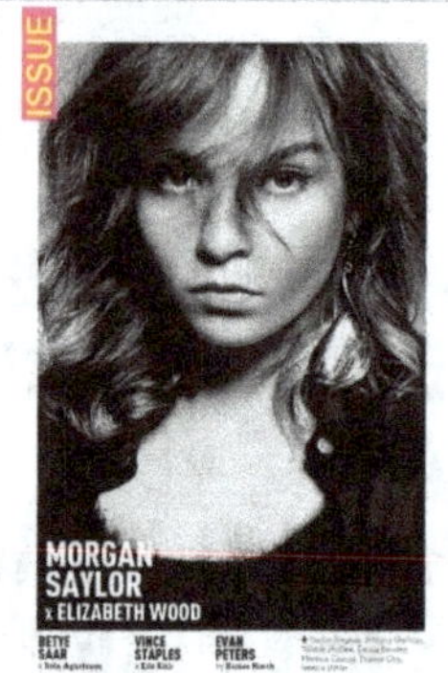

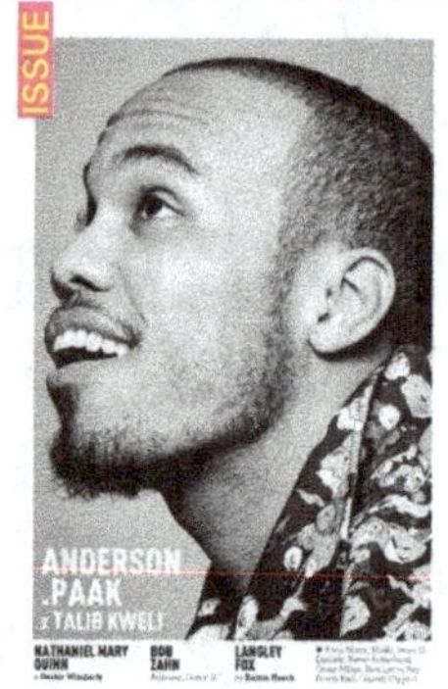

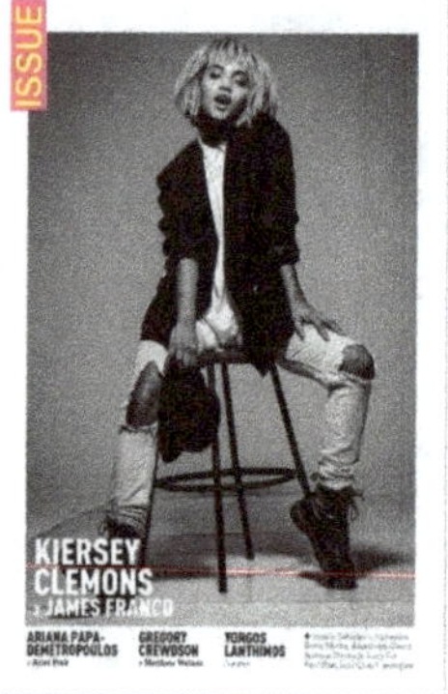

ALL PAST ISSUES AVAILABLE ONLINE AT ISSUEMAGAZINE.COM

FOUNDER & EDITORIAL / CREATIVE DIRECTOR Jan-Willem Dikkers

EDITORS Jess Cornelius, Shannen McKee, Aly Wicker

CONTRIBUTORS Tiffany Boone, Sophie Caby, Jenn Champion, Jess Cornelius, Gillian Deeds, Lukas Dhont, Jan-Willem Dikkers, Jess Gabor, Lola Kirke, Kilo Kish, Alice Phoebe Lou, Kevin Morby, Victor Polster, Esther Povitsky, Olan Prenatt, Marlon Rabenreither, Jon Ronson, Kendrick Sampson, Anna St. Louis, Chris Stein, Sunny Suljic, Aly Wicker, Breeda Wool

THE LATEST AND LEGENDARY IN ART, FILM, AND MUSIC

MADE IN LOS ANGELES

9 780974 512433